Jimmy Reid

A Clyde-built Man

W.W.J. Knox and A. McKinlay

Liverpool University Press

First published 2019 by
Liverpool University Press
4 Cambridge Street
Liverpool
L69 7ZU

Copyright © 2019 W.W.J. Knox and A. McKinlay

The right of W.W.J. Knox and A. McKinlay to be identified as the authors of this work has been asserted by them in accordance with the Copyright, Designs and Patents Act 1988.

All rights reserved. No part of this book may be reproduced, stored in a retrieval system, or transmitted, in any form or by any means, electronic, mechanical, photocopying, recording, or otherwise, without the prior written permission of the publisher.

British Library Cataloguing-in-Publication data
A British Library CIP record is available

ISBN 978-1-78962-083-2 cased
ISBN 978-1-78962-084-9 limp

Typeset by Carnegie Book Production, Lancaster
Printed and bound in Poland by BooksFactory.co.uk

JIMMY REID

Contents

List of Illustrations — vii
List of Abbreviations — ix
Acknowledgements — xi

Introduction — 1
1 Beginnings: 'I'm from Govan' — 15
2 Apprenticeship — 41
3 Cadre — 67
4 UCS Work-in — 95
5 Transitions — 139
6 Leaving — 159
7 Strike — 193
8 Reborn — 223

Bibliography — 243
Index — 251

Illustrations

1 Isabella with baby James (courtesy of Eileen Reid) — 22
2 James with his sisters (courtesy of Eileen Reid) — 23
3 The Reid family at Ettrick Bay, Bute (courtesy of Eileen Reid) — 23
4 Clydeside apprentices' strike (courtesy of Brian McGeachan) — 50
5 23rd Congress of the Young Communist League (courtesy of Brian McGeachan) — 50
6 Backcourt communist (courtesy of Eileen Reid) — 51
7 The Reid family in protest 1965 (courtesy of Eileen Reid) — 93
8 The Right to Work march, Glasgow 1971 (courtesy of Scran) — 115
9 Reid addressing a mass meeting of UCS workers (courtesy of Scran) — 116
10 Reid in his rectorial robes (courtesy of Scran) — 141
11 The mature Reid (courtesy of Scran) — 141
12 Addressing the Congress of the Romanian Communist Party (courtesy of Brian McGeachan) — 150
13 Robert Courtney Smith (courtesy of John Hume) — 151
14 The *Ailsa*, the last ship launched by UCS (courtesy of John Hume) — 151
15 Moscow, 1971 — 170

Abbreviations

AES	Alternative Economic Strategy
AEU	Amalgamated Engineering Union
AUEW	Amalgamated Union of Engineering Workers
BL	British Library
CEA	Clyde Employers' Association
CLP	Constituency Labour Party
CLPD	Campaign for Labour Party Democracy
CND	Campaign for Nuclear Disarmament
CPGB	Communist Party of Great Britain
CTC	Clydebank Town Council
DTI	Department of Trade and Industry
EC	Executive Committee
EEC	European Economic Community
GCA	Glasgow City Archives
GCU	Glasgow Caledonian University
GLC	Greater London Council
GUA	Glasgow University Archives
IRA	Irish Republican Army
JSSCC	Joint Shop Stewards Coordinating Committee
LLY	Labour League of Youth
MEP	Member of the European Parliament
MSP	Member of the Scottish Parliament
NATO	North Atlantic Treaty Organisation

NCB	National Coal Board
NEC	National Executive Committee
NEDS	North East Debating Society
NUM	National Union of Mineworkers
PLP	Parliamentary Labour Party
PPC	Prospective Parliamentary Candidate
RAF	Royal Air Force
SIB	Shipbuilding Industry Board
SLP	Scottish Labour Party
SNP	Scottish National Party
SPC	Scottish Precision Castings
SSP	Scottish Socialist Party
STUC	Scottish Trades Union Congress
TGWU	Transport and General Workers' Union
TUC	Trades Union Congress
UCS	Upper Clyde Shipbuilders
USA	United States of America
USSR	Union of Soviet Socialist Republics
YCL	Young Communist League

Acknowledgements

Any work of history is a collaborative effort. The historian draws on the work and research of previous generations of scholars, as well as that of contemporaries. Thus, many individuals and institutions, both materially and intellectually, have played a large part in facilitating the writing of this volume. We hope that we have conveyed an accurate and fair account of their ideas and works to past and existing members of the academy and to the wider reading public. We also extend our appreciation to the 70 or so interviewees who gave their time generously and hospitality freely. Space denies us the chance to mention them all, but a full list of names is included in the bibliography.

Of course, researchers need the support of efficient and helpful archivists. Thankfully, we have in Scotland several institutions in which these qualities are to be found in large measure, including the staff of Glasgow University Archives and Business Records Centre, the National Library of Scotland, and Glasgow Caledonian University Archives and their wonderful archivist Carole McCallum. Further afield were the British Library, London and the People's History Museum, Manchester. These archivists and institutions have helped in so many ways that it would be impossible to list them all. All we can say is thank you for making research such an enjoyable and rewarding experience. In this vein, we would like to extend our thanks to Brian McGeachan and John Hume and to Eileen Reid's family for their kind permission to reproduce photographs from their private collections.

Brian was also generous in giving us access to recordings he made with Jimmy Reid in the last years of his life. We benefited greatly from his helpful insights and feedback on any materials we sent him for comment. Without Brian's knowledge and input the book would not have had the same depth and range. Others have helped too: Dougie Napier unlocked hidden treasures at the BBC for us; David Chidlow allowed us access to the recordings he made with the Reid family and Jimmy's former comrades at UCS; likewise, Paul Ryan gave us access to his recordings of Reid's involvement in the Apprentices' Strike of 1952; Alan Campbell and John McIlroy allowed us access to material and recordings of their massive study of communists in Britain; John Foster and Willie Thompson provided insights into the culture of the Communist Party which could not be had simply by picking up a book on the subject. Gregor Gall, of the Jimmy Reid Foundation, provided practical help as well as a great deal of encouragement.

Our thanks also go to Hugh Murphy, commissioning editor for Liverpool University Press, who read the typescript with diligence and thoughtfulness. His comments and almost encyclopaedic knowledge of shipbuilding history were so helpful, especially when writing the chapter on the UCS work-in, as was his belief in and encouragement of the project. The same is true of Alison Welsby, editorial director at LUP. We would also thank James Mitchell for generously reading and commenting on the final draft of the biography, and not forgetting the three anonymous referees who provided excellent constructive feedback.

Some people gave their time freely and carried out unpaid research for us: John Boyle, who did some sterling work in nailing down the Reid family tree and for unearthing other material regarding Leo Reid's early life; Ewan Knox, who provided material on the UCS work-in; and, lastly, Sandy Ross, who carried out some early interviews. Thank you, lads; your efforts are much appreciated. Of course, we could not have hoped to have written this biography without the co-operation and support of the Reid family, particularly Jimmy's widow Joan and his eldest daughter Eileen. A massive thank you to you both.

To end on a personal note: we wish to express our thanks and gratitude to Joyce and Linda for their unflagging support, their occasional criticisms, and their love.

Introduction

Why write a biography of Jimmy Reid? What did he achieve that makes for compelling reasons to chronicle his life? He was, it is almost universally agreed, a great orator: 'the most authentic, radical, working-class political orator north or south of the border', according to the *Guardian's* Martin Kettle.[1] Alex Salmond, the former First Minister of Scotland, said of him that he was 'Scotland's great rallying figure over the last four decades and was one of the few Scottish political figures who can genuinely say that they provoked real change for the better in society'.[2] The late Tony Benn claimed he was 'a great figure of the labour movement',[3] and, according to others, he was the best MP that Scotland never had.[4] In the arena of industrial relations he achieved heroic status as the symbol of working-class defiance of market forces which manifested itself in the Upper Clyde Shipbuilders (UCS) work-in during the months of 1971 and 1972. Reid, as Gregor Gall states, secured his place in the pantheon of the left because, along with fellow Communist Party members, such as James Airlie and Sammy Barr, 'he led not only one of the most important post-war struggles but one which did not end in glorious defeat'.[5] This fact alone would provide enough reason to write a biography of him; but for the struggles of the shipyard workers, shipbuilding on the Clyde would have disappeared. As former Prime Minister Gordon Brown said, 'the fact there is still a shipbuilding industry in Scotland today is in large measure because of

---

1 *Guardian*, 12 August 2010.
2 *Scotsman*, 11 August 2010.
3 *Scotsman*, 11 August 2010.
4 *Telegraph*, 11 August 2010.
5 *Guardian*, 12 October 2010.

the inspirational campaigns that he waged'.[6] But Reid also matters as a political figure, not just for UCS, but because his political journey from communism, to Labourism, and ultimately to Nationalism (a political life in three acts) not only speaks of the complexities of left politics after 1945, but also illuminates and facilitates our understanding of 'particular institutions and forms of social change' by showing how they had been 'understood and negotiated' by a particular individual.[7]

Act One: Communism, 1945–1976

He began his political life as a young communist. Indeed, Jimmy Reid was almost the archetypal post-war communist: born in 1932 into severe and communal poverty; a father exposed to the uncertainties of dock work; a mother struggling to maintain her family in decency; a widely read autodidact; and a skilled engineer, drawn to radical politics because of its promise of a fundamental reordering of society. The only departure was the absence of family succession: neither of his parents was active in the labour movement.[8] The Communist Party was not only a vehicle for the political restlessness for change, but a way of life for Reid and others. Being a communist involved the complete immersion of one's self in a political culture whose ties extended way beyond the factory floor or the conference hall. It even provided a spouse. His wife, Joan Swankie, was a Party member, as was her mother Emily, who had taken part in the hunger marches of the National Union of Unemployed Workers in the 1930s and had stood as a Communist Party candidate in municipal elections in Clydebank. The marriage confirmed and at the same time advertised the singular importance of family and fraternity to Communist Party members: one married into a family and the family linked one in profound ways to the Party.

The founding of the Communist Party in 1920–1 had owed much to the networks of radicalised engineering shop stewards that emerged during the First World War, and engineers remained the bulwark of the Party until the mid-1970s.[9] Skilled craftsmen were not just numerically

---

6 *Guardian*, 11 August 2010.
7 B. Caine, *Biography and History* (London, 2010), 23.
8 See, for instance, recent autobiographies by Alexi Sayle, *Stalin Ate My Homework* (London, 2010), David Aaronovitch, *Party Animals: My Family and Other Communists* (London, 2016) and J. Kay, *Red Dust Road* (London, 2010).
9 R. Samuel, *The Lost World of British Communism* (London, 2006), 190–1.

important but also held national leadership offices. Until at least the second half of the 1960s, skilled working men defined the culture of grassroots communism, and were, in the main, deeply suspicious of new social movements and adhered to a politics of factory and class.[10] Reid remained wedded to the conventions of skilled, male, working-class culture. As a skilled engineer with obvious gifts of oratory, Reid rose through the ranks of the Party as, first, a full-time official with the Young Communist League (YCL), and later as Scottish Secretary of the Party. While a Party member, Reid faced no difficulties in reconciling his personal life with his politics; they were one and the same thing. However, after the UCS work-in had ended in September 1972, he began to express serious doubts regarding his Party membership and his philosophical attachment to Marxist/Leninism.

The work-in had catapulted Reid on to the national stage as the voice of the Clydeside workers; indeed, he was almost a household name through frequent appearances on radio and television. Reid was feted by the liberal media and became the poster boy of British communism. However, his appeal was to be tested in the 1974 general election when he contested as a communist the new constituency of Central Dunbartonshire. His rejection by the electorate came as a hammer-blow to Reid's political ambitions and forced him to reconsider his future as a Party member. As one activist put it, 'I think he felt party membership was an encumbrance to the use of his undoubted talents in a higher sphere of responsibility'.[11] Whether the result of a political epiphany, or from frustrated ambition, Reid took the momentous decision to leave the Communist Party in 1976. This was not a decision taken lightly, as to relinquish your Party card was much more than a political act: it was to become an apostate, to reject a way of life, to break from a circle of friends.

Act Two: Labourism, 1976–1997

Reid's break from the Communist Party paved the way for him to join the Labour Party two years later. In many ways, the policy differences between the left wing of the Labour Party and the Communist Party were

---

10 M. Waite, 'Sex 'n' Drugs 'n' Rock 'n' Roll (and Communism)', in G. Andrews, N. Fishman and K. Morgan (eds), *Opening the Books: Essays on the Social and Cultural History of British Communism* (London, 1995), 213.
11 *Guardian*, 15 August 2010.

negligible. The latter had given up being a vanguard revolutionary party since the publication of the *British Road to Socialism* in 1952; indeed, the only thing that distinguished communists from the Labour left was their continuing uncritical support for the Soviet Union, and even that could not be guaranteed after the invasions of Hungary in 1956 and Czechoslovakia in 1968. As Reid told the *Guardian*: 'People had the party wrong when they said it was a menace to capitalism'; it was precisely because it wasn't that he made the break.[12] However, Reid was never able to escape from his political past in the same way that other former communists, such as one-time Labour Chancellor Denis Healy had done. Selected as Labour candidate for Dundee East in 1979, he was soundly defeated by the Scottish National Party (SNP) candidate in what for the Nationalists was a disastrous general election. From there he began a lucrative career as a journalist and broadcaster, but controversy was never far away. Embracing Labourism, he became the scourge of the sectarian left even to the point of losing what comradely feeling was left for him by criticising in the right-wing press the leadership of the miners' strike in 1984.

Act Three: Nationalism, 1997–2010

All through the 1980s and 1990s Reid excoriated the Tory governments led by Margaret Thatcher for rewarding the rich and punishing the poor. The desire to end poverty, born of the memory of losing his three baby sisters to it, is the leitmotif of Reid's political history; it is what brought him into politics and what sustained him politically during his life. Even while writing for the right-wing *Sun* newspaper, Reid used his weekly column to attack the free-market philosophy behind Thatcherism. Thus, it came as a political bolt from the blue to him when the Labour Party under the leadership of Tony Blair began to espouse similar views on the market economy to that of the Tories. Blair and his Chancellor Gordon Brown both shared a belief that they had uncovered a solution to the boom-and-bust cycle of capitalism. Reid turned his wrath on them with ferocious denouncements of their social and economic policies. He also criticised them for drowning dissent within the Party – jobs were for the boys and girls but only if they toed the New Labour line.

It became apparent to Reid as it had done to previous radical voices in the Labour Party, such as the Red Clydesiders John Wheatley and

---

12 *Guardian*, 9 October 1976.

James Maxton, that it was beyond reform. He resigned his membership in 1998 and joined the Scottish National Party (SNP) seven years later. He had always had a belief in some form of home rule for Scotland, but had shied away from support for outright independence, calling it 'infantile' during the 1979 general election.[13] However, the market-orientated policies of the Blair administration pushed him further into the hands of the Nationalists, and, as with many, the second Iraq war was the final straw, straining Party commitment beyond the level of endurance.

Thus, the biography of Jimmy Reid is in many ways a collective biography of the British left since 1945 in as much as it examines the trajectory of his political journey against the background of the wider political culture, examining in turn the ideological shifts and the debates that laid the basis for such movements.

Sources

A wide variety of sources, both primary and secondary, have been used to chronicle the life of Jimmy Reid, although obviously some are of more importance and more plentiful than others. Several different methods were also used to collect and prepare the materials on which to reconstruct his life. Oral history was one of the most important methods used in building a narrative of events and the subject's participation in them, and how these events were internalised and understood by the active and the onlookers. We bear in mind the novelist Gabriel García Márquez's observation in his highly unreliable memoir – *Living to Tell the Tale* (2002) – that it is not only important that an event is remembered, but equally significant is *how* it is remembered. To that end, both family and friends were interviewed over a period of years as were former colleagues and comrades. Their stories, anecdotes and observations were crucial in constructing the foregoing narrative, but while oral testimony may supply insights not found in printed texts and offer different ways of interpreting events and responses to them it cannot by itself provide a definitive analysis of a subject's actions, as on its own it has no way of disentangling the often conflicting memories of events; though oral historians view remembrance conflict as one of the strengths of oral history. Tony Green, folklorist, argued at one of the first British oral history conferences for the subjectivity of memory and the ways that 'individuals and groups

13 *Dundee Courier*, 17 April 1979.

experience the same event in totally different ways'.[14] While conflicting interpretations may lay the basis for further research for historians into the role of memory in history, it is agreed and appreciated that memories can be distorted through the prism of time. Therefore, solely relying on this method of reconstructing the past is questionable as the accuracy of memory can be a highly problematic area for the historian. As people become distanced from the event or events memories become hazier and sometimes confused in regard to dates and participants: conversations are partially remembered, who did what becomes confused, and the narrative is reconstructed from the interviewee's point of view.

These caveats also apply to meaning which is capable of generating distortions arising from changing values and norms. They act to alter perceptions and the magnitude of distortion increases in proportion to the distance from the subject to the event.[15] Thus, if we take Reid's decision to leave the Communist Party in 1976: at the time, it generated understanding and hostility in equal measure among his erstwhile comrades. But, if we had interviewed the same people who had been witnesses to those events 30 years later, and in the full knowledge of the collapse of communism, the responses would probably have been very different, and less partisan in relation to a changed political environment. So, while recognising the vital role oral testimony performs in constructing the life of an individual, other sources have to be considered if we are to arrive at a more inclusive and objective study of the subject.

For historians, the most important historical artefact is the document. But while oral history proves problematic in terms of objectivity the historical document is no less value-free. In the past, the production of documents was in the hands of an educated elite. They decided on the survival or destruction of the historical record. Their exclusionary methods are best seen in political histories. They were generally written to glorify or justify some individual ruler or state. Indeed, political elites had an especial interest in promoting a certain kind of history: one that legitimised their position in the body politic and at the same time emphasised their part in the achievements and continuity of the constitution. This still remains the case. Attempts to persuade MI5 to release documents relating to the UCS work-in under Freedom of Information legislation have gone unanswered, in spite of the fact that the events occurred over 40 years ago. Thus, not

---

14 T. Green, 'The Leicester Conference on Oral History: Four Impressions', *Oral History*, 1 (1971), 10.
15 P. Thompson, *The Voice of the Past: Oral History* (Oxford, 1978), 129.

only can documents be open to wildly different interpretations, denying full access to them can create unintended distortions on the part of the biographer by leading the historian down a prescribed path of analysis through a structured conspiracy of silence. That silence can also extend to former comrades uncomfortable or unwilling to discuss the past and their relationship with the subject. Arthur Scargill, who was subjected to vilification by Reid in the press for his leadership during the miners' strike of 1984, refused to be interviewed for this book, such were the deep emotional scars that remain with him to this day unhealed.

Even at the micro level, the preselection of material bequeathed by the deceased to future generations may result in a narrative of that life being fully controlled beyond the grave. In spite of our adherence to objectivity, biographers can find themselves colluding with the dead or acting as their agents in conveying a set of images of them that they have actively influenced and one which they may even have approved of. In the case of Jimmy Reid, the possibility of controlling the narrative through the document is proportional to his organisational abilities, which were to say the least limited. His filing system constituted his brain and his top pocket; indeed, many of his most important speeches, especially during the UCS work-in, were spontaneous rather than well-thought-out responses to external events. There is no significant cache of letters or diaries with which to recreate his intimate thoughts, record his doubts, detail his turmoil and disappointments, or alternatively his moments of joy and happiness. However, there does exist an autobiography of sorts in published form,[16] as well as an unpublished one. But it has to be remembered that although an autobiography may be important in providing biographical detail of the subject it remains a form of self-justification for one's past deeds and decisions. This can be offset to an extent if the writer adopts a confessional mode in the attempt to seek self-knowledge, but Reid eschews this approach in favour of a social and political chronicle rather than a psychoanalytical examination of his past behaviour. Thus, it is doubtful if his autobiography can speak for the experience of humanity at a particular period, far less provide an honest and truthful chronicle of his life, as there exists too many elisions of the personal kind in his short account.

While the inner Reid may be an elusive quarry, we are on much firmer ground with Reid the political animal. In the arena of politics there is a wide and voluminous array of published sources in the form of Communist Party documents detailing his membership, his activities,

---

16 J. Reid, *Reflections of a Clyde-Built Man* (London, 1976).

his speeches and contributions at annual conferences as well as on the NEC. There is some archival material relating to Reid deposited with the University of Glasgow Archives and Business Records Centre, Thurso Street, Glasgow, but the content is largely random and heavily skewed towards his media activities. It consists mainly of drafts of television scripts: there are no diaries or personal or political letters or papers. However, Thurso Street offers much more in relation to the UCS work-in, particularly the recordings and transcripts of the interviews with the leading stewards carried out by Charles Woolfson as part of his doctoral thesis.[17] There are also transcripts of taped meetings of the shop stewards' committee deposited by Jimmy Cloughley, which are essential reading, as is the diary of the liquidator, Robert Courtney Smith. These can all be found in the DC65 series in the Records Centre. For understanding the political culture of the Communist Party in Scotland, the Archives and Special Collections held at Glasgow Caledonian University have a host of material covering such things as membership rolls, Party reports, election analyses, and more besides. For a wider perspective, Manchester Museums have an archive devoted to the CPGB which consists of the minutes, memoranda and correspondence of the Central Executive Committee, 1943–91, the Political Committee 1946–91 and the Economic Committee 1946–87. There are also personal papers of leading activists, such as John Gollan. All of this can be consulted online. The Marx Memorial Library and the Workers' School in Clerkenwell, London also carries the papers of some leading activists as well as complete runs of the *Daily Worker* and *Morning Star*. There is also a recently published biography of Reid by the former Justice Secretary (2007–14) in the devolved Scottish parliament, Kenny MacAskill. But while engagingly written, the style is journalistic rather than scholarly. Under-researched, the volume fails to capture the complexities of Reid's at times tortuous political life, or, indeed, provide any insights into the culture of British communism. For a historian, the absence of footnotes, or a fully annotated bibliography to compensate for this deficiency, necessitates inevitable caution as to any observations made, or conclusions reached, by the author.

Newspapers are also an invaluable source for examining Reid's views on a huge variety of subjects, from popular culture to the 1984 miners' strike to the royal family. As a weekly columnist at various times for the *Glasgow Herald*, the *Daily Mirror*, the *Daily Record*, the *Sun* and

---

17 C. Woolfson, 'Working Class Culture: The Work-in at Upper Clyde Shipbuilders' (unpublished PhD thesis, University of Glasgow, 1982).

the *Scotsman* we can trace the evolution of his political thinking from communism to labourism to nationalism in his writings.

Content

Chapter 1 discusses the appalling socio-economic circumstances of poverty and squalor into which Reid was born in 1930s Glasgow and how this impacted on his attitude to towards capitalist society. As part of this we look at the problems faced by his father in providing for his family and his mother's ability in a hand-to-mouth culture to use the meagre resources in such a way as to ensure food and clothing for her children. We stress the fact that music and literature were embedded in the family. Reid himself became the personification of the autodidact. We emphasise that it was the library rather than the classroom which moulded and shaped him culturally and politically. After engaging with a number of youth organisations, Reid joined the YCL at the age of 15, the year he began his working life in a stockbroker's office before leaving to become an apprentice engineer.

Chapter 2 examines the making of a communist activist, focusing on the 1952 apprentices' strike in Britain: an event that accelerated Reid's rise within the CPGB. Drawing on autobiographical material of various activists, we emphasise the fact that being a communist involved the complete immersion of one's self in a political culture whose ties extended way beyond the factory floor or the conference hall into wider society. Mutual assistance, socialising and politics were fused in Party lives. All of this in a small, embattled political party produced an intimacy that stretched across generations. This helps to explain why leaving the Party, as he did in 1976, was such a 'heart-wrenching' moment for him.

Chapter 3 examines Reid's elevation in the Party. When he finished his national service, Reid became a full-time officer of the YCL, which entailed a move from Govan to London. From the provincial working-class culture of Govan he found himself rubbing shoulders with the metropolitan elite, which included Michael Foot, Claude Cockburn, James Cameron and others. The first test of his commitment to the Party came with the Hungarian Uprising of 1956. The event provoked high-profile resignations of some leading Marxist historians, such as E.P. Thompson and Christopher Hill, but was not enough to shake Reid's belief in the Party and its leadership; indeed, it strengthened it. The chapter also deals with Reid's domestic life in London, as he married in 1958 and became a father soon after. A full-time official's salary was too meagre to raise a family forcing Reid to resign his post and return to Glasgow.

Chapter 4 deals with the UCS work-in: an event to which Jimmy Reid owes his fame and his place in the pantheon of Scottish radicalism. Although he was not the only leader of the workforce, it was his powers of communication and leadership which became the symbol of the coalition of resistance that developed on the Clyde in response to the Tory government's attempt to close the down the yards and throw the men on the industrial scrapheap. The decision by the leadership to stage a work-in rather than go on strike or stage a sit-in caught the imagination of constituencies of people way beyond the geographical parameters of the upper reaches of the River Clyde. The chapter challenges the received triumphal narrative in several ways: first, by stressing the role of the forgotten liquidator, Robert Courtney Smith, in keeping the yards open and the men working, and, secondly, by examining the legacy of the work-in, arguing that although it undoubtedly constituted a victory of sorts for the UCS workers the road ahead proved a rocky one. The analysis differs from previously published material on the event in as much as it is the only study to utilise the transcripts of meetings and interviews with the UCS shop stewards' committee and the only one to establish the chain of relationships between the CPGB leadership, the local cadres and the work-in.

Chapter 5 focuses mainly on two events: the rectorial campaign of 1971 and the general election of 1974. Because of his leadership of the UCS work-in, Reid became the poster boy of the CPGB, the human face of British communism. He was probably the only communist that most people in Britain had ever heard of. The media could not get enough of him and he appeared on talk shows such as *Parkinson*. Wider recognition came with his installation as Rector of Glasgow University in late 1971. As part of the process the Rector gave an Address. Reid chose the subject of alienation and his speech not only electrified the audience but reverberated around the world. But while at his zenith in terms of popularity doubts were beginning to surface regarding membership of the CPGB. Undoubtedly, the Soviet invasion of Czechoslovakia in 1968 played a part, but a much more important event we argue was the general election of 1974. Reid stood as candidate for Central Dunbartonshire, which had at its heart Clydebank – the centre of shipbuilding in Scotland. Although considered a shoe-in by the press, Reid was defeated by the Labour candidate in the first and the second elections of 1974. He was the victim of a largely sectarian campaign run by the Labour party, but it was clear that he would never be elected as a communist. We now are reaching the moment of the unmaking of a communist.

Chapter 6 covers the years 1975 to 1976, which proved so momentous for Jimmy Reid. It was during this brief period that he re-evaluated where he stood politically. He had experienced at first hand the Party's impotency in the political arena, he was now to experience it in the industrial field too. This chapter explores his vain attempts to be elected as a full-time national official of the AEU defeated by the right wing of the union's leadership. It also exposed the organisational deficiencies of Reid; a man capable of motivating and inspiring workers but unable to build a mass power base within the political or industrial arenas. It then discusses the 'heart-wrenching' moment, critically examining Reid's narrative concerning the road to leaving the Party as well as the reception to his decision both within the media and among the membership. We contend that international events such as the Prague invasion were secondary influences. Rather, we argue it was events nearer to home that were more influential. Thus, we discuss how the rejection of the concept of the revolutionary party by the CPGB in favour of broad-based parliamentary alliances narrowed the ideological chasm between communists and the Labour left. Indeed, the only issue dividing them was the continued support by the former for the Soviet Union; something that Reid had begun to reject. The other factor was his dissatisfaction with Party democracy. Reid left in 1976 and joined the Labour Party two years later. Fast-tracked by the left, he stood as Labour candidate in 1979 in Dundee where he suffered the same fate as in 1974. We examine the reasons why he was never able to shake off his political past, as former communists like Denis Healy and John Reid had done, and how this undermined his election campaign. The campaign is also important as it exposes the opposition to Reid within the Scottish Labour Party.

Chapter 7 is set against the background of the election of the Thatcher government in 1979, an event which triggered a series of heroic and sometimes futile struggles by the labour movement over industrial relations reform, the Poll Tax, poverty and unemployment, symbolised in the miners' strike of 1984. From discussing his unusual pathway through journalism to television we examine Reid's ideological shift away from Marxism towards a social democratic economic model. Reid was looking for a third way between communism and capitalism: one which would combine the efficiencies of the market with social justice and rights for individuals. His new philosophical outlook was tested to the full during the miners' strike of 1984. This was the road to Damascus for Reid. The struggle between the miners and the NCB and government over jobs that ensued in many ways mirrored the UCS demand for the 'Right to Work', and as such it might have been expected that Reid would have been in the forefront of the campaign, shoulder to shoulder with the miners and their leaders. The issues of trade union democracy are discussed, and its relationship to the leadership of the National Union of Mineworkers (NUM) under Arthur Scargill. We argue that Reid misunderstood the strike, its origins and its prosecution, by turning it into a psychodrama between Scargill and Thatcher and ignoring the roles of history, of gender, and of organisation within mining communities. His opposition gained him the opprobrium of many on the left who felt his actions comforted the strike's opponents and divided its supporters.

Chapter 8 is set against the background of Labour's political metamorphosis from a left-wing party to a centre-right one, repudiating in the process past cherished principles and policies. Nationalisation was out, and the free, or social, market, as Tony Blair would have it, was in. The intention was to allow a strongly deregulated market to flourish using the extra wealth it generated to fund improvements in public services: it became known as 'New Labour'. The question is how far would Reid, given his political record during the 1980s, coalesce with Blair's new vision for Labour's future? The short answer was not far. Reid's view was this was Thatcherism dressed up in new clothes. He became a critic of New Labour mainly on two counts: first, on the level of control freakery in the party, and second, of its over-friendly relationship with big business. His criticism led to disenchantment, brought to a head by the 2004 Iraq war. From there he shifted towards a radical form of nationalism and joined the SNP in 2005. We discuss the rise of the nationalist vote in Scotland and place Reid in this context, arguing it was not such a remarkable step for him to take as some would have it. Reid could argue that he had been a consistent supporter of self-government for the Scottish people throughout his active political life. In an article in the *Morning Star* as far back as February 1968, he was calling for a political initiative to unite the 'great mass of the Scottish people around the demand for a Scottish parliament'. However, in the past he did not support the idea of separation, but now he saw it as the only way forward.

However, by 2005, Reid was in his seventies and although still active he was a spent political force estranged in Rothesay, Isle of Bute. He died in 2010. The chapter concludes with an examination of his legacy. We argue that Reid was undoubtedly one of the great figures of the British left – at one time the most well-known communist in the world with the exception maybe of Fidel Castro – but he was in many ways a maverick, an individual, who found the discipline of party and movement difficult. For someone like him, being a communist and complying with the high standards of discipline and commitment demanded by the party must have been hard, and leaving was a form of liberation. In his life, he inspired many and repulsed others in equal measure; he was never less than controversial. Two images sum up the man: the first was his father on Old Year's Day holding Reid's dead youngest sister in his arms while crowds of revellers in the street below sang 'Auld Lang Syne'; the second was standing in the rain sharing an umbrella with the UCS liquidator Robert Courtney Smith outside James Airlie's (his one-time close comrade) funeral. Reid never stopped battling against poverty and inequality; the memories of his childhood were always present guiding him in this struggle. Finally, his journey from the left to the centre of British politics and from there to a radical nationalism only served to emphasise that he was an individual, an outsider, a man of restless intellect, an idealist, who could never quite come to terms with the compromises, discipline and organisation needed to succeed in the cutthroat world of politics.

1

Beginnings: 'I'm from Govan'

Apparently, when asked where he was from, Jimmy Reid wouldn't say Scotland, or Britain, or even Glasgow, he would reply spontaneously, without thinking: 'I'm from Govan: I'm a Govan man'.[1] This conscious affirmation of local identity begs the question: what was or is a Govan man? How are we to define the character of such a man? The simple answer is that a Govan man was born in adversity and was unmistakeably shaped by it. He had to face the seemingly never-ending problems of poverty, unemployment, squalor and ill health, and still manage to put food on the table for his family. If he was anything, he was a provider, a family man whose status in the community he lived and worked in was judged by his performance in the crucial area of provision. That provision could also extend to neighbours and friends: people stood by each other in times of hardship in a community largely built on scarcity. As Reid put it:

> I had tremendous warmth for the people around. I mean, if you saw a woman with a pot going into another house you knew there was somebody ill in that house and they were sharing the soup they'd made … I'm not trying to glamorise it, it was diabolical. But the one saving factor was a kind of solidarity of the poor, even in terms of anybody's ill they all go across … but that's … that is not fanciful … It was a community. It was a community in poverty but it was a community.[2]

Reid had personal experience of the community in action when he managed at the age of four to get lost trying to find his way to the docks to 'see if I could get some work to help … to try and get four hours, four hours' work,

---

1   Barry and Linda Atherton, interview with Knox (2015).
2   Jimmy Reid, interview with Paul Ryan (2006).

to bring the money home to my mother. I was only tiny at the time. Lost for hours, the place was in uproar. Not just my mother, all the people, the neighbours, were hunting ... Eventually the policeman brought me home'.[3]

Community feeling also derived from less-materialistic factors. Govan men and women, many of whose origins lay in the Scottish Highlands, had a strong sense of distinctiveness and independence from greater Glasgow. The burgh, with a population of 91,000, was the fifth largest in Scotland in the early twentieth century. It was incorporated against fierce opposition from Govanites into Glasgow in 1912; indeed, such was the level of hostility in the burgh to incorporation, a large number of municipal employees left their positions rather than serve Glasgow.[4] However, while strongly family orientated, it was a culture which was overwhelmingly patriarchal: a man's world. The hard, sometimes back-breaking, graft of the shipyard and the long hours spent there impacted on the male psyche in ways that were not always positive. Drunkenness and wife-beating were common at weekends in Govan as they were in other industrial enclaves and small mining villages throughout the west of Scotland.[5] But gender was not the only divisive issue; there was also the question of sectarian hatred between Catholics and Protestants to contend with.

However, adversity had gradations; some places were worse than others. The Gorbals district of Glasgow, where Reid's parents were married in 1921, was even more downtrodden and ghastly than Govan. Economically, it was 'a bustling district of small workshops and factories'; socially, it had 'a great many pawnshops and pubs and little shops ... public baths and a wash-house, many churches and several synagogues. The streets were slippery with refuse and often with drunken vomit. It was a place of grime and poverty'.[6] Throughout the 1930s, the Gorbals was often referred to in the national press as the most dangerous place in Britain: 'Hell's Hundred Acres' or 'Little Chicago on the Clyde'.[7] Razor gangs, most notably the Protestant Bridgeton Billy Boys and the Roman Catholic Norman Conks (Conquerors) made famous in the novel *No Mean City* (1935), and casual street violence were rife. Reid always considered the portrayal of the Gorbals as somewhat exaggerated, saying:

---

3   Jimmy Reid, interview with Ryan.
4   E. King, 'Foreword', in G. Rountree, *A Govan Childhood: The 1930s* (Edinburgh, 1993), iii.
5   P. McGeown, *Heat the Furnace Seven More Times* (Motherwell, 1967), 41.
6   R. Glasser, *Growing Up in the Gorbals* (Thirsk, 2001), 18–19.
7   R. Kenna, *Heart of the Gorbals* (Ayr, 2004), 19.

> Well, the Gorbals was a rough area at one stage. But it was grossly exaggerated, because of that book, *No Mean City* that was written in the 1930s. There were gangs, of course, but I used to play in a brass band in the Gorbals … We used to walk home at night, from the Gorbals back home to Govan, and there was never any trouble. I think Glasgow got a bad reputation, but, it was gangs, fighting gangs. If you weren't in the gangs, then no one touched you. I used to walk up Neptune Street, in Govan, which was a helluva street. They called it 'The Irish Channel'. I'd be walking to school, and they'd be saying, How's it goin' Jimmy, or James?[8]

Indeed, Glasgow was not Chicago. Gangland slayings in the 1920s in the latter city numbered over 500, while Glasgow's gangsters killed hardly anyone. Much of their activities were focused on sectarian fighting, petty thieving and extortion from local publicans and shopkeepers.[9]

The fatalities from intercommunal conflict may have been slight, but the Gorbals, with its complex mix of immigrant communities, could still be a dangerous place. One gave way to the local 'hard men' (read psychopaths), crossed the street rather than pass them by, avoided eye-to-eye contact – 'the stare' – and the dreaded question, 'Are you lookin' at me?' Reid said of one such hard man:

> A guy in Neptune Street called Cut-the-Lugs Riley. Mick Riley, was his name, but they called him Cut-The-Lugs because he was a razor slasher. He wasn't really a gangster, but, like many young men around that time, he tried to be. He would say to some of the local bookies that he'd give them protection, but bookies had their own men, and Riley was a bit of a bampot. He was mad. He fell out with some bloke and began searching for him all over Govan with a bayonet.[10]

One thing that was not exaggerated was the degree of poverty. Reid himself in an interview with the journalist Kenneth Roy in 2003 said that the 'Gorbals was riddled with slums and disease and Glasgow had the highest infant mortality rate in the western world'[11] – a view shared by contemporaries. The English folk singer and journalist A.L. Lloyd, visiting

---

8   Jimmy Reid, interview with Brian McGeachan (2009).
9   See A. Davies, *City of Gangs* (London, 2014).
10 Jimmy Reid, interview with McGeaghan.
11 Jimmy Reid, interview with Kenneth Roy (2003).

Glasgow in the late 1940s, remarked that 'Nearly 40,000 people lived in the Gorbals often six or eight to a room, often thirty to a lavatory, and forty to a tap'.[12] Prior to this, a Gorbals Ward Committee in a report on a tenement in Commercial Road told of the appalling conditions: 'There were no lights on the landings, and you had to grope your way to the doors in darkness. There was one lavatory on the landing to serve fifteen adults and twenty-two children'.[13] Ralph Glasser, in his highly evocative memoir *Growing Up in the Gorbals* (1986), further highlighted the appalling nature of tenement life, especially for children:

> On the common staircases, six or eight flats shared two lavatories, each tucked in a tiny intermediate landing between floors. You had to hold its decrepit door shut with your foot or wedge it with a lump of wood. And when the flush system did not work or the soil pipe was blocked, which was often, the floor was soon awash and the overflow spread freely down the staircase. Going to the lavatory we had to remember to carry a supply of newspaper, not only for use as toilet paper but also to clean the soles of our boots of excrement and urine before going back into the flat.[14]

As late as 1951, two-thirds of the population of the Gorbals were still living in one- or two-roomed houses, and out of 10,000 households only 5 per cent had exclusive use of a bath.[15]

There was also the problem of unemployment to contend with. 'Out of a population of roughly 40,000, the Gorbals Ward had in 1935 no fewer than 13,220 people dependent on public assistance'.[16] As Reid said: 'I was a down and out at birth. My brother was a down and out. So were my sisters. Our parents were definitely down and outs. Our neighbours too. So far as we knew the whole of Scotland was down and out'.[17] These were the circumstances in which Reid's father Leo, the son of an Irish immigrant from County Tyrone and an unskilled labourer, had to put food on the table. Leo's father, Michael Reid, was a tram car conductor, while his mother, Mary or Maria née Carroll, at the time of marriage in

---

12 A.L. Lloyd, *Picture Post*, 31 January 1948.
13 Kenna, *Gorbals*, 77.
14 Glasser, *Gorbals*, 9.
15 R. Baird, 'Housing', in J. Cunnison and J.B.S. Gilfillan (eds), *The Third Statistical Account of Scotland: Glasgow* (Glasgow, 1958), 463.
16 Kenna, *Gorbals*, 81.
17 Jimmy Reid, interview with Roy.

1892, was a sewing machinist. Leo was only three when his father died prematurely in 1903 after three days in a coma, aged thirty-five, an event which pushed his widow and five children into penury. Within two years of Michael's death the family were forced to apply for poor relief from the Parish of Govan. Applications for Michael, John, Margaret, Anastacia and Leo were lodged on 16 February 1905, but not for the eldest child, Maria, who presumably was in work of some kind. As Michael John was the oldest of the children at this time, most of the revealing information about the state of the family unit was contained in his record. It was noted that the Reid family were no strangers to poor relief as 'Mary Carroll or Reid was on the Roll of the Parish from 26 October 1893 until 28 October 1904 when she was offered Poorhouse for observation'. Furthermore, it was stated that: 'when sent to the Poorhouse she had been drinking'. Clearly, the mother was unable to cope and that caused a breakdown in family cohesion. This is further emphasised by the Inspector's observations: 'These children are utterly destitute and without any means of sustenance the mother desires them back to Industrial school' – an in-house training school or reformatory to keep poor children away from crime and at the same time providing them with skills to earn a livelihood.[18]

By seeking poor relief the family was liable to be broken up and thus Leo and his older brother and sisters were discharged from the Govan Poorhouse in August 1905 and boarded out with Mrs Mary Higgins of 31 Montgomery Lane, Ardrossan, Ayrshire. He took with him three shilling a week from the Parish of Govan to support his needs. There is no record thus far of the whereabouts of Leo's mother after 1905, but his marriage certificate of March 1921 records her as deceased. However, Leo's stay with Mrs Higgins proved only temporary and in January 1906 he was transferred to Mrs Emily Gordon of 7 Wellpark Road, Salcoats, Ayrshire, where he remained until his fifteenth birthday. There is a gap in Leo's biography between 1914 and 1921. But from a later poor relief application the record reveals that he claimed to have been in the army fighting for king and country from July 1915 until January 1919. If correct, this partially fills the missing four-year gap in Leo's history; however, a search of various military sources thus far indicates the absence of any service record for him.

We pick up Leo's life once more in August 1921 when he applied again for assistance to the Parish of Govan; this time he had a wife and

---

18   Poor Relief, Govan, Glasgow City Archives, Mitchell Library, D-HEW17/546. Nos. 72561, 72562, 72563, 72564.

a child on the way. Just as in the 1905 application, the 1921 poor relief application contains a little socio-economic information, including details relating to his employment status, his wife's condition, their health, previous work activity and the scale of unemployment relief awarded to him (15*s*. a week). Leo had no choice but to resort to claim poor relief as he had no alternative source of income, having 'stopped work'.[19] Prior to redundancy, he was employed as a labourer in Yarrow's Scotstoun shipyard, but as the restocking boom of the immediate post-war years came to an abrupt end, and unemployment began to rise alarmingly, he found himself, like thousands of others, out of work. Shipbuilding was particularly hard hit as unemployment ran at an average rate of 29 per cent between 1920 and 1929 before rocketing to 42 per cent in the 1930s.[20]

As the depression began to bite more deeply, even skilled workers were thrown on to poor relief. Things were more difficult for Leo as he 'had no trade and had to take whatever jobs he could pick up – at the docks or the pits usually'.[21] However, at times, economic activity could border on the criminal. People living on the margins of society, the surplus population, the 'outcast' groups, were forced through cyclical and casual unemployment to survive in what might be called the 'illegal economies of the cities'.[22] Leo was no stranger to the more questionable techniques of survival. As such, he developed a close connection with the illegal street bookmakers that were ubiquitous in working-class areas like the Gorbals in the 1920s and 1930s: 'My father used to take me to the horses when I was a kid. He worked in industry, but he was also a tick-tack man (conveyed betting odds by signs). And he used to run a bus [to the races] from Govan for all the local bookies'.[23]

If his father had to shoulder the burden of provision, then his mother Isabella had to use all her imagination and ingenuity to stretch the meagreness of what was on offer to feed and clothe a family of seven children. But even her capacity in this area was at times beyond

---

19 Assistant Inspector's Report, Parish of Govan Combination, 31 August 1921, Glasgow City Archives, Mitchell Library.
20 J. McGoldrick, 'Crisis and the Division of Labour: Clydeside Shipbuilding in the Inter-War Period', in T. Dickson (ed.), *Capital and Class in Scotland* (Edinburgh, 1982), 164–5.
21 *Glasgow Herald*, 26 June 1977.
22 L. Hunter, 'The Scottish Labour Market', in R. Saville (ed), *The Economic Development of Modern Scotland* (Edinburgh, 1985), 483–4.
23 Jimmy Reid, interview with McGeachan.

resourcefulness. The under-nourishment, the overcrowding and squalid living conditions took their deathly toll. In the mid-1930s, the Gorbals Ward had an infant mortality rate of 109 per 1,000 births.[24] Hardly a family was untouched by the tragedy of the premature death of a child. Of Reid's siblings, three died in infancy, all of them girls. The death of one of them was particularly poignant, as he described it:

> Slowly forwards and backwards on her stool by the fireplace, softly moaning. another of my sisters died in the dawn of the New Year. *Auld Lang Syne* rang out from the surrounding slums as people tried to drown out the miseries of the old year in cheap booze and mawkish sentiments. While this was going on my father had his dying daughter cradled in his arms beseeching God to save her life.[25]

To Reid, his sisters 'had been murdered – that whatever it said in the death certificate, they should have put down "Social conditions" as the cause. Or, in my opinion, capitalism'.[26] He held this view all his life and in a later television programme he recalled as a child seeing his 'mother … weep for her dead children'. As a result, he 'came to hate the social system that killed innocents and made mothers weep'.[27] It was the devastating impact of poverty and the desire to eradicate it that shaped his politics from an early age. As he put it: 'I couldn't understand myself, let alone anyone else doing so, without reference to those early years. My values. My politics. My philosophy. What I'm about, were shaped in those years. But I don't live in the past. I've never lived in the past. My early experience of life made me a dedicated advocate of change'.[28] Even in his last years he never ceased to be emotional when the bells rang out to announce the arrival of the new year.[29]

However, with the death of his sister Sally, Reid, who was born on 9 July 1932, became the youngest sibling of four children; the others were John, Isa and Betty (Figures 1–3). To his family he was always James never Jimmy. His mother became 'obsessed with keeping [him] … alive', an obsession that was in danger of proving transitory when at eight years

---

24 Kenna, *Gorbals*, 81.
25 J. Reid, unpublished autobiography (2006), Glasgow University Archives.
26 Jimmy Reid, interview with Roy.
27 *Moscow Gold*, 1992, Glasgow University Archives, ACCN37/17/16/5.
28 Reid, unpublished autobiography (unpag.).
29 Joan Reid, interview with David Chidlow (2012).

1   Isabella with baby James (courtesy of Eileen Reid)

Beginnings: 'I'm from Govan'   23

2 James with his sisters
(courtesy of Eileen Reid)

3 The Reid family
at Ettrick Bay, Bute
(courtesy of Eileen Reid)

of age he was diagnosed with the highly contagious and potentially lethal diphtheria bacterium. Reid was carried down the stairs of the tenement swaddled in a blanket and 'rushed into a fever hospital'. His thoughts, however, were for his mother, who, in spite of his tender years, he recognised was 'hurting more than me'. Reid resolved 'there and then to get better and never be ill while she lived',[30] a vow that he was fortunately able to keep up to her death in 1984.

It was understandable that men and women hardwired into misery and pain would from weekend to weekend seek some kind of escape in alcohol: engaged in as much as to dull the memories of such losses as to find a momentary but illusory happiness. However, drink was not only a means of escaping into a false and very temporary Shangri-La, it was also an important ingredient in defining masculinity in working-class communities. The world of the public house, the sawdust floors and spittoons, 'half an' halfs', remained closed to women in this period, which only serves to reinforce the male-bounded nature of public drinking and the patriarchism it reflected. By 1900, the most common cause of crime in Scotland was drunkenness and the ensuing breach of the peace, while crimes against property only accounted for 7.5 per cent of the total. Indeed, 58 per cent of the prison population in Scotland in 1904 were there for drunkenness and/or breach of the peace.[31] It was still just over 40 per cent in 1930, in spite of mass unemployment and widespread poverty.[32] Reid's father was no different from other working-class men in Glasgow. As his son said, 'He drank too much. He was a gambler'. Leo was perhaps a rogue, but clearly a lovable one.

Gambling was something that Reid inherited from his father. As he said: 'That's where I got my interest in horse racing, from my old man'.[33] And it rubbed off in later life: 'I go to the horse racing when I can, and I have a punt when I can. But not excessively'. Reid had a rather generous view of street bookmakers, who, in his opinion, were providing 'a social service' rather than what they were actually doing: sucking the life-blood out of poor working-class communities.[34] The impact on his own family was not always happy. A number of times Reid would find

---

30 Reid, unpublished autobiography (unpag.).
31 A.B. McHardy, 'The Economics of Crime', *Juridical Review*, 14 (1902), 48.
32 Criminal Statistics (1930), United Kingdom Parliamentary Papers, Cmd 3963, 17.
33 Reid, *Reflections*, 3–4.
34 Jimmy Reid, interview with McGeachan.

his mother in tears and hungry: emotions brought on by the economic uncertainties of living with a gambling man. Leo sometimes won but he also lost: a gambler who would occasionally place his entire wage on a horse. The losses were borne by his family; the luck was celebrated with family and friends. One Christmas Eve, the Reid family sat waiting on Leo's return with something left of his wages or, even less likely, some winnings. His arrival home was heralded by cheers: he had arrived home and with chickens, fruits and sweets for the other nine families in his Kintra Street tenement out of his winnings.[35] A decade or so later, the 15-year-old Reid won £60 (around £2,500 at today's value) at the dog track: riches to be savoured and shared. His friends were treated to double nougat bars before his mother took charge of what was left of Reid's small fortune.[36]

Isabella was the respectable face of squalid living conditions. One of a family of six, her father, Hamish McLean, was from Mull, and had migrated to Glasgow to work in the docks. Although Hamish was a staunch Presbyterian, he married a Highland Catholic girl, Elizabeth Motherwell, in January 1894. On her deathbed in December 1907, aged only 37, she asked him 'to bring up the ... children in the Catholic faith ... and he did just that'.[37] At the time of her marriage to Leo, in March 1921, Isabella was a tramcar conductor apparently so popular with the passengers that they sang a song about her: 'Fares Please, Fares Please ... She's Bella McLean From Petty Coat Lane, The Caur Conductress ...'.[38]

Unlike the McLean family, most of the Catholics living in Scotland were of Irish extraction. Having fled the great famine of the mid-1840s, they made their way over the Irish Sea to Glasgow. Theirs was a shameful history of discrimination and hostility from the host, largely Presbyterian, population. Poorly educated, underfed and underpaid, the Catholic Irish occupied the lowest rungs on the employment ladder in the nineteenth century. Any hope that the shared experience of the First World War might marginalise these religious hatreds and tensions was lost as competition for work in Scotland intensified after the restocking economic boom ended in 1920 and provided fertile soil for the resurfacing of sectarianism in its most virulent form. Churchmen

---

35 Eileen Reid, interview with McKinlay (2016).
36 Joan Reid, interview with McKinlay (2013).
37 Jimmy Reid, interview with Roy.
38 Jimmy Reid, interview with McGeachan.

and Protestant rabble-rousers, such as Alexander Ratcliffe of the Scottish Protestant League, who claimed his job in life was to 'Kick the Pope!', as well as some Nationalists and political commentators, fuelled these faith-based rivalries by claiming that the Catholic Irish were denying native Presbyterian Scots the opportunity to find work. The Tory Lord Scone summed up the position of the anti-Irish coalition when he claimed that 'If the Irish in Scotland were reduce to even a quarter of a million, the unemployment problem in this country would be so small as to be negligible'.[39] In 1923, the General Assembly of the Church of Scotland published a pamphlet entitled *The Menace of the Irish Race to Our Scottish Nationality*, and the influential Scottish intellectual Andrew Gibb, in his book *Scotland in the Eclipse*, underscored the feelings of the church when he claimed that the Irish were 'responsible for most of the crime committed in Scotland, which otherwise would be the most law abiding [country] in the world'.[40] Such views expressed by what might be deemed respectable opinion stirred enmity on the local as much as the national level and gave credence to the more extreme Protestant organisations.

The Reid family were indifferent to sectarianism: by the time Jimmy had reached young manhood there was 'no association with any church as distinct from Christianity'.[41] Although nominally Catholic, the deaths of his three daughters seemed to have destroyed Leo's faith in God and the Church, although he went 'through the motions' for his wife's sake, but in 'later years my father made us promise that when he died there would be no clergyman or religious service at his funeral'.[42] The teenage Reid's ever more frequent absences from church earned the family a visit from the priest. Bella flung the priest out of the home for having the temerity to suggest that they should put Reid out of the house. Only Bella attended church after that. But Reid's detachment from the Catholic faith did not mean he had rejected the underlying social values of Christianity. He was no militant atheist. So far as he was concerned, the New Testament was 'a book which proclaims human rights and human decency, which to all intents and purposes agrees with what I consider to be a correct attitude to life'. This meant that he was 'insured' against 'the nihilism of many

---

39 T. Gallagher, *Glasgow: The Uneasy Peace* (Manchester, 1987), 137.
40 Quoted in W.W.J. Knox, *Industrial Nation: Work, Culture and Society in Scotland, 1800–Present* (Edinburgh, 1999), 201.
41 Reid, *Reflections*, 3.
42 Jimmy Reid, interview with Roy.

hard-nut atheists'.[43] Similarly, Reid assumed that there was a historical Christ, 'a propagandist for a rebel Jewish sect'. Christ's dangerous message was that 'we're all sons of the one father – that one person is not superior to another'.[44]

An important text in shaping his attitude to religion was George Bernard Shaw's satirical fable, *The Adventures of the Black Girl in Her Search for God*. Written over 17 days in South Africa, it was first published in 1932. The story tells of the lone girl's search for God. She begins by leaving behind the comfort of certainty and during her travels through the jungle she meets dangers and pleasures, scientists and mystics, conjurers and poets. All had knowledge, none had wisdom; all were specialists whose unfounded certainty was matched only by their arrogance. For Reid, the parable established that it is the search for meaning rather than the attainment of belief that develops the individual intellectually, socially and politically. Reid's political life was, in one way or another, a search for meaning. The story itself provoked a storm of criticism from religious bodies and it was banned by the Irish government six months after its publication;[45] but the tone was agnostic rather than atheistic. While dismissing the Bible to be a book without divine authority, Shaw was at pains to stress the ethical importance of the work as well as its historical significance. In shaping his agnosticism, Reid also was heavily influenced by the writings and speeches of the American orator and lawyer Robert 'Bob' Ingersoll – 'a great rationalist',[46] and a great advocate of free thought and humanism.[47] The influence of these thinkers on Reid's views on religion is pretty transparent given his lifelong humanism and free thought.

The grinding poverty and squalid living conditions were alleviated slightly when at an indeterminate age the Reid family moved from the Gorbals to 42 Whitefield Road, Ibrox, a sub-district of Govan, just a few closes away from Rangers Football Club's ground – to 'two room[s] and kitchen with an inside toilet', a 'palace' compared with where they had moved from.[48]

43   Reid, interview with Roy.
44   Reid, interview with Roy.
45   M. Holroyd, *Bernard Shaw* (London, 2011), 672.
46   Jimmy Reid, interview with Roy.
47   For a selection of Ingesoll's speeches, see T. Page, *What's God Got to Do With It? Robert Ingersoll on Free Thought, Honest Talk and the Separation of Church and State* (Hanover, NH, 2005).
48   E. Reid, 'The Lessons My Father Taught Me', *Sunday Herald*, 6 July 2014; *Glasgow Herald*, 11 March 1998.

But while an improvement, Reid's abiding memories of the interior of Whitefield Road were 'the bare floors, [and] furnishings that were minimal'.[49] Things improved even further when the Reids moved a few blocks to 30 Kintra Street, a three-room apartment, before their final move to Priesthill Road.[50]

Govan had an economy that was quite different from the small business enterprises of the Gorbals. Although the economy of the burgh originally was based on salmon fishing, handloom weaving, silk making, pottery and farming, from 1850 it became tied to the development of shipbuilding, marine engineering and allied industries. The biggest of the shipyards were Fairfield, Stephens, and Harland and Wolff. It was said that it was impossible to 'get beyond the sound of the hammer. From early morning till late at night we hear the continuous hum of industry'.[51] The physical and cultural impact of the yards on the Govan community was immense. As Reid remembered:

> Well, first of all there was the clamour ... There was a noise. Now, the noise in the yards was diabolical. First time I ever went into a yard, I thought I was in hell ... The noise was deafening, you were holding your ears. That's why a lot of the old guys are deaf ... the shipyards were ... right up with, upsides with the tenements, because the bosses built the tenements for all these workers ... You could see ... in the bigger vessels, the superstructure rising above the tenements ... it was impossible to be unaware of it. In these yards, the great majority of the men worked in the yards. When the yards came out it would be like a river of men, usually with bonnets, caps, walking down the road ... and children, particularly boys, would be looking for their fathers ... in the midst of all these people ... the time of the day was dictated by the yards ... the horn would go – that's you going into work, lunchtime by the same, the same when you finished at night ... the rhythm of life was interwoven with the yards to an extent that I don't think applied in any other industry.[52]

---

49 J. Reid, *Power without Principles: New Labour Sickness and Other Essays* (Edinburgh, 1999), 272.
50 *A Place in my Mind*, BBC Radio Scotland, 7 June 1998.
51 P. Donnelly, *Govan on the Clyde* (Glasgow, 1994), 10.
52 Maritime History, BBC Scotland, 25 September 2003.

It was the hardship and dangers of yard life that were fundamental in forging the characteristic solidarity of the shipbuilding community. As Reid explained:

> People died in shipbuilding, there was always dangers about. You always had to depend on one another and so there was a kind of natural solidarity ... you lived cheek by jowl with your work, so the community, the part of Govan I lived in, was a shipyard community ... And if you had a problem outside the yards, that might have called for some social action, in crisis you could depend on the men inside the yard to take the initiative to try and resolve, or sort out or win a point that was troubling them at home. So you had this ... marvellous relationship between the community and the workplace and on occasions ... when a real problem arose to do with landlords ... the workers ... would use their industrial power to supplement ... the women that were concerned about rents ... what you had here was a culture sprung from the industry by which men earned their living and the family were able to live. It, it's quite significant.[53]

However, that natural solidarity was severely tested with the collapse of world trade and the growth of protectionism which saw the demand for shipping fall catastrophically in the interwar years. The loud and abrasive daily serenade or hum during the late 1920s and for most of the 1930s fell silent as two-thirds of shipyard workers on Clydeside found themselves unemployed. The mood music became one of sullen desperation; the workforce more fatalistic as they waited along with management for 'the expected upturn in trade'. One of the investigators of the Carnegie United Kingdom Trust caught the fatalism of the skilled workers, remarking that they had:

> acquired the art of patience. They had longer and more frequently recurring experiences of unemployment. With drooping shoulders and slouching feet they moved as a defeated and dispirited army. They gave their names, signed the necessary forms and shuffled out of the [Labour] Exchange. This, twice a week, was the only disciplined routine with which they had to comply.[54]

---

53 Maritime History, BBC Scotland. The rents issue referred to by Reid is the Rent Strikes of 1915. See J. Melling, *Rent Strikes: People's Struggle for Housing in West Scotland, 1890–1916* (Edinburgh, 1983).
54 T.C. Smout, *A Century of the Scottish People, 1830–1950* (London, 1986), 115.

In Govan, Reid was enrolled in August 1937 with another 553 pupils in St Saviour's Primary School. One of his classmates, Freddie Shiach, recalled that Reid 'was always late for school', even though he had found a 'shortcut through the girls' playground'.[55] He was far from a model pupil and received the 'belt (tawse) like everyone else'; indeed, when he dared to laugh at the singing of a Gaelic song the music teacher 'hit him across the face'.[56] For the education authorities, school discipline was best enforced through corporal punishment. Although the use of the cane was prohibited in Glasgow schools, the tawse, or leather strap, was permitted for use on unruly scholars,[57] but striking a child across the face was stretching this a bit far.

In August 1944, after seven years at St Saviour's, Reid was enrolled in the newly opened St Gerard's Senior Secondary School, where later the famous Scottish comedian Billy Connolly was also a pupil. The school roll was about 1,000 pupils and it seems to have had a fairly good reputation for sports. The School Report of 1945–6 states that 'The corporate life of the school is in a flourishing condition. There is a good choir … Games are well-supported: there are four school football teams, and rugby and hockey have been introduced recently. Cricket, netball and swimming also receive full attention'.[58]

In what was a broadly positive report, the only black mark was the acknowledged difficulties in 'bedding in' inexperienced teachers. However, by 1949, the school roll was 1,270 and St Gerard's was providing courses 'for all categories of secondary pupils' from the most able like Reid to the least able.

According to Reid, he was already 'known as a communist' in secondary school, even although at that point he had 'never met one [and] knew nothing about communism'. In spite of this, 'if a teacher made a snide remark about communism (which was not unknown, for at least one was a fanatical anti-communist) then heads would turn to stare at me as if I was personally responsible for whatever atrocity they had concocted'. If he was a communist, then it was by instinct rather than intellect. Reid said that he always felt 'that communists were for the workers. Nobody had to tell me we were living in a society of the rich against the poor and

---

55 F. Shiach, interview with McKinlay (2013).
56 Shiach, interview with McKinlay.
57 Glasgow City Council, *Education Handbook* (1947), 84–5.
58 Glasgow City Archives (D-ED7/218/1/1).

that there was a class struggle. What I needed was to be taught how to wage and win that struggle'.[59]

Perhaps reflecting the improving Reid family circumstances, at least as far as housing, Jimmy's academic range was added to through learning to play a musical instrument. As he said, 'My father was a great believer in his sons learning about music, and being able to read music. My brother played the sax, I played the trumpet'.[60] But instruments had to be bought, lessons had to be paid for; a cost far too high for those on the 'the dole' or reliant on casual labour, but not, perhaps, for those engaged in the illegal economy of the streets. Another aspect of what might be called self-improvement was literature. From an early age, Reid developed a passion for reading, saying: 'I can't remember when I couldn't read. Yet there must have been such a time. I don't remember anyone teaching me to read; but there must have been. All I know is that from the beginning of time, my time, I have read. It became compulsive'. At first it was boys' comics, but he outgrew them quite quickly, as he put it:

> At some stage I started reading through boys' comics. All my pals read them. But they were about boys at public schools that were really private fee paying schools for the sons of the rich. The plots were all the same and the characters were all stereotypes though I didn't know that word at the time. We were supposed to fantasise that we were them. I could dream but couldn't fantasise. For reading, I wanted something stronger and found it in the adventures of Robert Louis Stevenson. To this day I am an RLS enthusiast.[61]

His enthusiasm for literature was shared by his older sister who was a voracious reader of detective stories.[62] One can only conclude that in the Reid household books were not an unusual feature of daily life; something that for a family dependent on the wages of a casual labourer was surprising.

It was to be expected that Reid's passion for literature would mark him out academically. Indeed, the extent of his reading for such a young boy was insanely ambitious. By the age of 12 he was able to call himself

---

59 Notes for a speech 1964, Jimmy Reid Collection, Glasgow University Archives (uncatalogued).
60 Jimmy Reid, interview with McGeachan.
61 Reid, unpublished autobiography (unpag.).
62 Shiach, interview with McKinlay.

a Shavian, having devoured a great many of the works of the Irish playwright George Bernard Shaw, although it would take another three years for him to read the whole canon. Other influential authors, apart from the previously mentioned Stevenson, included Walter Scott and Charles Dickens.[63] Reid apparently could recite from memory pages of Tom Johnston's *History of the Working Classes in Scotland* (1920). With the pocket money his mother gave him from his first wage packet, Reid bought his own copy of Johnston's *History*. This purchase earned him an exceptional reprimand from his mother: after all, why squander his money on a book he already knew by heart?[64]

But while obviously gifted, Reid's academic horizons were limited partly by economic necessity, and partly, but more importantly, culturally. Scottish education in the 1930s was highly elitist even in the state sector. Pupils were split into those small numbers destined for higher education and those, the majority, who did mainly vocational subjects intended to equip them for skilled and unskilled occupations. Institutionally, this was expressed in those pupils who attended higher secondary schools and those who attended lower. Which door a pupil went through was decided upon at the age of 12 when he/she sat what was known as the qualifying exam.[65] Reid was streamed for university, having passed his qualifying exam by 99 per cent. This put him in the elite cohort of Scottish pupils, but although he studied 'Greek, French and Latin', his 'expectations never involved higher education. I did not know anybody who went to university from the streets of Govan'.[66] In the end, Reid did what all his classmates did: leave school at 14 to find work without any qualifications, which he did on 30 June 1947. The exceptions were a couple who were sent to an approved school, one or two for medical reasons, and a handful who moved away.[67] This was the general rule in Scotland: in 1951, 87 per cent of the occupied population between the ages of 20 and 24 had left school at age 15 or younger.[68]

His intellectual precociousness and rigorous study regime made Elder Park Library, Govan, his second home. As Sir Alex Ferguson said at his funeral, 'our education was football, his education was the Govan library

63 Reid, *Reflections*, 5.
64 Joan Reid, interview with McKinlay.
65 Smout, *Century*, 226–7.
66 Reid, *Reflections*, 4.
67 Admission Register, Glasgow City Archives (D-ED7/218/2/4); Reid, *Power without Principles*, 198.
68 Smout, *Century*, 228.

Beginnings: 'I'm from Govan'

– he was never out of there'. Once he was asked by Jonathan Miller, the theatre director, at which university he'd been educated; Reid told him, 'Govan public library'.[69] Reid himself said of Elder Park Library that it 'represented more to me than a university'. Just 300 yards from the shipyard gates, he would return time and time again from the Workers' Educational Forum with the – sometimes muddled or misheard – names of philosophers to be puzzled over by the librarian.[70] The reading habit was to last all his life; indeed, before sleeping, he had to read something no matter how late he got to bed. As his wife Joan remarked, 'he was always reading'.[71]

But Reid was not detached from the popular culture of his parents and that of his peers. His father, who 'was a music hall buff', took him regularly to all 'the theatres in Glasgow'. He claimed that 'Some of my fondest childhood memories are of Dave Willis, Tommy Morgan and other[s] … whose names are enshrined in Clydeside's equivalent of vaudeville'.[72] During the war years, his mother and he were mostly on their own, and as a result they often frequented the cinema: 'I became an expert on Hollywood movies circa the 1940s. Don Ameche, Alice Fay, Ann Sheridan, James Cagney, Fred Astaire and Dorothy Lamour. The latter was the first to create some kind of sensation in my groin. I hadn't a clue what the hell it was but mysteriously sensed it would be better not inform others of this happening'.[73]

Reid was also (briefly) a member of the Boy Scouts, but his rebellious side soon was apparent as he

> was drummed out of the Boy Scouts for refusing to wear the pointed hat of those days. Other youngsters luxuriated in what was for them the uniform of the 'Mounties', yet I steadfastly refused to place the offending headpiece on my cranium. I can remember being ordered from the Scout hall and shouting back to the leader: 'Pointed hats are for people with pointed heads, ya big bampot'.[74]

That rebellious spirit was being nurtured as Reid's restless intellect sought some explanation for the poverty and squalor he saw all around him.

---

69 *Sunday Herald*, 15 August 2010.
70 *Jimmy Reid: My Britain*, ITV, 1992.
71 'The UCS Work-in and Jimmy Reid', 5th Annual Lecture, Research Collections, Glasgow Caledonian University (2007); Joan Reid, interview with McKinlay.
72 *Glasgow Herald*, 14 March 1981.
73 Reid, unpublished autobiography (unpag.).
74 *Glasgow Herald*, 6 December 1982.

The outbreak of the Second World War in September 1939 would lead to millions of deaths through fighting, systematic bombing, starvation and the Holocaust, and would culminate in the atomic bombs dropped on Hiroshima and Nagasaki, making the war one of the most brutal and horrific in the history of the world. Never had science and technology been so effectively harnessed to achieve such deadly and destructive ends. Ironically, despite the slaughter of military and civilian personnel on a mass scale, Reid claimed his family was healthier and wealthier than they had been in peacetime. As he put it:

> Suddenly every man and woman had a job. Indeed, work became a patriotic duty. Food was rationed but the rations were much more than we ate before. In war we bloomed. The affluent, whoever they were, complained about the hardships of rationing while we remembered the cruelties of peace. War was terrible but peace, for us, had been more terrible.[75]

One might also add that, thanks to the intervention of Tom Johnston, Secretary of State for Scotland, medical services were opened up to the public on a treatment-on-demand basis from 1943 onwards until the founding of the National Health Service in 1948.

Reid's first memory of the war was being bundled by nurses in the fever hospital down to a cellar which was being used as a makeshift bomb shelter as the phoney war ended and the sustained bombing of Clydeside began by the Luftwaffe. As he recalled:

> Warships under repair in the river were firing at the German aircraft. The noise was frightening. The hospital was only a few hundred yards up the river on the south bank from Clydebank. It sounded as if we were under attack. The building shook. Children cried. I was about to join them but my nurse squeezed me reassuringly. I think this comforted her too.[76]

Beginning in March 1941 the impact of the German bombing was devastating. Only seven houses out of approximately 12,000 were undamaged, 528 people were killed and 35,000 made homeless.[77] The response of the authorities was to evacuate thousands of children from

---

75 Reid, unpublished autobiography (unpag.).
76 Reid, unpublished autobiography (unpag.).
77 R. Ferguson, *George Macleod: Founder of the Iona Community* (London, 2001), 197.

Clydeside to the surrounding countryside. Perhaps it was his illness that exempted Reid from being evacuated but there is no evidence of him being sent to the safe havens of rural Scotland. His second memory was his Aunt Mary, a widow with six children, being bombed out of her home in the Clydebank blitz and being taken into his parents' home on 30 Kintra Street, as 'they were family and that was that'.[78]

The war years were also a period of profound political debate regarding post-war reconstruction. What kind of society was Britain to be? It was a question that the young Reid became passionately interested in:

> The war years invoked a ferment of political and philosophical debate on Clydeside and I was a schoolboy in the midst of it, with eyes and ears wide open. Soaking it all up. The war, of course, was hotly discussed. It was, after all, by definition, an anti-fascist war. This gave the Left an advantage, for its opposition to fascism, both at home and abroad, was more constant. But the debate ranged further and wider and embraced thoughts about the kind of society we wanted to see when the war was over. One thing was certain; the men and the policies of the thirties had to go. And they did in the 1945 General election.[79]

The war had a radicalising effect on the British people and Labour was elected by a landslide in July 1945. Reid's parents celebrated with their neighbours at the news; indeed, his father sent out for a bottle of whisky: 'It was like Hogmanay'.[80] Caught up in the massive wave of political enthusiasm that had brought Labour to power and laid the basis for the establishment of the Welfare State, Reid made the leap from passive listener to active participant. Probably the first and arguably the most important influence in the making of Reid as political activist was his association with the Revd George Fielden MacLeod's Iona Community mission. MacLeod, heir to a baronetcy, was educated at Winchester and Oriel College, Oxford. A captain in the 12th Battalion of the Argyle and Sutherland Highlanders, he was a decorated war hero who had seen action at Ypres and Passchendaele, for which he was awarded the Military Cross and the French *Croix de Guerre* with palm for bravery. However, his disillusionment with war and the failure of mainstream politicians to create 'a land fit for heroes' saw McLeod gradually move towards

---

78 *Sun*, 11 July 1989.
79 Reid, unpublished autobiography (unpag.).
80 Reid, unpublished autobiography (unpag.).

supporting socialism and pacifism. At the age of 35 he exchanged his position as the collegiate minister of St Cuthbert's, a society church in central Edinburgh, for the ministry in Govan Old Parish Church, where his equally charismatic great-uncle John MacLeod – 'the Pope of Govan' – had had a remarkable ministry in the late nineteenth century. In much the same way as his great-uncle, George Macleod fired up the Govanites through 'a huge programme of social action, service, and open-air preaching'.[81] Reid described him as 'a great man'.[82] While others saw poverty and degradation, MacLeod saw a community, which, although dirt poor, was based on mutual aid. He later wrote:

> [T]here is more practical Christianity on the common tenement stair than in the eight long terraces in Kelvingrove. Someone always carried up the kindling sticks for the lonely widow. The child of the jailed was everyone's child till the man came out again. The down and out was up and in provided only he was honest. The cripple lad was carried pick-a-back to the boys' club along five long streets; and the rota never forgot its order for this chore.[83]

Given the social conditions in 1930s Govan, politics was never far away from theology so far as MacLeod was concerned. To this end, he established a Youth Parliament in which Reid was made Labour Chancellor of the Exchequer. He was a highly unusual choice since there was a wide disparity in terms of age between Reid and the other members of the parliament: 'Some of them [were] much older than me, there was a big disparity, there was guys of twenty and … me at fourteen and the guy's twenty, it's big … it's not like being twenty and twenty-six'.[84] His choice was put down to the fact that he was working in a stockbroker's office (see below). He prepared for his role by 'making speeches in front of the mirror' in his home.[85] The 'budget' he produced was 'lifted' partly from the Attlee government's programme of economic and social reforms as well as from the pages of the *Daily Herald* and the *Daily Worker*, but it was carried. However, the careerism of some of

---

81 D.B. Forrester, 'MacLeod, George Fielden, Baron MacLeod of Fuinary (1895–1991)', *Oxford Dictionary of National Biography* (2004).
82 Jimmy Reid, interview with Ryan.
83 Ferguson, *George MacLeod*, 113.
84 Jimmy Reid, interview with Ryan.
85 Shiach, interview with McKinlay.

the members of the Youth Parliament soon led to Reid's disillusionment with the mainstream. He was in politics to change the world in order that other children, unlike his three sisters, did not die in infancy. As he put it:

> [T]hey were all older than me but they were all wanting to be councillors and then MPs. And they wanted careers in Parliament and all that. Now, I had a bitter mistrust of career politicians. See, I was in politics in order to build a society in which children didn't die in their infancy because … that's what I was in for. I'm suddenly surrounded by these guys who are all talking about their career prospects. And I remember we were talking about … they were in the Labour party rooms near Hampden Park … this is the Parliamentary group of the Labour party. And they were all talking about this, I'm going to be this, I'm going to be that. No mention of what they were in politics for. And of course I was a young Wallace. And they were walking out and one of them, Gregor Mackenzie, who ended up in the government, he said, 'Jimmy are you going to the toilet?' I said, 'No Gregor, I'm leaving the toilet', and I left the toilet.[86]

In any case, the day after he presented his budget he was 'sacked'.[87] The Youth Parliament was only one of several political possibilities for engagement and education open to Reid. Although too young, he forged his date of birth and joined the Labour League of Youth (LLY) in 1945.[88] The League had been established in 1926 as a counterweight to the Young Communist League (YCL), although in practice it seemed to operate as a preparatory school for membership of the latter organisation. Reid himself took this route, joining the YCL in 1946. The desire for change; the restless quest for social justice again clashed with the careerism openly displayed by some in the LLY: 'Politics after all was not a career. It was a mission, a dedication. Careerism was a poison that would finally corrupt the body politic of the Labour Movement'.[89]

Another part of Reid's political education was his regular participation in the Workers' Open Forum every Friday night in Glasgow's Renfrew Street. There, in a smoke-filled room full of autodidacts, literature and

---

86 Jimmy Reid, interview with Ryan.
87 'The UCS Work-in and Jimmy Reid', 5th Annual Lecture.
88 Jimmy Reid, interview with Roy.
89 Reid, *Reflections*, 8.

philosophy, topics ranging from Jane Austen to existentialism, were discussed in a semi-structured way. He later recalled:

> I went on Friday evenings to the Workers' Open Forum in Glasgow, where debates on philosophy, economics, politics and the social sciences were held. I think the average attendance would be about 250, which by today's standards would be deemed a mass meeting. The participants looked elderly, but then at that time I considered anyone over 25 to be elderly. They were all well-read, and to call them working-class intellectuals would have been no exaggeration. Their contributions were spattered with profuse quotations from Hume, Marx, Mills, Nietzsche, Adam Smith and others too numerous to mention. They taught me about dialectics from Greek philosophers through to Hegel and Marx. They argued about the inherent contradictions in everything and how the resolution of contradictions was the dynamic force of change, and not just in abstract thought but in life. Thesis – antithesis – synthesis. The general approach was based on scientific methodology. A hypothesis would be debated. Was it true? Did it work? Did it need modification? Or was it rejected because it was fundamentally flawed? They were against dogma, and rightly so.[90]

But the elitism and the patronising attitude shown by most of the speakers – men 'with a thinly veiled contempt for the great mass of the working people' – again proved a turn-off for Reid.[91] However, it was there he was first introduced to Marxism. Reading Emile Burns's *What is Marxism* (1939) proved to be an intellectual milestone for him. As he said later: 'it was Marx, and in particular his economic analysis, that was beginning to make sense out of the turmoil of ideas and contradictions threatening to engulf me'.[92]

The end of the war saw Reid leave school and enter the labour market. After a series of dead-end jobs, he began his serious working life with a small stockbroking firm in Glasgow's Renfield Street – Kilpatrick and Robertson. The senior partner, David Robertson, was also chairman of the Glasgow Stock Exchange and politically what Reid called a 'Liberal Conservative', or one-nation Tory. It appears that the young left-wing

---

90 *Scotsman*, 13 May 2002.
91 Reid, *Reflections*, 9.
92 Reid, *Reflections*, 9.

firebrand struck up a considerable rapport with Robertson. The latter took a paternal interest in young Reid, occasionally taking him to the Conservative Club in Bothwell Street, where he met 'the rising stars of Scottish Conservatism'. Robertson would introduce him apparently without a hint of irony: 'This is James. He's a young socialist'.[93] He would also engage politically with Reid in a non-serious, almost knockabout way, asking him to bring in the *Daily Worker* and *Forward* to discuss its contents with him. It was probably Robertson's opinion that socialism was just a 'youthful' phase in Reid's political journey and that he would eventually outgrow it as he became more and more embedded within the firm in particular and finance capitalism in general.[94] But there was no doubting Reid's warm feelings for his boss, as he said: 'I really liked old Robertson and he liked me'.[95]

Robertson recognised Reid's considerable ability and afforded him a highly responsible position in the structure of the firm. At the age of 15, and after only eight months with Kilpatrick and Robertson, he had become the youngest transfer clerk on the Glasgow Stock Exchange, dealing with men as much as four times his age.[96] Essentially, being a transfer clerk involved monitoring the buying and selling of share capital between firms of stockbrokers. Reid's job was to ensure that the books balanced at the end of the month, as he explained:

> In those days [on] the stock exchange, you'd buy and sell shares but you didn't settle up until the end of the month … what you did is you've got an account with another stockbroker. And you buy so many shares of this, that and the next thing and the cost of them and he buys from you. So you don't go into the whole way of paying for everything. At the end of the month he either owes us or we owe him.[97]

By this time Reid felt that his socialist convictions and membership of the YCL was incompatible with working in a stockbroking firm. Indeed, there is an anecdote regarding his decision to leave Kilpatrick and Robertson. Apparently, on one of the training courses he was sent on, the lecturer claimed that 'The Stock Exchange will last as long as the present

---

93 Jimmy Reid, interview with McGeachan.
94 Jimmy Reid, interview with McGeachan.
95 Jimmy Reid, interview with Ryan.
96 Jimmy Reid, interview with McGeachan.
97 Jimmy Reid, interview with Ryan.

socio-economic system'. Reid, who at that time believed that capitalism was on its last legs, retorted: 'We deserve more job security than that'. For that reason, he decided that getting a trade behind him would offer more economic security than working in a stockbroking firm, whose future prospects it seemed were, at best, slim. Robertson did his best to persuade Reid not to leave, holding out to him the offer of a future partnership. But Reid's mind was made up and all his boss could say to him was 'all the best'.[98] He left without any bad feeling; indeed, he felt that the 'prejudice about all stockbrokers being grasping and vicious' was wrong. 'They weren't vicious at all. They were lovely men. And I think even if I stuck to my politics, I think they could accommodate that'.[99]

His experience of working for Kilpatrick and Robertson also left its imprint on his psyche in ways both practical and political. Practically, it gave him a rudimentary understanding of the workings of finance capital which remained with him for the rest of his life. As he put it, 'I've always been able to read the stock exchange, and in debates with people it has come in quite useful'.[100] Politically, his relationship with David Robertson taught him the virtue of tolerance: not 'to treat all who were in the opposite side from me in politics as if they were beasts … I've known Tory ministers … I was really friendly with them, really friendly. And actually worked with them about doing things during the Thatcher years to try and circumvent some of the policies'.[101]

However, Reid left the world of finance behind and headed for the Labour Exchange where he asked for an application for an apprenticeship in engineering. The making of a communist activist was about to be set in motion.

---

98 Jimmy Reid, interview with Ryan.
99 Jimmy Reid, interview with McGeachan.
100 Jimmy Reid, interview with McGeachan.
101 Jimmy Reid, interview with Ryan.

2

Apprenticeship

The decision to turn his back on a career in stockbroking was to prove momentous for Reid. By opting to take up an apprenticeship in engineering he was catapulted almost from the outset into the heady world of industrial politics. Industry was a university of sorts where the lecturing staff was made up of 'philosophers in overalls': self-taught men who were incredibly well-read and mainly communist in outlook. Reid himself opined that 'all the best shop stewards were communists'.[1] Indeed, Amalgamated Engineering Union (AEU) members made up 50 per cent of the delegates during the Second World War at Party congresses, and it remained high at 30 per cent in the 1960s. All were 'class one' or 'time served' men.[2] Contrary to the received image of the hard-line, intolerant and sectarian image of communists, those encountered by him gave 'every indication of being open minded and tolerant. Anyway, I was quite impressed by them. They were not the dogmatists I had anticipated'.[3] Thus, under the tutelage of these workplace philosophers, Reid began his fledgling career as a young communist activist.

His working life in industry began in 1950 when he found himself the only apprentice in the tool room of a small firm called Scottish Precision Castings (SPC) based in Hillington, Glasgow. Even as an apprentice, Reid remained cosseted by his mother. Few apprentices left for work wearing a coat warmed on the door of the range by their mother. 'His mother always put his pieces (sandwiches) in his pocket in case he forgot them'.[4]

---

1   Jimmy Reid interview with Brian McGeachan (2009).
2   R. Samuel, 'Class Politics: The Lost World of British Communism, Part Three', *New Left Review*, 165 (1987), 59, 74.
3   Jimmy Reid, interview with McGeachan.
4   Joan Reid interview with Alan McKinlay (2013).

The fact that as a Catholic Reid had been able to acquire an engineering apprenticeship was remarkable, as sectarianism in the west of Scotland in the 1950s and 1960s still played an important role in determining one's life chances. Unspoken embargoes still existed on employing Catholics in occupations as diverse as banking, the fire service, quantity surveying, as well as, of course, shipbuilding and engineering.[5] Alex Ferry, later president of the AEU, highlighted the way in which religion could maintain craft exclusiveness, recalling as a young Catholic male in the 1940s that:

> It was still much more difficult for a RC to be employed in the craft trade than it was for others ... I discovered that myself when I was trying to find an apprenticeship. The employer ... would ask you which school you had gone to ... if you tried to cover it up, you were then asked about the Boy Scouts and the Boy's Brigade ... Notwithstanding that, I managed to get an apprenticeship in one of the less desirable engineering companies in Clydebank ... when I moved to the Singer Sewing Machine Co. in 1954 ... the effects of discrimination were even more glaring. The tool room, where I was, employed around 300 people ... You could have counted the Catholics on the digits of your two hands and, in the shop in which I worked, I was the only Catholic.[6]

However, having leapt over the sectarian barrier into what he later described as 'four or five years of drudgery',[7] Reid was no sooner started when he was faced with redundancy as SPC went into liquidation. His apprenticeship was for the time exceptionally fragmented, as in the post-war years interrupted apprenticeships affected under 8 per cent of apprentices, the overwhelming majority serving their 'time' with the same employer.[8] From SPC he transferred to Weirs of Cathcart, but was sacked within months, which, he claimed, was 'blatant victimisation'. The Weirs shop stewards were highly politicised but deeply divided and proved unable – or unwilling – to negotiate his reinstatement. This was another hard political lesson: communists were always pragmatic and strategic in their actions, even if this meant sometimes losing one of their own. Reid's experience was not unique: Eric Park, an apprentice draughtsman, and

---

5   Kenna, *Heart of the Gorbals*, 268.
6   T. Gallagher, *Glasgow: The Uneasy Peace* (Manchester, 1987), 252–3.
7   Jimmy Reid, interview with McGeachan.
8   T. Ferguson and J. Cunnison, *The Young Wage-Earner: A Study of Glasgow Boys* (Oxford, 1951), 108–10.

another YCL activist, was also dismissed from Weirs in the same year. Park was sacked for insubordination, for having the audacity to challenge a foreman on the shop floor about whether Weirs could afford a pay rise. Unlike his foreman, however, Park could quote figures from Weirs annual report to its shareholders.[9] No foreman who hoped to maintain their personal authority could tolerate being publicly bested by an apprentice. By issuing a letter noting that dismissal was due to insubordination, the employer reduced the chance of the apprentice being hired elsewhere and so hoped to force the chastened trainee to ask for his job back.

Although Reid only worked in Weirs for a few months this experience was to prove a profound part of his political education. Weirs, Cathcart, was a factory with a radical tradition that stretched back to before the First World War. The young communist Harry McShane served his political apprenticeship in Weirs; and the Scottish Marxist John McLean's hugely popular education classes on economics included Weirs workers. On the other side, William Weir and his chief lieutenant J.R. Richmond were key figures among Clydeside employers. The former had been a leading adviser to the government on munitions production during the First World War and was unusual among Clydeside industrialists in his willingness to dabble in the most modern American management techniques. Weirs developed a strategy of working closely with some shop stewards to reduce the influence of radicals inside the Cathcart factory. As part of this strategy, older, long-term stewards were invited to regular teatime meetings with management. Needless to say, those younger Weirs stewards who were part of John McLean's circle ridiculed what they termed the 'fish supper' stewards. But Weirs was in many ways an industrial anomaly in that period: a factory with an aggressive modernising management and a highly skilled, highly unionised workforce.

However, the long interwar depression reduced the vibrant shop stewards' movement of the First World War to little more than a shadow of its former self. While AEU officials despaired of the limited presence and ambition of Clydeside shop stewards, Weirs was to prove an exception to the prevailing mood of despondency as the Cathcart factory sustained continuous shop steward organisation even in the depths of the interwar depression. During these years, the shop stewards' priority was keeping the union intact. In Weirs, they were careful not to confront management in case it produced a backlash that threatened the AEU's fragile presence in the factory. Passivity, however, began to be replaced by assertiveness in

9   *Daily Worker*, 4 March 1952.

the late 1930s with the beginning of rearmament. By the early years of the Second World War, younger, more radical shop stewards began to emerge in Weirs, including a small group of able communists centred around John – 'Jock' – Sheriff.[10] The strong impression they made on the young Reid was revealed in a later radio programme in December 1971 hosted by Robin Day. David, a 14-year-old boy from Slough, wondered why Reid had joined the Communist Party and not some other political party. He replied:

> I decided to become a communist, because I found that communists were, in the main, the most incorruptible fighters for socialist ideals, and for the cause of the working class. In the early days of my joining the communist movement, that was what impressed me most of all … the dedication and incorruptibility of communists in their socialist ideals.[11]

Sheriff was a big, handsome man, standing to his full, commanding height he would have stood out in any crowd. Somewhat surprisingly, given his stature, he was quietly spoken, pressing home his argument with persistence, logic and detail. Sheriff was no less visible as a communist and as the public face of the AEU in Weirs, organising sales of the *Daily Worker* in the factory and regularly standing outside the gates before starting-time asking workers if they had any issues for him and for the union. He embodied a different type of trade unionism: radical and, above all, *publicly* representing the Cathcart members. This put him at odds with most of the Weirs shop stewards whose main concern was with the earnings of their workmates rather than with the workforce as a whole. Sheriff was determined that the union should speak with one voice and represent *all* workers in the factory, rather than just the toolroom elite. The toolmakers were the labour aristocrats of every Clydeside engineering works: they produced the jigs, tools and fixtures needed throughout the factory, which gave them an understanding denied to other workers of how the works as a whole operated. So important was the toolroom to factories like Weirs that it was managed with the lightest of touches. As toolmakers were highly skilled and difficult to replace, they were less exposed to victimisation and could move about the factory without management raising so much as an eyebrow – a real bonus for a shop steward. The toolroom was also the heart of shop steward organisation, a place where work was less hurried and left gaps for doing union business.

10 John Sheriff, Obituary, *Herald*, 11 October 1997.
11 *It's Your Line*, BBC Radio, 3 December 1971.

Inside Britain's factories post-1945 the Communist Party tried hard to maintain shop stewards as a national movement to modernise industry. Apprenticeship was singled out as a key issue by the Glasgow Organiser of the Communist Party in 1946. British industrialists were deeply opposed to giving workers – especially communists – *any* voice in shaping their policies on new technology, training or productivity. Clydeside employers were not just opposed to including workers in discussions about boosting productivity, but hostile to the very existence of shop steward organisation. The powerful Clyde Employers' Association (CEA) tried hard to introduce a blacklisting system against union activists, especially communists: 'to keep out these undesirables' and was always ready to warn other firms in danger of hiring one of 'the subversive element'.[12] However, a desperate shortage of skilled labour made it difficult for employers to root out shop stewards. Blacklisting was nearly impossible when firms could see around a quarter of their workforce leave inside a year. Of course, high labour turnover also made it awkward for unions to build stable networks of shop stewards. Employers responded to these challenging workplace problems with a variety of tactics designed to make life hard for shop stewards, especially for those in their first few months of employment. Newly arrived shop stewards – or those who generally made themselves 'pests to management' – found themselves given the dirtiest jobs on the oldest, crankiest machines or shifted between jobs without warning. Employers tried almost any tactic to disrupt shop steward organisation. The hope was that a new shop steward would quickly tire of such petty victimisation and simply leave for a job elsewhere. As the CEA noted on many occasions – 'with regret' – that some of their member firms were so glad to see an active shop steward leave that they did not have 'the courtesy' to inform his next employer.

Jock Sheriff was singled out by Weirs for similar treatment. Management announced their intention to transfer Sheriff out of the toolroom and onto mainstream production where they anticipated that he would have much less time for union business. Also, he would be working alternate weeks on day and night shifts, making it impossible for him to represent the factory as a whole. It was hoped that these petty, vindictive tactics would lower Sheriff's personal profile and his

---

12 A. McKinlay, 'Management and Workplace Trade Unionism: Clydeside Engineering, 1945–1957', in J. Melling and A. McKinlay (eds), *Management, Labour and Industrial Politics in Modern Europe: The Quest for Productivity Growth during the Twentieth Century* (Cheltenham, 1996), 180–2.

authority amongst the shop stewards. Indeed, before implementing them management had taken the precaution of sounding out those shop stewards considered 'loyal' to the firm and were assured that they would be 'glad to see the back of him'. Privately, Weirs told the CEA that singling out Sheriff would drive a political wedge into the factory's shop steward committee. Moving – or, better still, sacking – Sheriff was considered so important that Weirs were prepared to risk a factory-wide strike of up to six weeks. Such an expensive shutdown was regarded as a worthwhile investment in disorganising and dividing the union in the factory. The payback was that Weirs would have demonstrated their 'right to manage' and consequently the AEU would be tamed.[13] Faced with such a determined and calculating management, Sheriff accepted his move to another department. His decision left the union intact inside Cathcart and avoided any risk of a long and divisive strike. Management's petty victimisation of him, however, did not stop there. He was put on an antiquated grinding machine to make long turbine shafts with twelve different diameters along their length. Set up to fail he was sacked for incompetence within the year. The union represented Sheriff through official channels but his was a lost cause. It was no surprise that he was unable to find work in another Glasgow factory. After a year unemployed, he was elected as a full-time AEU official.

Sheriff was 'very influential' on the teenaged Jimmy Reid.[14] He cited Sheriff as a guide on how to think and act as a grassroots communist: learning never to hide the fact that you are a communist, always to co-operate with others – if at all possible – and to accept that your commitment will be tested and that you risk victimisation. Sherriff represented the depth of personal commitment and the risks of being a communist. 'That's what it took to be a communist'.[15] The young Reid would also have learnt a sense that to be a leader – as a communist – sometimes meant accepting pragmatic retreat: peoples' livelihoods were far too important to be jeopardised unless there was a good chance of success. The grassroots communism of Jock Sheriff was to prove in the long run much more important in Reid's political apprenticeship than the writings of Joseph Stalin, and their close association continued in the years to come, as we will discover in the next chapter.

13   Clyde Employers' Association, Correspondence re Dismissal of J. Sherriff, Shop Steward, 1951, Glasgow City Archives, TD1059/A52/157.
14   Sheriff Obituary.
15   John Quigley, interview with McKinlay (2017).

Reid joined the Communist Party as it adopted the *British Road to Socialism* and reaffirmed – or, rather, returned to – its commitment to a 'united front' strategy' to work with other groups and parties to form progressive alliances. The first Scottish Party Congress Reid attended in 1950 was dominated by this issue. Co-operation with local Labour parties and trade unions was essential. The first, however, in working towards a 'united front' strategy was unpicking the insularity of grassroots communists: 'we've got to end rapidly this sectarianism, this sitting in our Ivory Tower, secure in our "superior" knowledge, regarding everybody else as hopeless and reactionary'.[16] Again, this was a crucial formative influence on Reid's politics. The Marxism that the Communist Party aspired to was expressed most clearly in a series of primers, such as *What is Marxism?* written by Emile Burns. For Reid these texts were revelatory. Marxism not only explained the long-run dynamics of global capitalism but also the day-to-day realities of life in any community or factory. Marxism went beyond moral indignation to provide an intellectually coherent world view. More than this, Marxism was a tool to be used in the normal conversations on the factory floor. Far from being dry dogma, it was an open, dynamic way of thinking about the world. Perhaps just as important were how grassroots communists were to conduct themselves in their everyday lives. In argument, communists were to be tolerant as well as assertive: to keep a dialogue going was more important than winning a debate if that involved humiliating a workmate. Equally, the politics of the communist shop steward stressed co-operation with all sorts of other organisations. The strategy was to build alliances, a realistic strategy that always involved being hard-headed about campaigns including being ready to step back if there was a danger of becoming isolated. Communists had a deep ethos of what we might call public service: they understood that any authority they might have in the workplace would be derived *only* from their effectiveness in negotiations, not their political convictions.

The sacked – but unrepentant – Reid moved on to a firm called Daniel Varney; however, it soon closed as well and he moved to British Polar Engines (BPE), Helen Street, Govan to complete his apprenticeship.[17] The ease with which Reid moved between employers, despite his sacking, owed everything to the chronic shortage of apprentices in the metalworking industries. Clydeside employers estimated that the shortfall in engineering

---

16 Communist Party of Great Britain, Scottish Congress (1950), 12, Glasgow University Archives, ACCN37/7/4/1.
17 Reid, *Reflections*, 13.

apprentices was around 44 per cent. Nor was that of passing importance. For, as the employers fully appreciated, fewer apprentices in the short term meant long-term shortages of skilled labour which would alter the balance of power in Glasgow's factories and shipyards.[18] In BPE, Reid established 'one of the few' YCL factory branches and became active in the engineering union's Junior Workers' Committee for Glasgow.[19] Polar Engines proved to be a more settled move for Reid, and he began his training as a marine engineer. Apprenticeship in engineering had been degenerating for some time in terms of the all-round knowledge needed to qualify as a 'time-served man'. The two main branches of the craft were fitting and turning, both of which had become more specialised during the interwar years due to the introduction of new machine tools: a phenomenon which lowered the range of skills required of the operative. This had a knock-on effect on apprenticeship. According to the AEU, throughout the interwar period apprentices had been used as a source of 'cheap labour for the bosses'. The charge had some substance as even the engineering employers recognised that 'large numbers of boys and youths are not apprenticed but are learning and eventually taking their places in the skilled categories in the same way as apprentices. This movement ... will be encouraged by the tendency of the industry towards simplification and sub-divisions of operations'.[20] Such was the degree of dissatisfaction felt by apprentices/learners over specialisation that during the 1937 apprentices' strike on Clydeside they not only demanded higher pay but also the opportunity 'to become brilliant mechanics, a chance which their employers denied them'.[21]

Reid was fortunate in his time at BPE. When asked in an interview with Paul Ryan whether he had received 'an all-round training', he emphatically replied:

> Oh, yes. All around engineering skills. Put me all over the place, yeah. I got quite a bit of machine experience in the tool room. There was less machining done in the shipyard. They've got an engine shop you understand and there are more specialists work in the engine shop. You know, lathe operators etcetera, etcetera.

18 Clyde Shipbuilders' Association, 'Recruitment of Apprentices', 1949, Glasgow City Archives, TD241/12/603.
19 Reid, *Reflections*, 19–20.
20 R. Penn, 'Trade Union Organisation and Skill in the British Cotton and Engineering Industries, 1850–1960', *Social History*, 8 (1983), 50.
21 *Challenge*, 8 April 1937.

But I was fortunate to have the benefit of the Polar Engines ... I got a broad training.[22]

Reid's transient apprenticeship provided him with the beginnings of a contact network in factories across Clydeside, a network consolidated and extended by his YCL and union activities. This was to be of crucial importance in the 1952 apprentices' strike (Figures 4–6).

The 1952 strike was not the first major strike by engineering apprentices. There had been others: in 1912, 1937 and 1941. However, they had not produced any individuals who achieved lasting local prominence, far less a national reputation. The 1952 strike was different. Four of the strike's leadership achieved important roles in the labour movement: Dick Douglas became a Labour MP and subsequently a SNP MP after leaving Labour over the poll tax, while Gavin Laird and Alex Ferry became national leaders of the AEU and the Confederation of Shipbuilding and Engineering Unions respectively. For Reid, although only *one* of the group who organised and led the 1952 strike, this was the moment that propelled him to national attention inside both the AEU and the Communist Party.

The 1952 apprentices' strike echoed earlier youth disputes. Launched in Glasgow and the west of Scotland, locally based, highly participative, centrally co-ordinated, it spread rapidly to other areas.[23] The 1952 strike was defined by wages, the apprentices' right to union representation and improved training (unlike the 1912 apprentices' strike, which contested new state forms of national insurance, or the 1937 campaign, which was solely about wages). The dispute was triggered by the 1951 11*s*. pay award to adult male engineering workers, of which apprentices received a percentage, but not the full award they had hoped for. The 1951 percentage award to apprentices continued a practice that had increasingly disappointed apprentices from 1941 onwards.[24] Reid was one of the BPE apprentices who contacted other apprentices in neighbouring factories, through night schools and the engineering union's junior workers' committees.[25]

---

22 Jimmy Reid, interview with Ryan.
23 P. Ryan, 'Apprentice Strikes in the Twentieth-Century UK Engineering and Shipbuilding Industries', *Historical Studies in Industrial Relations*, 18 (2004), 19.
24 See P. Ryan, 'The Embedding of Apprenticeship in Industrial Relations: British Engineering, 1925–65', in P. Ainsley and H. Rainbird (eds), *Apprenticeship: Towards a New Paradigm of Learning* (London, 1999).
25 *Challenge*, 23 February 1952.

4 Clydeside apprentices' strike (courtesy of Brian McGeachan)

5 23rd Congress of the Young Communist League
(courtesy of Brian McGeachan)

6 Backcourt communist (courtesy of Eileen Reid)

Before the strike, the AEU's official apprentices' organisation was virtually moribund. The apprentices' demand was for a £1 wage rise for all apprentices. Their slogan was 'the pound, the whole pound and nothing but the pound'.[26] The local union made only half-hearted attempts to exercise control over the nascent grassroots apprentices' organisation. Reid was brought before the union's district committee and 'instructed' to 'direct his energies towards the official apprentices' organisation'. The committee was composed of experienced activists and their instruction can be read as a tacit endorsement of the apprentices' actions disguised as a mild rebuke. In any case, Reid showed no sign of being cowed by being called to account: he 'assur[ed] the Committee that he will give their advice his serious consideration'.[27]

Major Clydeside employers, especially in shipbuilding and engineering, were active members of the rabidly anti-communist Economic League. The Economic League noted with alarm the growing support for the Clydeside Apprentices' Committee (CAC), chaired by Dick Douglas 'of Fairfields and James Reid of British Polar Engines'.[28] For Clydeside employers, it was essential that the unofficial apprentices' committee was ignored, and the authority of union officials restored. Stories were dripped into Glasgow's popular press that the apprentices were being misled by their unofficial leadership, but these had little effect. The first meeting of the campaign was attended by 114 'delegates' from 31 Clydeside factories who decided by 111 votes to 3 to stage a one-day token strike and march through Glasgow's city centre. The strike started on the south side of the city spreading quickly as youths marched from factory to factory. In Weirs, the first few lads who walked out of the factory had to pass through a gauntlet of 'gaffers, cursing and swearing'.[29] After this meeting, Reid was elected as Secretary of the CAC; however, recognising his flair for public speaking, he was quickly shifted to the 'Propaganda and Factory Organising Committee', which also included Dick Douglas and Alex Ferry. Eric Park replaced Reid as campaign secretary. This was an amicable redivision of labour designed to free up Reid's time for propaganda. Together, Park and Reid represented the traits of successful

---

26 *Daily Worker*, 15 February 1952.
27 Amalgamated Engineering Union, Glasgow District Committee, Minutes, 16, 30 January 1952, Glasgow City Archives, TD241/13.
28 Economic League, Scottish Area, Monthly Letter, January 1952, Glasgow City Archives, TD241/12/163/II.
29 Shiach, interview with McKinlay.

communist activists. On the one hand, performing essential, often mundane, organisational tasks, and, on the other, developing 'their own voice to enthuse their workmates', not repeating a dry Party line. The Apprentices' Strike Committee was organised in three sections: co-ordination, finance, and propaganda. Maximising fund-raising and apprentice participation in demonstrations, social and sporting activities was essential to the strike's success. As in previous apprentice strikes, fund-raising was critical, especially for apprentices whose families lived outside the Glasgow region and who had to pay for their lodgings. Funds were also important to rent a strike headquarters, fund daily briefings and pay any fines for apprentices arrested during demonstrations. Reid became the face and the voice of the strike. Addressing a rally of 5,000 striking apprentices, he articulated the apprentices' campaign in terms of fairness and turned the wage demand into a potent image: he described current apprentice wages as less than the cost of keeping a dog in a kennel for a week. That telling image was early evidence of Reid's ability to turn personal experience into political gold.

Apparently, it came to him as a result of his mother's need to kennel the family dog while on holiday on the Isle of Bute. As Reid explains:

> I've always been a dog man and I'd a dog [called] Glen ... in those days all the people in Bute moved out of their houses and let them out for the summer. I don't know where the hell they slept but they slept somewhere ... And the woman wouldn't let a dog in ... didn't want a dog in the house. So my mother put [it] into the cat and dog home. I was quite upset about it but nonetheless. And when she told me what it cost her, I was saying, 'Christ Almighty, that's twice as much as I'm getting in wages, you know'.[30]

The obvious inference was that an apprentice engineer was worth half a dog![31] But they ate more! Amusingly, national union officials used the hearty appetites of teenage apprentices as one of the reasons justifying a wage increase: 'many lads between the age of sixteen and twenty-one are *at least* as costly as a grown man to keep. They certainly do not eat less than an adult, and in many cases they eat a good deal more'.[32]

---

30 Jimmy Reid, interview with Ryan.
31 Unfortunately, Glen died while Reid was living and working in London in the 1960s; something that upset him greatly (see Chapter 3).
32 Report of Confederation of Shipbuilding and Engineering Unions, Central Conference, 6 March 1952, 4, Glasgow City Archives, TD241/13/149.

Reid was also able to draw support from the Iona Community mission in Glasgow:

> The Community House put its facilities at our disposal. It's an amazing place for an organisation ... they just give us the facilities for nothing. And so we've set up... they had to get a structure you understand. So we got facilities in there and then we got facilities from the Christian Institute. It doesn't matter, we had two facilities. Because we wanted to keep a grip in the organisational sense. So we met every morning as the representatives ... every factory was represented. It was a big, big meeting, that's why we had to go to the Community House ... but we had to keep everybody informed ... we had to keep the pot hot.[33]

The Clydeside activists visited other engineering centres, laying the groundwork for a national campaign. A national meeting of apprentice activists overwhelmingly endorsed the recommendation to strike from 10 March 1952. From the core of factories in which the Apprentices' Committee had contacts, the Glasgow strike spread rapidly, primarily by groups marching to neighbouring factories and shouting 'out, out, out' to those working inside.[34] The procession of strikers rendezvoused in Glasgow city centre and each factory was asked to send two delegates to a meeting at strike headquarters that afternoon.

Reid had gone as a delegate to the AEU's annual junior workers' conference in March to put a resolution supporting the strike. During the summing up, he was interrupted in a completely unconstitutional way by the 'silver-tongued' president Jack Tanner, who referred to his syndicalist past to convey his empathy with the striking apprentices, but insisted that unofficial action was an act of bad faith that breached the voluntary codes that regulated collective bargaining.[35] This led to a heated argument between the two men. The 19-year-old Reid in response accused the president of failing properly to represent the apprentices, saying:

> We're getting nothing for year after year after year ... Now we might get something because you've taken action. And what you (Tanner) should be doing, you should be taking advantage of our strike in order to maximise the pressure on the employers

---

33 Jimmy Reid, interview with Ryan.
34 M. Park, interview with McKinlay (2011).
35 *Guardian*, 21 March 1952.

and get us a decent settlement. The whole bloody place was off their seat.[36]

Tanner's response was to ingratiate himself with the young firebrand from Govan; first, by securing a seat at the top table next to him at the conference dinner; and, secondly, offering a future position within the AEU. Reid's recollection of the conversation that took place was as follows:

> 'Are you interested in a trade union career?', he (Tanner) says. 'If that's what you're interested in you've got to work with the forces of importance.' He meant himself. I said, 'Are you trying to corrupt me?'[37]

To Tanner's embarrassment, the *Daily Herald* the next day had a banner headline, 'Apprentice Reid versus President Tanner'. 'And there was a photograph, I think a photograph of me and Tanner'.[38] Reid had made the front page of a national newspaper for the first time and the strike had received a great deal of publicity. Indeed, it took the Eastbourne conference intervention before he was even mentioned by name in the *Glasgow Herald*, and then it was a perfunctory 'J. Reid of Glasgow'. There was even a sympathetic article by the industrial correspondent of the right-wing *Daily Express*.[39]

By the strike's second week, over 20,000 apprentices were out, and apprentices' committees existed across Britain. In Manchester, a meeting of a thousand or so apprentices was encouraged by a Clydeside speaker, 'to fight for your pound which was being spent by fat employers with their limousines and cigars in Monte Carlo'.[40] Growing financial support from grassroots trade unionists and the craftsmen's refusal to complete apprentice jobs increased the pressure on employers, both because of the importance of components made by apprentices and the build-up, as Reid observed, of 'the menial, irksome and usually filthy jobs that no self-respecting Tradesman would look at'.[41] The apprentices' Glasgow demonstration of 27 March included around 200 shop stewards. The

---

36 Jimmy Reid, interview with Ryan.
37 Jimmy Reid, interview with Ryan.
38 Jimmy Reid, interview with Ryan.
39 Jimmy Reid, interview with Ryan.
40 *Manchester Guardian*, 18 March 1952.
41 J. Reid, *Youth in Overalls*, Clydeside apprentices' four-page celebratory newspaper (1952), 2.

Strike Bulletin declared: 'The support of shop stewards and working engineers was a decisive blow in our campaign. In the apprentice strikes of 1937 and 1941 the adults took action. We are now on the offensive. Let us go forward to smash the employers'.[42]

There is, however, no evidence that shop stewards or Party activists were more than occasional mentors. Reid himself said that they received little or no advice.

> I don't recall sitting ... saying to somebody, 'Were you in the strike, how did you go about it?' And so on. First of all the wartime strike was so unusual it was doubtful if any experience could emerge from that.[43]

After a three-week strike the apprentices voted to return to work – with some reluctance – on the understanding that an improved offer would be negotiated by the Confederation of Shipbuilding and Engineering Unions and the Employers' Federation.[44] The employers themselves had refused to negotiate directly with the apprentices' representatives claiming that 'it was a national issue and it was going to be handled in London'.[45] They had tried unsuccessfully to intimidate the striking apprentices by sending letters to boys' parents reminding them, as the managing director of the North British Locomotive Company did, that 'by the introduction of indentures ... Strike action may well be regarded as a break of the agreement and I hope you will support me in the efforts I have already taken by advising the apprentices to press the claim in a constitutional way'.

The AEU officials were also pleased it was over, 'as they', according to Reid, 'were not happy about these strike leaders in Govan who were usurping their power. It was a threat to their positions'.[46] Indeed, the apprentices published an 'Open Letter' to J.T. Byrne, district secretary, accusing him of 'lining up with a Tory Lord Provost against the present strike action of the apprentices' and acting as the 'voice and servant of the employers'.[47] The April award fell short of a flat £1 rise – a graduated rise from 5*s.* 6*d.* for first-year apprentices to 11*s.* for final-year apprentices

---

42 *Strike Bulletin*, 7, 20 March 1952.
43 Jimmy Reid, interview with Ryan.
44 *Challenge*, 5 April 1952.
45 Jimmy Reid, interview with Ryan.
46 Jimmy Reid, interview with McGeachan.
47 Clydeside Apprentices Strike Committee, Open Letter to Mr J.T. Byrne, Clyde District Secretary, Confederation of Shipbuilding and Engineering Unions, 27 March 1952, Glasgow City Archives, TD1049.

was accepted under protest. The offer did bring them nearer into line with apprentice wages in the building trades, which averaged £3 17s. for youths under 21.[48] For the Clydeside apprentice leadership, the pay rise represented a significant breakthrough in that the employers had confirmed the unions' right to negotiate for apprentices.[49] The AEU annual junior workers' conference, just after the strike, cemented Reid's reputation as an audacious activist. Despite attempts by the union president, Jack Tanner, to stop any discussion of the apprentices' strike, Reid's speech received 'thunderous applause'.[50]

After the return to work, the Clydeside apprentices issued a four-page celebratory newspaper, *Youth in Overalls*. Eric Park described how apprentices should organise themselves at factory level in readiness for future campaigns, a contribution which reflected his organisational role. It was, however, far too optimistic as the apprentice organisation collapsed almost as soon as the strike was over. From October 1951, Reid recalled, Govan had become the hub of a loose network of AEU junior workers' committees, galvanised by the 'disappointment' of receiving only a fraction of the 11s. rise awarded to adult engineers:

> It was not enough waging our own little wars inside our own particular factory with our own individual employers, for in that way the cards are stacked on the side of the Employers who operate through their Employers' Federations. So we organised ourselves in our factories, and became a dynamic force that had to be reckoned with.[51]

Much later, Reid observed that the 1952 strike was 'an education for me in so many different ways':

> It was the first time I got involved in the leadership of a movement in which you, without even thinking of it, became a voice of thousands of others. And I rarely spoke to notes, it was all there. And I was not intimidated because there's a movement there, you're articulating that movement. And I was fearless in a certain sense and I wasn't interested in what kind of figure I was as long as I was presenting (as well as I could) the issues in the case. And so you developed an enormous sense that a movement was speaking

---

48 *Daily Worker*, 7 March 1952.
49 *Challenge*, 26 April 1952.
50 *Daily Worker*, 21 March 1952; *Socialist Advance*, April 1952.
51 Reid, *Youth in Overalls*, 2–3.

through you. And it's exhilarating. It's the only way I can describe it, exhilarating. Same thing happened to me in the UCS.[52]

For Reid, the 1952 apprentices' strike was formative in several respects. First, that whatever the personal 'exhilaration' of speaking for others, only by remaining connected to *their* concerns conferred authority, not rhetorical gifts. Secondly, that authority could only be based on the routine, preferably continuous, involvement of those on strike. Thirdly, that 'mass leadership' was based on a division of labour: organisation was necessary, but dutiful organisational work was not his strength. Fourthly, that successful campaigning entailed taking the message outwards, making the case as public and popular as possible while directly engaging with critics, a practice Reid was to deploy throughout his political career. Fifthly, a virtue of the apprentices' strike was that they had successfully asserted their independence and refused to remain dependent on the whims or self-interest of others, whether employers or trade unions. *Only* independent, participative mass action could provide workers with a glimpse of their potential power. Lastly, that official union leaderships inevitably tried to subvert mass action and attempted to corrupt grassroots leaders through careerism. Conversely, his experience of his role in the strike leadership was proof positive that to be a communist was to be part of a movement capable not just of providing leadership but of being personally transformative. The role of Party activists during the strike confirmed the plausibility of vanguardism as they had formed an alternative leadership; a leadership made possible by the combination of Reid's oratory and the careful administration of others.

On a personal level for Reid, the strike stood out for two reasons: first, his clash with the right-wing leadership of the AEU, in particular Jack Tanner, something that would leave an indelible mark on his career; and, secondly, his arrest for causing an obstruction, for which he spent 30 minutes in a police cell and was later fined with three others (one named Karl Marx McCulloch!) a pound.[53] They

> were put into single cells while some of the lads outside scrambled round for bail money. We … refused to pay bail and a vigil started to develop outside the police station. Wee Karl started singing 'The Red Flag' and some of the lads joined in. A few hours before we

---

52 Jimmy Reid, interview with Ryan.
53 Reid, *Reflections*, 18; *A Place in My Mind*, BBC Radio Scotland.

were young lads celebrating the end of an industrial dispute. Now we were in prison singing.[54]

Reid's union and political contacts were the dominant features of his social group, but were far from being its only component. A group of the apprentice activists remained friends after the strike, and maintained something of a network across Clydeside engineering. One of them wrote:

> We'd go to the football. We'd go to the Citizens' Theatre in Glasgow, and the dancing, and we'd talk, seriously talk. We were all reading poetry. We weren't trying to be clever. We were just young industrial workers, normal young men. But when I look back I feel an inordinate pride in that group of young men of which I was a part.[55]

These sentiments were echoed by Reid too:

> [W]e used to meet on a Saturday and then decide … meet in the community house … they'd a cheap restaurant there for down and outs. We were down and outs. I'm talking about after the strike. We'd go for a pint. We would pick a match, they've got a group of us, we'd pick a match we'd go… none of this Rangers and Celtic, we'd go, you know. And we would meet on a Saturday night maybe and have a drink and we'd go to the dancing. I would go … chasing the women, chasing the lassies and that. We'd be talking and somebody would say, 'Listen, I've stumbled on a poet …' I mean, the apprentices' strike radicalised us, sure, but it did more than that. Somehow or other it opened minds to pursuits that would hitherto have been considered intellectual.
>
> So we'd meet in … just ordinary boys but we would talk about politics. You know, I did in my teens become tremendously enthusiastic about the English romantic poets, about Shelley and Byron and Lee Hunt and, you know. Now … they're all Burns men … and they're influenced by Burns and all… we'd talk about things. I really look back and say that either through experience of the struggle or experience of the struggle plus the fact that they were genuinely bright guys, bright boys but good boys … they'd

---

54 B. McGeachan, *Jimmy Reid: From Govan to Gettysburg* [one-act stage play] (Glasgow, 2007).
55 M. McDonell, 'Life-long Dream Still Fans the Flame', *Scotsman*, 1 October 1990.

> not a lout among them, you know what I mean? And yes, they were... I don't know whether we were just fortunate or whether the experiences also... maybe a combination of both. But, yeah, they were very good, good boys. Intelligent guys.[56]

The earnest young communists, affectionately referred to by their Party elders as 'wee cut doonies', created a social life that involved dancing as much as dialectics. Reid's life – whether in terms of friends or reading – *always* extended beyond the Party. He 'was an all right dancer, not as good as was a talker', laughed one female contemporary.

The 1952 apprentices' strike was, however, only one part of Jimmy Reid's political apprenticeship. His industrial activism was paralleled by his deepening involvement in the Communist Party. In the decade after 1945, the Party lapsed into a torpor, with no organisational innovation and experiencing electoral decline.[57] Nationally, the experience of the YCL mirrored that of the parent body. Membership rose sharply, peaking in 1949, before steadily falling away as the Cold War intensified. However, the League's experience in Scotland was different from other parts of the UK. The Scottish region's main difficulty was organisational: simply sustaining the branch network through members' own efforts proved difficult. In spite of this, the membership in Scotland rose by 40 per cent from 1950 to 1952: from 481 to 673.[58]

Reid played his part in this. Betty Meth (née Stewart) was the daughter in 'a Party family': her father was 'not quite a foundation member' but joined the newly formed Communist Party in 1921. The 15-year-old Betty was recruited into the YCL by the 17-year-old Reid. She recalled with a smile:

> Jimmy was always mature, in his speech, in his manner. Party people thought he was great because he knew all these big words and could talk about Marxism. A lot of people were in awe of him because of the way he carried himself. No problem was too complex or too big to be solved. Even older comrades looked up to Jimmy.[59]

Jimmy Reid's personal file held by the Communist Party contains a scrap of paper reporting on his performance at a YCL training school in 1952:

---

56 Jimmy Reid, interview with Ryan.
57 K. Morgan, *Harry Pollitt* (Manchester, 1994), 155–6, 164.
58 N. Rafeek, *Communist Women in Scotland: Red Clydeside from the Russian Revolution to the End of the Soviet Union* (London, 2008), 61.
59 B. Meth, interview with McKinlay, 2013.

Jimmy Reid – Scotland. Acted as group leader and did a very good job as such. Made very useful contributions, which less developed cadres commented on as being helpful. Future perspective needs careful consideration. Can become a powerful mass leader in his present job. This is an outstanding cadre with tremendous potentiality who will merit the most careful assistance.

But the young Reid was not without his flaws. He was responsible for organising neighbourhood sales of the YCL newspaper *Challenge* that took place every Sunday afternoon. This was an important ritual, binding young communists together. But it was also a way of developing – and demonstrating – the organisational skills required of grassroots communists, especially those singled out as having leadership potential. 'Jimmy would set the time and place to meet but then – lo and behold – Jimmy would nae show up (laughs). Routine wasn't Jimmy's forte. But he could always get by because of his charm.' Not all his young comrades were charmed: his failure 'to muck in, as we all did', was interpreted as a failure really to grasp his leadership responsibilities. After all, every *Challenge* sold opened up the possibility of recruiting a new comrade.

There seems little doubt that Reid was one of the 'splendid new cadres … [providing] really good leadership' reported to be emerging in the YCL in 1950. Nevertheless, in 1951, just months before the 1952 apprentices' strike, the Scottish District reported to the Party's headquarters that although 'some advances have been made in the sphere of trade union youth activity … the work at factory level is still very weak'.[60] The successful apprentices' strike changed the mood as the 1953 Scottish Congress was positively euphoric regarding the role played by the YCL activists:

> There are many fine and capable young comrades in the leadership of the YCL and they deserve every bit of assistance that the Party can give. The outstanding role of some of our YCLers during the great apprentice strike in March 1952 was a great credit to the YCL and the Party.

The apprentices' strike was used to vindicate the Party's 'turn outward', to seek alliances around single issues with other civil society organisations. Reid had been consistently mentioned by name, along with several others in *Challenge*'s reports of the strike. However, *only* Reid remained visible

---

60 Communist Party of Great Britain, Scottish District Report (June 1951), 14–15, Glasgow Caledonian University.

in *Challenge* after the strike ended: the 12 April *Challenge* singled out Reid by name in a front-page headline as one of the key speakers at the Whitsun Youth Peace Festival. The British 1952 YCL Congress gave Reid 'a tremendous ovation ... for his leading part in the apprentices' strike last March'. Reid, 'who has won many young engineers to the YCL', replied: 'We can't build a mass YCL where youth are inactive. But where they are fighting the boss, on the factory floor, there they will turn to us if we go to them with our policy of change'.[61]

His triumph saw him elected National Chairman of the YCL that year. This placed him at the centre of the Communist Party's hopes that youth recruitment would revitalise the party.[62] But even if successful it would be double-edged: recruitment to the YCL continued to come mainly from those in the skilled trades; there was little attempt to broaden the social base.

However, in making that commitment to the Party, Reid was expressing not just an allegiance to a political cause, to an ideological position, but, for want of a better phrase, to a way of life. Being a communist was not simply a case of paying one's subscriptions, going along to monthly branch meetings, canvassing at elections; rather, it involved the complete immersion of one's self in a political culture whose ties extended way beyond the factory floor or the conference hall. Loyalty to the Party, perhaps especially when its integrity was under attack, was about fidelity to comrades, family and friends. Raphael Samuel's brilliant evocation of a 'lost world of British Communism' takes the tired cliché of communism as a secular religion and examines its meaning in terms of communist lives, stating that:

> To be a Communist was to have a complete social identity, one which transcended the limits of class, gender and nationality. Like practising Catholics or Orthodox Jews, we lived in a little private world of our own ... A great deal of our activity ... might be seen retrospectively as a way of practising togetherness.[63]

The Party's 'ways of practising togetherness' structured the individual's family and social life. The poet Jackie Kay's memoir *Red Dust Road* is partly about being raised by communist parents in the Glasgow of the 1960s and early 1970s:

---

61 *Challenge*, 1 November 1952.
62 W. Thompson, *The Good Old Cause: British Communism, 1920–199* (London, 1992), 121–2.
63 Samuel, 'Class Politics, 59.

> The Party was ... a group of like-minded people who shared each other's company and shared similar values. ... the Party seemed like an extended family. Because we had very little money, the Party butcher made us a packet of meat on a Saturday for a fiver that would last us the week. ... The Party carpenter would fit bookshelves for next to nothing. When the plumbing went in the bathroom, the Party plumber came and fixed it for next to nothing too.[64]

For communists, 'branch life' was both intensely personal and deeply social.[65] Mutual assistance, socialising and politics were fused in Party lives: 'your friends were comrades and your comrades were friends'.[66] All of this in a small, embattled political party produced an intimacy that stretched across generations. Jackie Kay remembers the thrill of hearing her 'Uncle Jimmy' address the UCS work-in, a thrill heightened by her knowledge that he was a member of a particularly close extended family.

A comrade was measured in terms of their selflessness. To be a communist was to have a vocation. The good communist was 'disciplined' and 'organised', terms which signified that the individual was reliable, mannerly, dedicated and loyal. For the full-time Party worker such as Reid, these qualities were extraordinarily heightened. Jim Whyte recalled his time as a full-time Party worker from the mid-1950s until hardship forced his return to shipyard work in 1968:

> [B]ecause the Communist Party put such stress on having full-time officials, raising money to pay the wages of the full-time officials was a huge part of the YCL and the Communist Party. That meant making sure dues were paid on a regular basis and every activist in the YCL had what was called a 'dues run': they had to go out every week collecting dues from the members and they had to raise additional monies through donations and so on. ... You simply didn't have any time off: seven days, seven evenings, virtually every week. And you'd be travelling to Aberdeen or Dundee for branch meetings. All the time you were doing meetings. It was an absolute requirement of every full-time Communist Party official to do a factory-gate meeting every

---

64 Kay, *Red Dust Road*, 35–6.
65 D. Denver and J. Bochel, 'The Political Socialization of Activists in the British Communist Party', *British Journal of Political Science*, 3 (1973), 69–71.
66 N. Grieg, interview with McKinlay, 2011.

single day of your life. So you always had a factory-gate meeting pencilled into your activities on every working day of the week, every month of the year … It was exhausting: it was a huge, huge amount of work … The Communist Party made huge demands of you but in the process of making these demands, it made more of you in every way.[67]

Reid was accepting of the intense level of commitment demanded of Party members and especially that of officials. However, his period as National Chairman of the YCL lasted about as long as his time in SPC as he was called up for National Service in 1953; coincidentally, the same year he completed his apprenticeship at Polar Engines.

National Service was introduced by an Act of Parliament in 1948. Under the terms of the Act, healthy young men of 18 years or more were obliged to serve in the armed forces for 18 months. This was later increased after the outbreak of the Korean War in 1950 to two years – more demanding than anywhere else in Europe. National Service affected all men born between 1927 and 1939, who six weeks before their eighteenth birthday would receive their call-up papers which included a travel warrant and a postal order for 4s. in lieu of wages. Although conscription was abolished in 1957, it continued until 1960, and the last conscripts were not demobbed until 1963. Every fortnight some 6,000 youths were conscripted, with a total of 2,301,000 called up over this period. The army took 1,132,872 and the Royal Air Force (RAF) much of the rest, with very few going to the navy. After discharge, conscripts remained on the reserve force for another four years, and were liable to recall in the event of an emergency. The story of conscription is one of mind-numbing square-bashing, petty and vindictive acts of cruelty, miserly pay, lack of privacy and mindless rules imposed without consent.[68] But to many young men from deprived working-class backgrounds the bleakness of employment in places like Glasgow made national service something of a welcome respite. Some picked up skills and found, for the first time, discipline and structure in their otherwise chaotic lives.

Reid was called up to the RAF where he served nominally as a flight engineer. He never took National Service very seriously. As he himself admits, he was a rotten soldier. 'I made a half-hearted attempt at the spit and polish bit, but mostly while the others rubbed away at everything in sight, I

---

67 J. Whyte, interview with McKinlay, 2011.
68 R. Vinen, *National Service: Conscription in Britain, 1945–1963* (London, 2014).

would be on my bed reading'.[69] Jock Sheriff, his mentor at Weirs, kept him supplied with food parcels and bundles of left-wing literature. He was to be posted to Malaysia to fight against the communist insurgency, but with his political leanings it was thought better to send him to Shrewsbury where he spent the last eighteen months of his National Service as a member of a band. His time in the RAF was not devoid of humour and incident and many situations provided the basis of an entertaining anecdote or two. As he said: 'I had a great time, in terms of not being remotely involved in any heavy action'.[70] The only 'unsettling incident' for Reid was being asked to break a strike in the docks. He point-blank refused to comply with the order, saying that he was 'a trade unionist': a line that a number of other conscripts followed.[71]

One of the first things conscript Reid did was to set up a 'socialist school' on Friday nights in the NAAFI to counter the political education programme of the RAF regarding Britain's role in the world and the maintenance of the Empire. Reid proved to be a continuous thorn in the side of the officer class in charge of education. When they spoke about the exploitation of

> Malaysia ... countries in the Third World by the Russians. That raised my hackles quite a bit. 'Wait a minute, sir. The Third World is suffering from exploitation by whom? I'll tell you who ... Dunlop Rubber Company, all the big companies exploiting their mineral resources, cheap labour, with the connivance of the British, American and French governments. It ain't anybody else responsible for exploiting Asian and African but Western Capitalism' ... He'd never heard these arguments put forward before. He'd be about 21, same age as me ... but very different background. 'Show me any evidence where Russia is exploiting these countries, and I'll show you the companies, they're all registered on the London Stock Exchange'. Chaos, chaos, they couldn't continue ... You know, they ended up cancelling these political lectures, because every time one was held I was there. 'I'll contact my Member of Parliament if you're going to advocate blatantly biased politics in the British Armed Forces'.[72]

---

69 Reid, *Reflections*, 25.
70 Jimmy Reid, interview with McGeachan.
71 Jimmy Reid, interview with McGeachan.
72 Jimmy Reid, interview with McGeachan.

Reid was quite inventive when it came to challenging the authorities over Britain's role in international affairs. The tensions between the USA and the Soviets promoted the rearmament of Germany. It was acknowledged to be a military necessity for NATO to match Soviet forces, which still numbered some six million in Europe. Like other Party members, Reid was completely opposed to the rearming of Germany and the threat it posed to the USSR. He wrote a couple of verses to an old jazz standard, 'Ace in the hole', which he sung with a friend at informal RAF dances:

> If You Don't Want Arms for Nazis to Fight Their Bloody Wars,
> If You Want a Britain Prosperous and Free,
> If You're fed up With the Yanks, their H Bombs and their Tanks,
> Then Come on Boys Sing This Song with Me …
> Oh, We Don't Give a Heck for That Bastard Chiang Kai-Shek,
> Or the other Yankee stooge Syngman Rhee,
> Back in 1941 When the Bombs Began to Come,
> Just Remember What They Did to Us Then,
> So Churchill Go to Hell, Take Eden There as Well,
> Cos We'll Never Ever Arm Them Again![73]

Music came to dominate Reid's time in the RAF as he was asked by the camp commander at Shrewsbury to take over as conductor of the band.

> That was me, my last year in the RAF and I'm band conductor. We had to play in the village fetes. In England they have these village fetes … We had a great time. And at night, we used to have a march through the streets. As it started darkening we'd march to the tent to perform and the villagers would be feeding us drink. As a result, our hats were often off to the side! And if we'd been photographed we'd have been up on charges. It was a cushy number.[74]

In 1955, Reid's time as a conscript came to an end. So far as he was concerned it had been 'Great fun. A complete waste of time, mind you. But great fun',[75] and the first time 'that I had ever had a bed to myself'.[76] However, playing at soldiers was over and it was off with the uniform and on with the overalls as he re-entered the gates of Polar Engines.

---

73 Jimmy Reid, interview with McGeachan.
74 Jimmy Reid, interview with McGeachan.
75 Jimmy Reid, interview with McGeachan.
76 *Herald*, 29 November 1999.

3

Cadre

After 1952, Reid had been singled out by the Party's General Secretary, John Gollan, as someone with the potential to play a future leading political role in the Party or, more likely, in the AEU. This involved moving to London in 1958 and becoming a full-time official and a member of the National Executive Committee (NEC) of the CPGB. His move coincided with one of the most turbulent periods in the history of the Party. First, following the publication of the *British Road to Socialism* in 1951 there was a rejection of its role as a revolutionary party; secondly, the secret session of the 20th Congress of the Communist International in February 1956 saw the denunciation of Stalin by Khrushchev; thirdly, later that year the Soviet Union invaded Hungary. None of these momentous events shook Reid's belief in the Party or in any way diminished his support for the USSR. In many ways it could be argued it simply strengthened the ties between the Party and Reid as he came under the spell initially of Harry Pollitt, and, when he died, John Gollan. But in doing so, as we will see, he was forced to justify the unreasonable, the contradictions, the distortions and elisions of economic and political realities by the Party.

The *British Road to Socialism*, which sold over 200,000 copies, was mainly the work of Harry Pollitt, who was an advocate of the united front politics that had been Party strategy from the mid-1930s to the Nazi/Soviet Pact of 1941. This essentially involved working with progressive forces in society against Fascism and unemployment. In the 1950s, the Party claimed not to be a revolutionary party but 'a left-wing parliamentary party, in contest with right-wing Labour'.[1] It believed 'in a peaceful transition to socialism through parliamentary activity and pluralistic democratic

---

1   J. Eaden and D. Renton, *The Communist Party of Great Britain since 1920* (Basingstoke, 2002), 116.

socialism'.[2] Pollitt was not alone in the authorship of the *British Road to Socialism*; key passages were vetted and rewritten by Stalin. According to George Matthews, assistant general secretary of the Party, 'Stalin's role in initiating the preparation of a long-term programme for Britain ... was decisive'.[3] Although some members, like Harry McShane, left in protest at the seemingly rightward drift of the Party, in many ways this was forced on it as its support was steadily declining. In the 1945 general election, it had fielded 22 candidates, gaining 102,780 votes and winning two seats in parliament, with nine saving their deposits. Just five years later, it fielded 100 candidates of which only three saved their deposits, polling 91,815 votes and with both Communist MPs losing their seats.[4] Given its electoral impotence, the Party had to devise campaigns capable of mobilising those outside of the membership if it was to maintain some political influence and presence in post-war Britain.

Towards the end of 1955, prior to moving to London, Reid, along with other shop stewards at Polar Engines, organised a campaign among the workers there to provide Christmas aid for needy pensioners. This broadened the following year into a national campaign for higher old age pensions. It became, in Reid's words, 'one of the broadest united campaigns in the post-war history of Scotland. All the trade unions, every church organisation ... was affiliated'. He was elected secretary and as such he had to deal with the campaign correspondence in his workplace during the lunch break. A petition to increase the level of the pension was launched with over 300,000 signatures.[5] Reid pushed two arguments on the issue of pensions: first, that a society should be judged on how well it looked after 'the most defenceless sections of the community', and, secondly, pensioners during their working lives had been 'profit fodder' for the bosses, but now too old for this purpose 'then our society didn't care'.[6] The petition was delivered to Downing Street with delegates drawn from a cross-section of Scottish society. The pension was increased a few months later. The success of the campaign for higher pensions impressed on Reid the importance of seeking political alliances to achieve far-reaching social

---

2   K. Laybourn and D. Murphy, *Under the Red Flag: A History of Communism in Britain, c.1849–1991* (Stroud, 1999), 164.
3   P. Deery, 'The Secret Battalion: Communism in Britain during the Cold War', *Contemporary British History*, 13 (1999), 15.
4   Eaden and Renton, *Communist Party*, 109.
5   Reid, *Reflections*, 31.
6   Reid, *Reflections*, 32.

reform; something that was later to bear fruit in his attachment to the concept of a broad left.

Flush from his success on the pension front, Reid moved to London in early spring 1958 as a full-time national officer of the YCL – an appointment that for him came as a 'bolt from the blue'.[7] However, there was the feeling in the Party that the current leadership was too old: John Moss, general secretary, was 36, and Gerry Cohen, national organiser, was 38. The 1956 crisis had drained the Party of obvious successors, and others were suspect because of their criticisms of the British leadership. Reid had no history of dissent. Indeed, in 1948, he had organised a collection at Polar Engines that became part of the folklore of the YCL. The money was used to send a telegram to Stalin – 'The Great Leader of the International Proletariat' – on his 70th birthday.[8] Reid's potential as a mass leader had been shown in his leadership of the apprentices' strike and his selection as chairman of the YCL. A report on his performance at a YCL Training School in 1952 stated: 'This is an outstanding cadre with tremendous potentiality who will merit the most careful assistance'.[9] Although it was recognised that his talents were not administrative but as a public speaker of genuine ability, it was felt by NEC that he would be well suited to the full-time position of general secretary provided 'he had a good organiser beside him'.[10] Having fallen out with some of his Scottish comrades over accusations regarding his punctuality and attendance record at Party meetings, Gollan rather surprisingly invited Reid down to London to 'work for the YCL'. Reid said that 'he thought about it for a while, then agreed to do it much to the annoyance of a lot of people here (Scotland), because at that stage they were seeing me as having a role in the broader labour movement. I think it was a challenge more than anything else'.[11]

As a 26-year-old man who, national service apart, had rarely been out of Govan, he was now, as a member of the Political Committee, mixing with the 'giants' of the scribbling and chattering metropolitan left-wing elite: 'I was privileged to meet and know them, including James Cameron, Wilf McCartney, Claude Cockburn, Harry Pollitt, [Michael] Foot and others'.[12]

---

7   Reid, *Reflections*, 35.
8   Letter from Jim Whyte to Alan McKinlay, 4 October 2011.
9   Personal file, Communist Party of Great Britain Archive, People's History Museum, Salford (6/04).
10 Whyte to McKinlay.
11 Reid, *Reflections*, 151–2.
12 *Glasgow Herald*, 4 December 1996.

Although never known for lacking in confidence, even Reid must have been ever so slightly in awe of these important and influential figures of the left in Britain. It was a far cry from a couple of pints after work on a Friday, a football match on a Saturday afternoon and later a dance or two at one of Govan's ballrooms.

However, perhaps even more important for Reid's political development were the founder members of British communism: Pollitt, J.R. Campbell, Willie Gallacher and Peter Kerrigan. These men were the touchstones of how Reid thought about politics, leadership, and how one should conduct oneself as a communist and as a man. Reid thought deeply about his relationship with Pollitt and the affinities between their personal lives:

> These men helped found the Communist Party of Great Britain in 1920. They were outstanding intellectuals and deeply idealistic. ... Harry Pollitt was a superb man, and almost a second father to me in terms of his influence on me as a young man. He always illustrated his points with human experience and amusing stories he'd gleaned from decades of activism. A hard, industrious life. I was very close to Harry ... He had total integrity in his dealings with Party officials, and you never saw any dissembling. He'd say the same thing to you privately as he'd say in meetings at King Street.
>
> Harry came to communism from a hatred of capitalism. Like me, three of his siblings died in infancy. Harry never forgot that. It brought anger and compassion to your views and activism. In Harry's case – and mine – it was *absolutely* central to who we were.[13]

Reid identified with Pollitt's politics and, perhaps above all, with his personal integrity. Pollitt had been removed from his post as General Secretary in 1941 for his refusal to endorse Stalin's pact with Hitler: 'I think that if I had been an adult at that time and a member of the Communist Party, I would have been with Harry Pollitt'.[14] It is impossible to overstate the influence that Pollitt had on young cadres like Reid.[15] An everyday morality, a practical idealism underpinned this influence: a sharp contrast with the degrading careerism that the young Reid had been

---

13 Jimmy Reid, interview with Brian McGeachan (2010).
14 Reid, draft script, n.d. (1975), Glasgow University Archives, ACCN3717/4/1.
15 Morgan, *Harry Pollitt*, 119–23.

exposed to through his limited time with the Labour League of Youth and in the AEU. He said:

> Part of the atmosphere of the Party – and Pollitt was always clear about this – was that good workers were never victimised: be at your work, be on time, be a good workman, have all the qualifications necessary. And, of course, for full-time (Party) workers, he emphasised that, 'you're not getting a job for life'. Pollitt always kept his tools sharpened and ready in his box.[16]

Pollitt's advice that all communists should 'keep the tools ready' was personal and political, practical and symbolic. The practicality of being ready to return to a working life in the factory was what communists were and would always be. But this was nothing to fear for the communist activist. After all, going back to the tools was what he *was*. Nor was this a return that was likely to cause further hardship to a family accustomed to the poor, uncertain wages of a Party worker. This also spoke of an independence, a kind of freedom: that the individual was beholden only to his beliefs and not to a career. For Reid, to be a communist cadre reaffirmed this independence: his was a loyalty freely given rather than enforced through Party discipline. Being a communist developed the individual 'in terms of writing, in speaking, in self organisation. But the Party also provided a *moral* education, a *practical* moral education'.[17] This moral tone to *being* a communist was fundamental to Reid, but far from unique to him: '*being* a communist was about being the best human being possible. It was about living the *best* way you could'.[18] Thus, being a communist was not just a political affiliation but the cornerstone of who that person was and what they hoped to become.

The quiet authority Pollitt exercised over communists several decades his junior was paralleled at local level. Communism in Faifley, Clydebank was dominated by three veteran Party members – Finlay Hart, Arnold Henderson and Jock Smith – 'very respectable, old school communists'. Such veteran communists enjoyed enormous status in the Party and the community. One young communist recalled that the authority of these veterans was based solely on respect, never deference:

> They had lived their lives as communists, which is hardly the softest of options, politically or any other way. He never raised his

---

16　G. McLennan, interview with A. Campbell and J. McIlroy (BL 1049/98).
17　W. Thompson, interview with McKinlay (2013).
18　M. McGowan, interview with McKinlay (2017).

voice, he was always approachable, maybe a bit solemn. But he had led all sorts of campaigns, *as a communist*. He never hid what he was, what he believed in. People like Finlay, their entire life was about service to the community. People loved Finlay so much that they didn't care whether he was a communist or not.[19]

There was respect, too, for the devotion shown by the Faifley sisters who spent their winters deconstructing outgrown, damaged school uniforms to make 'new' trousers and blazers to be sold cheaply at the Party bazaar. The difference was that while both types of grassroots communism inspired respect for their selflessness, individuals like Hart – and Pollitt – had decades of commitment and leadership.

While domiciled in London, Reid got married on 9 August 1958 at Old Kilpatrick Register Office to Joan Swankie, five years his junior, and one-half of the folk duo the Swankie Sisters, who by all accounts were taking the 'London folk scene by storm'.[20] She later became a professional singer with the Steve Benbow Folk Band, considered one of the main influences behind the English folk revival in the 1960s. The couple had met at a *Daily Worker* dance in the St Andrews Halls, Glasgow, some two years earlier. Joan was born in Romford, Essex, to Scottish parents: John Swankie, blacksmith, and Emily Theresa Mairs, a boot repairer's assistant. Like her formidable mother, who had taken part in the hunger marches of the 1930s, and later had stood as a Communist candidate in municipal elections in Clydebank, Joan was a Party member. The marriage confirmed and at the same time advertised the singular importance of family and fraternity to CPGB members: one married into a family and the family linked one in profound ways to the Party. As Eric Hobsbawm put it: 'The Party was what our life was about. We gave it all we had. In return, we got from it the certainty of our victory and the experience of fraternity'.[21] A grassroots Glasgow communist said, less eloquently but in a more heartfelt way, 'the Party was a *warm* place: people cared for you'.[22] For another, Party life and personal lives were deeply entwined: 'Your friends were comrades and your comrades were friends'.[23] The Reids' wedding reception was riotous to say the least. Reid had sold his golf clubs (he was a pretty useless golfer, so it was no great

---

19 J. McGoldrick, interview with Knox (2013).
20 *Glasgow Evening Times*, 17 November 1961.
21 E.J. Hobsbawm, *Interesting Times* (London, 2002), 134.
22 J. Whyte, interview with McKinlay (2011).
23 N. Greig, interview with McKinlay (2011).

sacrifice on his part) to pay for the drinks. But he was mortified when the alcohol ran out; a cardinal sin in working-class communities in those days. Both families blamed the other for the situation, but when Reid's mother-in-law was carried out of the hall on a door, to Reid's further embarrassment, much the worse for wear, the pendulum of blame tipped towards the Swankies.[24]

Back in London, life was a constant struggle for Jimmy and Joan to make ends meet. As 'funds were low, almost non-existent. The party was operating on a shoestring … Joan was pregnant. The party guaranteed my weekly wage and without this it would have been impossible for me to continue'.[25] It took them three years to find a place of their own – a maisonette in south-east London.[26] Prior to this they had relied on the generosity of party members for accommodation, staying intermittently with Idris Cox, former editor of the *Daily Worker*, and his wife Nora, then Jim Jefferies, physicist, and his wife, before moving in with Colin Wilson, secretary of the communist front organisation the British Youth Festival Committee.[27] 'It *was* difficult', Reid recalled. 'But we were dedicated and there was a warmth and camaraderie about it all. Do I regret the hardship of those days? And it *was* hardship for us all … not at all. We were being true to our beliefs'.[28] On top of economic hardship and the nomadic lifestyle there was the loneliness experienced by Joan – a shy young woman with few friends in the metropolis. While Jimmy was out changing the world, Joan was changing nappies.

The fact that the Party was struggling had much to do with the Soviet invasion of Hungary in 1956. Because of the Second World War and the success of the Red Army against the Nazis, Hungary had been drawn into the Soviet sphere of influence. By 1948, the takeover by the communists was complete. The country was renamed the Peoples' Republic of Hungary and the monarchy abolished. However, the regime was never popular and there was growing discontent which spilled over into a spontaneous armed nationwide revolt against the communist government and its Soviet-imposed policies in October/November 1956. After announcing their willingness to negotiate the withdrawal of Soviet forces, the authorities changed their mind and moved to crush the revolution. On 4 November

---

24 Eileen Reid, interview with McKinlay (2015).
25 Reid, *Reflections*, 37.
26 *Glasgow Herald*, 18 December 1975.
27 Reid, *Reflections*, 36.
28 Reid, interview with McGeachan (2010).

1956, a large joint military force of the Warsaw Pact, led by Moscow, entered Budapest determined to crush the armed resistance. It was all over in a week: 2,500 Hungarians, mainly civilian, and 722 Soviet troops had been killed and many thousands more had been wounded.

The invasion brought international condemnation of the Soviet action, which bordered on the brutal, in silencing its Hungarian opponents. It also had severe repercussions for the unity of the Party in Britain. The CPGB lost a third of its members between February 1956 and February 1958; a third of the staff of the *Daily Worker* resigned over Hungary.[29] Anecdotal evidence from Scotland suggests that those leaving the Party tended to be 'younger recruits from during or just after the war'.[30] However, Lawrence Daly, future general secretary of the National Union of Mineworkers (NUM), also resigned, publicly tearing up his Party card. In alliance with the New Left he founded the Fife Socialist League as a political discussion forum and as a base from which to launch independent candidates in local and national elections until its dissolution in 1962.[31] There was also an outflow of high-profile academics, such as members of the Communist Historians Group (CHG), including E.P. Thompson, John Saville, Christopher Hill and the novelist Doris Lessing, although the historian Eric Hobsbawm remained loyal. Saville and Thompson had been unhappy for some time over the process of democratic centralism, saying that all it did was to rubber stamp the views of the Party's leaders. They were expelled from the Party for issuing an unauthorised publication – *The Reasoner* – which was critical of Soviet communism and capitalism. For them, the invasion of Hungary had simply forced the issue. The others resigned over the *Daily Worker*'s refusal to publish a letter criticising the Executive Committee's endorsement of the Soviet invasion, saying 'We feel that the uncritical support given by the EC … to Soviet action in Hungary is the undesirable culmination of years of distortion of fact, and failure by British Communists to think out political problems for themselves'.[32] Despite the anger over Hungary, resigning from the Party was a difficult

---

29 Laybourn and Murphy, *Red Flag*, 150.
30 K. Morgan, G. Cohen and A. Flinnet, *Communists and British Society, 1920–1991* (2007), 248.
31 C. Efstathiou, 'E.P. Thompson, the Early New Left and the Fife Socialist League', *Labour History Review*, 81 (2016), 25–48; J. McCrindle, 'Lawrence Daly: Obituary', *Guardian*, 30 May 2009.
32 W. Styles, 'British Domestic Security Policy and Communist Subversion: 1945–1964' (unpublished PhD thesis, University of Cambridge, 2016), 109. The letter was published in the *New Statesman* on 1 December 1956.

decision for many: 'Leaving the party was more than changing politics. It was abandoning one's faith and one's friends – for as Jack Murphy and Douglas Hyde could testify, old friends crossed the street to avoid you'.[33] The 'heart-wrenching' decision to leave would be Reid's to make 20 years later.

The year 1956 struck at the heart of the CPGB. At stake was 'the *absolute* necessity of the existence of the Communist Party'.[34] In Scotland, the Communist Party lost about one-third of its membership in the year after 1956; overall, John Callaghan estimates that 11,000 left the Party.[35] But it wasn't simply the sheer number of those who left: the communists who left were often among the most committed. For many, 1956 represented confirmation of long-standing unease about the Soviet Union. 'Very firm', 'thoughtful' comrades were, recalled Gordon McLennan, the Scottish organiser during the crisis, 'very unhappy about our Party. They only remained in the Party because of their experience of good Party people, building the Party, unemployed struggles … or the fight against fascism. But they were becoming increasingly unhappy and Hungary was the end point for them'.[36] Some returned, but far from all. The next decade was dominated by the need to rebuild the Party in terms of membership and organisation. Membership was, however, prioritised above all else. Increasing sales of papers and pamphlets, membership drives, home visits dominated the Party leadership's strategy.

In many ways, the Party in Scotland mirrored the British experience. Indeed, in Glasgow a layer of experienced activists resigned in protest over the revelations about Stalin's crimes in February 1956. Over the next year, because of the invasion of Hungary, yet more activists left, demoralised by having to spend all their time convincing members not to resign. Consider the experience of the Ashton brothers, Jack and Harry. They both joined the Party on 10 May 1947, a day and a date that Jack recalled *exactly* almost 70 years later. For a lifelong communist, the date you joined the Party was etched in memory, akin to a birthday or the date of your marriage. In 1956, Jack remained but his brother was part of the exodus and left in the October. That year 'shook lots of people to their

---

33 F. Beckett, *Enemy Within: The Rise and Fall of the British Communist Party* (London, 1995), 138.
34 McLennan, interview with Campbell and McIlroy (BL 1049/98).
35 J. Callaghan, *Cold War, Crisis and Conflict: The CPGB, 1951–68* (London, 2003), 18.
36 McLennan, interview with Mike Squires (1994).

foundation ... some people just disintegrated'. 'I was a full-time worker', remembered Jack, 'and it was like psychological warfare: every morning it was two or three more people resigning from the Party. These were people you *knew*'.[37] After 1956, for the next decade, even in thriving Party branches, only around one-third were active members, and many of them were regarded as at risk of allowing their membership to lapse at any time. Attendance at monthly meetings halved to around an average of ten. The social side of grassroots communism had all but ceased. Even the Glasgow annual bazaar was imperilled with just three months to go and 'only a few knitted items made'. In such a small party, even the temporary loss of local stalwarts placed enormous pressure on the organisation. In just one year the Paisley branch slipped from decades of stability to the edge of collapse. One activist had cut back his devotion to party work 'because Willie has another interest, ... but has never had occasion to discuss this hobby with me until last Sunday night'. Another willing comrade was under 'strict doctor's orders' for bed rest because of a slipped disc and just could not help, even in an emergency. Yet another member was extremely reluctant to collect dues outside his immediate family: 'reluctant to take on anything. Just reluctant – though a very genuine lad in many ways'. Despairingly, Duncan, the Paisley branch chair, said to the Scottish officials: 'I am faced with too many tasks – which is it to be?'[38] The Glasgow Party, after 1956, similarly 'lost a lot of good people'. Those who remained were consumed by 'everyday campaigning. There was such a lot of work to do. There was an onus on you to *do* something. One of the things about the Party was that you got found out if you were just a spouter because you weren't able to link action to words'.[39]

The Party hierarchy bore down on officials and grassroots activists to meet membership and financial targets. After 1956, rebuilding the Party's organisation and, above all, membership was a personal obsession for McLennan:

> He was always demanding certain targets to be reached. It was that kind of atmosphere – authoritarian, hierarchical, bureaucratic – that was cultivated. Very sharp with those that failed to meet their targets. There were those in the Scottish Party that would be inclined to fake their membership figures rather miss their targets.

37 J. Ashton, interview with A. Campbell and J. McIlroy (BL 1049/03/01/02).
38 Communist Party of Great Britain, Paisley Branch, 'Notes', 1966; AGM, 1972, Willie Thompson Collection, Glasgow Caledonian University Archives.
39 J. Kay, interview with McKinlay (2011).

I remember one occasion on the Glasgow Committee when the Secretary exploded at the number of ghost members. The rest of us could barely contain our laughter.[40]

Individual members, similarly, had 'targets, targets, targets. It was demanding. You were held to account'.[41]

The Party was severe on its own. Jack Ashton illustrated this by recalling travelling through Midlothian one snowy Hogmanay visiting the last four members to collect their dues before returning to Glasgow for the Bells. Ashton got two members' dues but had to return home to restore feeling to his frozen limbs in a hot bath. He was disturbed by a phone call from Gordon McLennan just before midnight who asked him to report on his collections. Ashton reported what he thought of as his success in collecting the dues of two members, despite being forced to turn back due to snow. There was a pause at the end of Ashton's report before McLennan replied: 'So you've failed comrade – happy new year'.[42] Reid's mentor Pollitt was demanding, but in a different way from McLennan. Pollitt 'was a slave driver with a flattering tongue instead of a lash'.[43] Perhaps something of Pollitt's charming pressure lay behind Reid's recollection that 'Harry once told me and Joan, my wife, that I would be the General Secretary of the Party. His tone of voice suggested it was the greatest honour in the world. There was a religious-like reverence for the post'.[44]

Reid, like many others, used the metaphor of religion to understand – and convey – the depth of commitment of communists to their beliefs and to their party. Later, during a long interview with Jonathan Dimbleby, in his Clydebank flat, complete with the sounds of an ice-cream van outside, Reid drew on a biblical-like phrase to explain that 'people like Airlie and me we're very much flesh of the flesh, and blood of the blood, of the British working class'.[45] Indeed, Pollitt rarely spoke without referring to the 'gleam' of socialism, a gleam that gained lustre the more distant it became. But there were two sides to this quasi-religious metaphor. First, and by far the most common, is that of blind faith, of individuals whose deep loyalty blunted their intellectual and democratic instincts. Of course, this

---

40   J. Foster, interview with McKinlay (2013).
41   M. Easedale, interview with McKinlay (2017).
42   D. Chalmers, interview with McKinlay (2017).
43   C. Cockburn, *Crossing the Line, Being the Second Volume of Autobiography* (London, 1958).
44   *Moscow Gold*, rough draft, 1992, Glasgow University Archives, ACCN3717/16.
45   Jimmy Reid, interview with Jonathan Dimbleby, *This Week* (April 1972).

metaphor was most commonly expressed by those heretics who publicly renounced their erstwhile faith, or by those bemused critics who had never shared it. Second, and often forgotten, was that this sense of a revolutionary vocation was based on hope, personal experience and a coherent political world view. The Party, in contrast to the highly disciplined public face, George Greig maintains, was 'full of *argumentative* people. Arguments brought people together. You got a real political education through argument'.[46] Paradoxically, argument was part of the fabric of grassroots communism but was not necessarily corrosive of Party unity, and maybe that is why such an individualist like Reid could tolerate and be tolerated. As Greig says:

> Argument created a great unity. That was our strength: what we were trying to do was make a better society, better for people. There was a tremendous feeling: we weren't doing this to get money or to advance ourselves in any way; it was about important principles. That was the basis of the great community you found in the Party. Of course, there were profound disagreements – we argued like hell, but *never* about principles. *That* was the basis of comradeship, *that* was the real discipline in the Party.[47]

This sense of revolutionary vocation was a deep resource for the Party, but one that could grate. One life-long communist, Willie Thompson, recalled a Glasgow meting led by Gollan and Reid in the early 1960s: 'we didn't like hype: too revivalist. It really set our teeth on edge. Too much like a religious rally. In taking the collection – multiple pounds; then pounds; then coins. Felt like moral blackmail. Plus, it felt like an evangelical rally'.[48]

For those that remained in the party fold rather than loosening ties with Moscow, steps were taken to strengthen them. Considerable sums of money were sent through the Soviet Embassy to finance the *Daily Worker*.[49] Reid described the cloak and dagger arrangement that was established to promote the flow of cash to King Street:

> The delivery was always on Hampstead Heath. At an appointed place, the deputy general secretary of the British Communist Party, a man called Reuben Falber, would wait. A car would draw

---

46 Kay, interview with McKinlay.
47 G. Greig, interview with McKinlay (2011).
48 W. Thompson interview with A. Campbell and J. McIlroy (BL 1049/143).
49 Laybourn and Murphy, *Red Flag*, 153.

up to the kerb. A window facing the kerb would be lowered. The KGB man inside would hand out a parcel containing cash in British currency. Only three people knew of this: these were Falber, and the general secretary of the Communist Party, John Gollan, and someone from the *Morning Star* newspaper whose name I can't recall. I was then in the leadership of the British Communist Party and knew nothing of this; neither did all the others except the three mentioned above.[50]

The party also reconfirmed its commitment to democratic centralism. Reid's mentor and 'hero' Harry Pollitt was particularly unapologetic. Echoing the Comintern line, as far as he was concerned the Soviet invasion 'not only saved Hungary from fascism, but also ... saved Europe from the menace of a new base for aggressive fascism and imperialism'.[51] Pollitt had also refused to be part of the chorus of disapproval of Stalinism. Resigning as General Secretary, he said that 'he was too old to go into reverse and denigrate a man who he had admired above all others for more than a quarter of a century';[52] indeed, he became disillusioned not with Stalin but with Khrushchev. Reid was convinced that Pollitt had known nothing of Stalin's crimes before 1953. But Pollitt continued to hang a portrait of the Soviet dictator in his living room, saying, 'He's staying there as long as I'm alive'. Pollitt died, aged 69, of cerebral thrombosis, after years of worsening health, while returning on the SS *Orion* from a speaking tour of Australia on 27 June 1960. He was cremated at Golders Green Cemetery, London, on 9 July. The degree to which both men had formed a bond of comradeship which went beyond politics can be deduced from Reid's reaction on hearing the news of his death. He was on holiday with his wife and first child at a caravan park somewhere in Ayrshire: 'I walked down the pier at the village called the Maidens to some deserted sand dunes, flung myself down and wept'.[53] Reflecting on his passing, Reid remarked:

> Looking back at the leadership of the party when I joined it ... one thing stood out. The old guard ... were almost without exception leaders, mass leaders in their own right ... they were not unresponsive ... of new information and knowledge, to new ideas

---

50 *Herald*, 22 January 2001.
51 J. Mahon, *Harry Pollitt: A Biography* (London, 1976), 408.
52 Laybourn and Murphy, *Red Flag*, 143.
53 Reid, *Reflections*, 41.

and concepts. But they could not implement them. Even if the will was there, age, and in some cases death, made sure of that.[54]

After Pollitt's death Reid grew closer to John Gollan, who had succeeded the former as General Secretary of the CPGB.

Another death that profoundly touched Reid and showed his sentimental side was that of Glen, his dog. As he explained:

> He was an ever-present companion during my childhood and a source of solace during my teens and early manhood ... One afternoon I was phoned at work by my sister, Betty.
>
> She started talking about every mundane thing under the sun. I was getting alarmed. After some prompting she got to the point. On the vet's advice Glen had been put down that morning. Those back home were worried about my reaction. I said something like it was better that than Glen should suffer. Betty sounded mightily relieved. When I put down the phone a million memories flooded back. I cleared my desk, left the office. Went to a bar across the road and ordered the first large whisky. Sometime later I walked down to Charing Cross station just off the Strand to get a train home. My train was due in 15 minutes. I went into the station bar to wait in 'comfort'. I missed the train and waited for another. Missed that too. I did get home eventually, couldn't find my key, had to knock the door. My young wife stood looking at her swain swaying on the doorstep. This man who was alleged to be a leader of men. All he could say in a trembling voice was: 'Glen's deid (dead)'.[55]

The Party's defiance on Hungary did no lasting harm as within a few years recruitment drives brought membership levels back to where they were before the invasion.[56] In fact, YCL membership at 4,666 in 1963 was the highest it had been since 1945.[57] New constituencies of potential members were also sought out by the Party. One fruitful area was support for nuclear disarmament. Communists had stoutly defended the USSR's right to possess a nuclear arsenal. Indeed, Hugh Kerr, former Labour MEP (1994–9), recalled, in his obituary of Reid, that he had first met him 'in the late 1950s when he came to Kilmarnock to recruit

---

54 Reid, *Reflections*, 41.
55 *Herald*, 28 January 1998.
56 Eaden and Renton, *Communist Party*, 122.
57 Thompson, *Good Old Cause*, 121.

a group of sons of communists to the Young Communist League. We asked him his policy on nuclear weapons and he defended Russia's right to the bomb – 'the workers' bomb'. We were into CND and decided to join the Young Socialists instead'.[58] Under Reid's leadership the YCL had moved from trying to act as a politicised mainstream youth organisation, akin to a youth club, to a more explicitly 'junior version of the Party'.[59] 'The YCL', Reid reminded the 1962 National Congress, 'exists to make communists: People who join our ranks are not ready-made Marxists. We have to equip them with a Marxist understanding'. Part of this political education involved finding ways to work with all sorts of community organisations:

> The character of our branch life must be broadened, social and cultural activities must be seen, not as sugar coating on the political pill but as an integral part of our political life and work. We are serious young men and women. We want to change the world. Our purpose is not only serious – it is exciting and exhilarating and enjoyable.[60]

Although growing in terms of membership and organisation, the YCL was in the long run under even greater strain than the Communist Party. In 1966, only 19 per cent of members were up to date with their dues; around half of Scottish branches had not met in the previous six months. Even those individuals singled out as likely to become communist activists, perhaps even full-time party workers, were not immune: more than a third of this select group had resigned or slipped away in the previous year.[61] Replacing lost members was a monumental job, let alone expanding the Party. The scale of the problem was highlighted by the activities of the Jimmy Reid Youth Brigade, formed to help his Clydebank campaign in the 1964 general election – its slogan was 'We Need Jimmy'. It was led by Willie Thomson and Donald MacKenzie and had between six and 12 members out every night for more than three weeks. Despite

---

58 *Guardian*, 12 August 2010.
59 M. Waite, 'Young People and Communist Politics in Britain, 1920–1991: Aspects of the History of the Young Communist League' (unpublished M.Phil. thesis, University of Lancaster, 1992), 27, 295.
60 Report of Young Communist League, 24th National Congress, 3, 4 November 1962, 14.
61 Young Communist League, Scottish Committee, 1966, Glasgow Caledonian University.

this heroic effort, the campaign report showed that: 'They sold 576 copies of *Challenge* ... [but] only 2 recruits for the Party and 3 for the YCL have been reported ... 6,700 people seen on doorstep, 2,800 heard the candidate ... 2,400 pieces of literature sold, 29,400 leaflets distributed and over £300 raised'.[62] But the campaign was ignored by senior party members, as the report noted: 'Key figures in area not yet won to participate e.g. A(rthur). Henderson – no contact with Jimmy at all ... F(inlay). Hart saw Jimmy once during [his] visit'.[63] Disappointment led to relentless self-reflection among the members. After relaxing at the Youth Brigade social – complete with 'fab goings-on' – young communists were asked to reflect on the scope, speed and effectiveness of their canvassing: 'working in a critical and enthusiastic manner, dissatisfied with previous standards and continually aiming to improve its performance'.[64]

The extent to which the YCL with Reid as general secretary had become an integral part of the parent body allowed Gollan to boast at rallies that he 'never had to discipline the YCL'. This did not spare him from criticism within the YCL. Stan Graham, in an open letter to delegates at the 1964 Congress, spoke of the lack of rigour in the branches regarding the study of Marxism, and accused Reid and Gollan of 'wholeheartedly support(ing) the crimes of Stalin', and of crushing internal debate by running the YCL on the 'basis of democratic centralism'.[65] It is revealing that when Reid was replaced by Barney Davies as National Secretary of the YCL there was a seismic shift in its outlook: from obedience to defiance on issues diverse as sex, popular culture and drugs.[66]

However, the CPGB, despite these criticisms, had showed itself to be open to change. It changed the name of the *Daily Worker* to the more inclusive *Morning Star* on 25 April 1966 in an opening ceremony performed by the actress Sybil Thorndike, and supported by Reid.[67] Also, after some fiercely fought debates, unilateralism became Party policy by the mid-1960s. The liaison with CND was fruitful; the alliance saw membership climb from an all-time low of 24,670 in February 1958 to

---

62 Young Communist League, Campaign Report, October 1964, Glasgow Caledonian University.
63 Young Communist League, Campaign Report, October 1964, Glasgow Caledonian University.
64 Young Communist League, Bulletin 2, Glasgow Caledonian University.
65 Jimmy Reid Collection, Glasgow University Archives (A2, 1/6).
66 G. Andrews, *End Games and New Times: The Final Years of British Communism, 1964–1991* (London, 2004), 32–7.
67 Callaghan, *Cold War*, 284.

34,281 in 1964.[68] The Party was also jettisoning its pro-Stalin position in favour of a much more transparently critical stance. This ideological transition was assisted by Khrushchev at the 22nd Congress in 1961, where he further denounced Stalinism and announced that the USSR would overtake the USA in material consumption by 1980; a prospect which did much to improve the image of communism and, along with unilateralism, helped to attract new recruits to the Party.[69] But, as a result, the composition of the Party was beginning to undergo a social transformation. Prior to the 1960s, the CPGB was a working man's party made up of cadres of the highest skilled workers. 'Communists were drawn exclusively from Class 1 (engineering) members, the "time served" … in the coalfields the party typically recruited face-workers … in the clothing factories … it was the cutters, a job elite of tailors … among the London busmen … it recruited its cadres from the drivers'.[70] From Keir Hardie down to Willie Gallacher, socialism or communism was seen as a political creed for the respectable, hard-working, decent and honest folk rather than the drunken, uneducated working poor. The journalist Ian Jack, writing of the nature of his father's socialist beliefs, captured the skilled worker's fusion of respectability with politics, remarking:

> For all his socialist convictions I don't think my father ever saw social division in purely political and economic terms … it was an older moral force which generated the most genuine heat in him, and the class conflict … was not so much between classes as internal to each of them; it was 'decent folk' versus the rest … A strict application of socialist theory would mean that we were bound to the Davidsons (crash, thump; where's ma fuckin' tea) and that we would be bound to them for life.[71]

The idea of a socialist society being inhabited by unrespectable beer-swilling wife-beaters, using expletives in place of decent language, was anathema to the politically conscious, and, as a result, they sought to distance themselves from the lumpen poor. Communists were utterly conventional, if not conservative, in their home lives: communism and male chauvinism were far from being incompatible. For male communists of Reid's generation, like their forebears, the disciplined communist cadre literally wore their

---

68 Eaden and Renton, *Communist Party*, 121; Callaghan, *Cold War*, 17.
69 Thompson, *Good Old Cause*, 119.
70 R. Samuel, 'Class Politics', 74.
71 I. Jack, *Before the Oil Ran Out: Britain, 1977–86* (London, 1987), 33.

convention as a uniform: a suit, white shirt, a tie and *always* well-polished shoes. To be a communist was to have a vocation. The good communist was 'disciplined' and 'organised': terms which signified that the individual was reliable, mannerly, dedicated and loyal. For the full-time party worker such as Reid, these qualities were extraordinarily heightened.[72] But conventionality and social orthodoxy were to become problematic for the Party in a post-war Britain that was experiencing far-reaching cultural change and the birth of consumerism.

First, the Party was ill-equipped to capitalise on the surge of student radicalism in the 1960s which was as much about lifestyle as it was about politics. Politically, in Britain, there were 5,000 members of the YCL in 1951 by 1958 it was 1,387. Eric Hobsbawm, in a report on the CPGB's relationship to young people, claimed that the Party was ignored by young people in favour of the New Left. Young radicals favoured the New Left-led causes against the nuclear bomb and anti-colonialism, which the Party, tied to the interests of Soviet foreign policy, was equivocal about. Hobsbawm highlighted the lethargy and appalling political ignorance in the CPGB as he could find no evidence that Party officials or even 'student and youth organisers' had been attending any 'meetings or activities' of the main New Left organisation: *Universities and Left Review*.[73] Culturally, it was no different. A small episode that demonstrates the Party's remoteness from the youth movement was that a YCL organiser in the 1960s was 'ordered to get his hair cut'.[74] Martin Jacques, the youngest member of the NEC, and later editor of *Marxism Today*, said: 'I felt like a Martian ... they would turn up in conservative clothes ... I was dressed in the style of the times, I'd turn up in a sweater. I'd go to Congress and I'd be the only man in the place not wearing a suit'.[75] When the YCL organ *Challenge* put the Beatles on the front cover of the December 1963 edition it elicited 'much criticism from Scottish YCLers'.[76]

Reid, who never considered himself dressed without a suit, collar and tie, was as much out of touch with youth culture as his older comrades. In a later interview with the journalist Ruth Wishart, his eldest daughter Eileen said that he was 'profoundly ignorant of popular culture', recalling

---

72 A. McKinlay, 'Jimmy Reid: Fragments from a Political Life', *Scottish Labour History*, 46 (2011), 38–53.
73 Callaghan, *Cold War*, 23.
74 Beckett, *Enemy Within*, 161.
75 Beckett, *Enemy Within*, 167.
76 Waite, 'Young People and Communist Politics in Britain, 1920–1991', 336.

that after an appearance on *Parkinson* he was introduced to Roger Daltrey, lead singer of *The Who*, but had no idea who he was.[77] Indeed, he was contemptuous of popular music: a medium he could barely understand. Writing some years later he claimed that he'd 'never bought or possessed an Elvis Presley disc or seen one of his awful movies … His light baritone voice was tenth rate. He couldn't swing and his face and personality reflected a mind permanently caught in the grips of infantilism … Then lots of people started raving about Bob Dylan. He sounded like an asthmatic tom cat "dressed" by the vet'.[78] His taste in music was summed up in 'two names – Beethoven and Basie'. 'In my book the symphony orchestra represents the sublime pinnacle of musical achievement. I also love jazz, the only genuine urban folk music … The "Come All Ye" folksy punters are essentially involved in the music of the rural past'.[79]

Secondly, it was also faced with the growing issue of women's liberation and the problem that posed for the party's class-based analysis of society. From the early 1960s, feminists were beginning to raise issues connected with sexuality, family, inequalities in the workplace in terms of wages and conditions, as well as official legal inequalities. In America, Betty Friedan (*The Feminine Mystique* [1963]) and Gloria Steinem ('A Bunny's Tale', an article in *Show* [May 1963]) were the trailblazers and their views concerning the oppression and exclusion of women in the workplace as well as in the home were imported into Britain in the 1960s, catching the imagination of radical women, mainly it must be said outside the CPGB. This shift towards analysing society in terms of gender rather than class became manifest in Britain in the 1970s in the works of Germaine Greer (*The Female Eunuch* [1970]), Juliet Mitchell (*Women's Estate* [1970]) and Sheila Rowbotham (*Hidden from History* [1973]). There was no explicit misogyny in the CPGB: women were welcomed into Party membership. A few joined but those that did tended to be relatives of existing male members.[80] Callaghan estimated that in 1955, out of a total of 32,681 members, there were 9,504 women members, of which two-thirds were 'housewives', and women were never less than a third of the membership.[81] But they were never encouraged to

---

77   *Daddy's Girl*, BBC Radio Scotland, 2008.
78   *Daily Record*, 8 August 1983.
79   *Daily Record*, 7 July 1986.
80   S. Bruley, 'Socialism and Feminism in the Communist Party of Great Britain, 1920–1939' (unpublished PhD thesis, University of London, 1980), 123, 295.
81   Callaghan, *Cold War*, 18.

take leading roles in the Party, nor to be active in making policy. At the 1952 Congress, out of 448 delegates, 72 were female, of whom 26 were described as 'housewives'.[82]

Thirdly, there was also the issue of deindustrialisation and the impact this had on the post-war composition of the workforce. There was a decisive shift away from heavy industry to the service sector where the party had little influence. That change was more evident in Scotland than in other parts of the UK as its economy was less diversified. The number of miners in Scotland fell by 60,000 between 1939 and 1970 and output was 45 per cent lower than it had been in 1913. Shipbuilding, the jewel in Scotland's industrial crown, had seen its share of world output fall from a respectable 12 per cent in 1951 to just 1.3 per cent in 1968. The Scottish textile industry lost 50 per cent of its workforce, or 92,700 jobs, between 1960 and 1978.[83] Everywhere the staple industries in Scotland, South Wales and the north-east of England were in retreat, if not in a state of collapse. These industries had in the past been the rocks on which party membership was built. It was now a house of cards liable to collapse completely at any time. By contrast, the service sector was growing rapidly, and by 1984 would account for around two-thirds of total employment in Scotland and 60 per cent of its gross domestic product. Even industrial Glasgow had nearly 73 per cent of its workforce in the service sector by that date. The economic transition was also reflected in the trade union movement. In 1960, the industrial section of the Scottish Trade Union Congress (STUC), which included mining, metals and machines and transport, accounted for 57 per cent of total affiliated membership, and the service sector, which included distribution, public employees and general workers, contained 26 per cent. Ten years later, the respective figures were 48 per cent and 42 per cent.[84] As industry shrank so did Party membership.

But lifestyle, feminism and economic change were not the only barriers to advance. The CPGB's commitment to following the Moscow line, although not as rigid as it had been during the 1950s, remained into the 1960s, and there was still a marked tendency to view foreign affairs through the eyes of the Communist International. Reid was not immune from this almost instinctive pro-Moscow reaction to world events. Introducing the *Political Report* to the CPGB's 24th National Congress in November 1962, he addressed the Cuban missile crisis of the previous

---

82 Callaghan, *Cold War*, 22.
83 Hunter, 'Labour Market', 177.
84 Scottish Trade Union Council, *Annual Reports* (1960, 1970, 1980).

month, in which the Soviet Union agreed to Fidel Castro's request to place nuclear missiles in Cuba to deter future harassment of the country by the USA: a situation that almost provoked a third world war. In the following highly partisan manner, Reid claimed:

> That we are meeting in Congress this weekend and not dead, or the mutilated victims of nuclear war, is above all a tribute to the peaceful policy and restraint of the Soviet government and people in the face of the maniacal provocations of Robert Kennedy, the Pentagon and the multi-millionaires of Wall Street … the plague on both your houses' brigades, those who argue that the blame for the danger of war and nuclear annihilation is shared equally by the USA and the Soviet Union, are talking through their hats.[85]

However, that certainty, that righteousness, was to be tested six years later when divisions once again re-emerged in the Party ranks due to the Prague Spring of 1968. The 'Spring' only flickered brightly for eight months before being extinguished by the invasion of the Warsaw Pact armies totalling around half a million men. It had begun with the installation of Alexander Dubček as First Secretary of the Czechoslovakian Communist Party in January 1968. He was committed to creating socialism with a human face and took steps to reform the economy, promote freedom of speech and assembly, travel, even considering a multi-party state. Unlike Hungary, there was no armed resistance to the invading forces, but a well-orchestrated campaign of civil disobedience was carried out. Compared with 1956, when thousands of Hungarians were killed, only 72 Czechs lost their lives. By March the following year, Dubček had been removed from office and 'normalisation' had seen the re-establishment of strict censorship, freedom of movement severely restricted and the re-centralisation of the economy.[86]

There was widespread criticism of the Soviet action in Czechoslovakia within western Communist parties. Both the French (*Parti communiste français*) and the Italian (*Partito Comunista Italiano*) parties condemned the invasion and denounced the occupation, as did nearer to hand the Finnish party. Dictators such as Enver Hoxha of Albania and Nicolae Ceaușescu of Romania also spoke in harsh critical terms regarding Soviet interference. Within the CPGB, the criticism by the Party leadership of the invasion

---

85 Speech to the 24th Congress of CPGB (November 1962), Jimmy Reid Collection, Glasgow University Archives.
86 B. Fowkes, *Eastern Europe, 1945–1969: From Stalinism to Stagnation* (London, 2000); T. Judt, *Postwar: A History of Europe since 1945* (London, 2005).

of Czechoslovakia 'opened up bitter divisions which never healed ... and formed the battle lines between the different wings of the Party through to its final demise in 1991'.[87] The traditional or Stalinist wing of the Party, which included the intellectual R. Palme Dutt, incredibly, given the changes that had taken place in the CPGB and the popularity of Euro-communism, still managed to attract 28 per cent of the vote of delegates at the 1969 conference to discuss Czechoslovakia. However, unlike over Hungary there was no mass exodus and few high-profile resignations. But, despite the leadership's and Reid's condemnation of the invasion, membership of the Party declined from 33,000 in 1967 to under 29,000 in 1971.[88]

In a practical sense, Reid's role in determining the CPGB's response was negligible. When the Soviet invasion occurred, John Gollan, the Party's General Secretary, was on holiday in a remote Scottish croft and could not be reached. The Party's all important Political Committee was immediately called to King Street for an emergency meeting. Reid, the Scottish Secretary, was called and asked to catch the first flight to London. For the British Party's leadership, their condemnation of the invasion had to be couched very carefully to maintain Party unity. Publicly to condemn the Soviet invasion would infuriate those steadfast supporters of the Soviet Union and those for whom any criticism had to remain inside the Party's ranks. Thus, publicly, the invasion was referred to by the leadership in more neutral terms as an 'intervention'.[89] Reid rang from Heathrow at 2 p.m. and approved the immediate release of the Party's statement to catch the evening news cycle. Gollan, irritated at the interruption to his holiday, rang at 6 p.m., completely unaware of the invasion. For Reid, the complex politics of maintaining Party unity were more hard lessons in the conservatism of the Communist Party.[90]

With the London leadership, apparently far from happy at his decision, Reid decided to return to Scotland in 1964 to what was described by one his comrades as a 'poor hoose' in Faifley council estate, Clydebank, which 'didnae hae nothing, but they didnae hae much'.[91] His daughter Eileen said of the accommodation: 'Our tiny tenement home was very poor. There was nothing in it that wasn't given to us. The floors were all lino. But we had

---

87 Eaden and Renton, *Communist Party*, 145.
88 Laybourn and Murphy, *Red Flag*, 164.
89 Andrews, *Cold War*, 38.
90 R. Faber, 'The 1968 Czechoslovak Crisis: Inside the British Communist Party', Socialist History Society Pamphlet, 5 (1996), 12–14.
91 Bob Dickie, interview with McKinlay (2016).

an upright piano. Despite us being very poor, my Gran and Grandpa paid for me to have piano lessons from age seven. That kind of thing happened in communist families'.[92] Another reason might have been the death of his father Leo in May 1962. Leo had provided a considerable amount of moral support for Joan and his grandchildren, while the Reids were domiciled in London, and with his demise life got harder and lonelier for her.[93]

Almost immediately after returning Reid was elected full-time Secretary of the Scottish Committee of the Communist Party, a position he held until 1969. Some of what he found on his return would have been familiar. The Glasgow Party was a 'very proletarian Party'. John Foster, who arrived in the city in 1967 from Cambridge University, recalled his first May Day in Glasgow: 'the Party contingent was *drilled* for the march, literally *drilled* by people who had served in the Spanish Civil War. We were in rows and columns representing the Communist Party'.[94]

However, the low wage Reid received as a full-time official was barely enough to keep him and his family, and when a third child, Julie, arrived in 1969, he quit his position for better-paid work. Throughout the 1960s, the Party fell short of its ambition to pay its full-time workers the average industrial wage. Not only were Communist Party workers 'paid buttons', their wages were always uncertain:

> [D]ripped their money, a little bit on a Tuesday, a little bit more on a Friday. You were always short of money. Party officials toured members' homes, updating comrades on campaigns but also collecting the dues that would pay their wages. On his return to Scotland, Reid became one of these revolutionary mendicants. There was no embarrassment involved in visits that were an accepted part of Party life. Reid, then, was not alone in feeling financial pressure but, if anything, the uncertainty for regional Party workers was even greater than for national officials.[95]

Full-time Party workers were typically family men like George Grieg, with 'rent to pay, provisions to buy. It was a hard struggle. I'm not bemoaning the life, but it was an imposition on the family. There was a limit on what you could sustain – we lost many good cadres like that'.[96] Greig

---

92 Eileen Reid, interview with McKinlay (2017).
93 Eileen Reid, interview with McKinlay.
94 Foster, interview with McKinlay.
95 P. Devine, interview with A. Campbell and J. McIlroy (BL 1049/41).
96 Ashton, interview with Campbell and McIlroy.

also experienced the strain of balancing sustained political commitment and the financial demands of raising a young family: 'That happened to us all. But you were so strongly committed to what you were trying to achieve that you made sacrifices that you'd never make for anything else. But you had *nae* money. It was difficult and that goes on year after year'.[97]

Despite being offered a wage increase by Gollan, Reid resigned his post as Scottish Secretary and found work at Upper Clyde Shipbuilders (UCS), Govan – the former Fairfield shipyard – as a fitter: he had returned to the tools. Jimmy Airlie was instrumental in arranging Reid's return to industry. Davy Cooper, a fellow communist and UCS shop steward, explained:

> He was an engineer, but he hadn't worked in the tools in years. So, he was an engineer of sorts, just don't ask him to tighten a nut. Jimmy had to be found a role. You can't just walk in the door and become a shop steward straightaway: he had to start working on the tools. We were outfitting a dredger at the time and it was decided that Jimmy should work alongside me in the depths of an engine room in a dredger. These were about the most inhospitable conditions you could get in a shipyard, and that's saying something. So, Jimmy came straight from the shirt and tie environment of King Street to the cold, wet depths of a ship's hull.
>
> Tea breaks were in a shed knocked up inside the ship. Sometimes the conversation wasn't too elevated: there was very little talk of dialectical materialism (laughs). Jimmy did his best to fit in and his knowledge of football and horses certainly helped.[98]

Reid was transferred to UCS Clydebank, formerly John Brown, with another Party steward, Frank McGowan. They joined a group of shop stewards that management observed with some unease, as younger, more collective and more strategic in their approach to industrial relations. By this time Reid was also Town Councillor for Clydebank's Seventh Ward and AEU Convenor and Chairman of the Outfitting Trades. As well as being active in local politics, and a leading shop steward, Reid was also a member of the Communist Party's Shipbuilding Branch that drew together activists from all the Clyde yards. In 1965, the Shipbuilding Branch had 31 members, of which between 18 and 24 regularly attended meetings. But, 'given assistance', Party officials were hopeful that the

---

97 G. Greig, interview with McKinlay.
98 D. Cooper, interview with McKinlay (2016).

Branch offered 'real possibilities' of development.[99] An important part of the Branch's activities was Marxist education, partly theoretical but always *practical*. John Foster, one of the Branch's tutors, explained the objectives of these classes:

> There was a particular character to Communist Party industrial work. The way that communists operated was quite different from those they opposed, the right wing in the trade unions. The mentality of Catholic Action, for instance, was that of deference, doing what their bosses said, working within the established order, using the established bureaucratic mechanisms: it was more or less the discipline of a regular army, so to speak. That explains the weaknesses of that type of group. The way in which communists operated – encouraged by Bert Ramelson and his predecessor Peter Kerrigan – was as guerrilla fighters, so to speak. Ramelson and Kerrigan had both fought in Spain so they understood guerrilla warfare in practice as well as in theory. You had to have people on the ground, in each workplace, who could think for themselves and have the education – the *political* education – and understanding to *act*: the basic principle of guerrilla warfare. … Communists were there for the long haul, embedded in a particular workplace. Communists were acutely aware that they couldn't operate as individuals but only as part of a collective. But they were always conscious that they were in a minority, typically a very small minority, and had to operate in terms of their *own* assessment of what was possible in that particular circumstance. An enormous amount of Party resources went into education that gave comrades that kind of *practical* theory.[100]

The Shipbuilding Branch was where strategy was debated, always in terms of what was considered practical within the shifting categories of sectionalism and solidarity. Decisions were not reached abstractly but were 'ruthlessly realistic'. If the communist activists were schooled in the tactics of guerrilla warfare, then they also schooled themselves in a language of solidarity that reached beyond craft divisions. The development of this language of solidarity took many forms but its most acerbic form was used by the engineer Jimmy Airlie, who never missed an opportunity to

---

99 Communist Party of Great Britain, Glasgow Branch Organisation, 1966, Glasgow Caledonian University.
100 Foster, interview with McKinlay.

pour scorn on the boilermakers' insistence that they were 'the kings of the river'.[101] This language of solidarity was to prove a crucial resource for the communist stewards during the UCS work-in. Airlie's jibes at the boilermakers' expense were designed not to ridicule and alienate but to produce solidarity where none had previously existed. The necessity for such rough humour was, on the other hand, a reminder to Airlie and others that any shipyard solidarity had to be made and was always precarious. The examples of Airlie, Reid and others in the Shipbuilding Branch also showed members how to hold a room, how to argue, and how to maintain solidarity despite differences of opinion.

The leadership of the Scottish Party was more practical than intellectual, with a deep understanding of the working-class communities and organisations they were part of. It was not so much insular as self-contained, and enjoyed considerable autonomy over its strategy and operations. Reid's time as Scottish Secretary had not been a great success, for although at the time of his resignation Scotland represented a quarter of Party membership, organisation was very poor. Local spikes in membership aside, it was experiencing managed decline. However, the Scottish leadership was not easily reconciled to the erosion of the Party's membership and influence. For them, the only answer was to redouble its efforts, to work a declining number of Party cadres still more. Reid was bitterly opposed to this as likely to prove counter-productive. Quietly, Reid was asked to resign his post since they were convinced the Party in Scotland needed someone to work even longer hours and not to spend the morning reading in bed. In reply, Reid said that he was 'lying in my bed doing what you buggers *never* do: think[ing]'.[102] To the British leadership, Reid posed the question: 'was our membership organised in a network of functioning branches?' The answer was an emphatic 'no ... the majority were limping along'.[103] Indeed, he was so concerned at the state of the Party that in his letter of resignation as Scottish Secretary in 1969 he told John Gollan of the grave personal and political difficulties of working in 'an atmosphere of constant crisis'. Such was the burden on Party full-timers that he feared that it would lead to 'a tired, faded cadre force, to branches that have had all the life kicked out of them and to serious breakdowns in the health of some comrades'.[104]

---

101 J. Kay, interview with Campbell and McIlroy (BL 1049/78/02).
102 D. Chalmers, interview with McKinlay (2016).
103 Reid, *Reflections*, 43–4.
104 J. Reid, Communist Party of Great Britain Archive, Peoples' History Museum, Manchester.

7 The Reid family in protest 1965 (courtesy of Eileen Reid)

But there was more to his resignation than failing Party organisation. Reid was, at best, an awkward fit for a Party of activism rarely sidetracked by reflection. In terms of internal Party politics, Reid was not closely identified either with the modernisers anxious to break with democratic centralism or the stalwarts reluctant to change. Reid remained very much on the sidelines, very much an individual sympathetic to calls for modernisation without being a vocal critic of the status quo: 'he had a reputation for being somewhat patient with the comrades who were more conservative although he clearly had reservations about the Party's culture'.[105] Reid's ambivalence was a recognition that the Party could not reconcile these contradictory impulses towards modernisation and pluralism, on the one hand, and discipline and democratic centralism, on the other. The redrafted *British Road to Socialism* that Reid helped write and launch in 1968 spoke to the need for communists to 'marry liberal democracy with socialist democracy', but the Party structure and culture remained stubbornly hierarchical and conservative.[106] However, it was evidence of the increasingly reformist nature of the CPGB as it moved

---

105 Foster, interview with McKinlay (2015).
106 'Moscow Gold', final draft, 1992, 17, Glasgow University Archives, ACCN3717/16/8.

from a revolutionary insurrectionist Party to a reformist opposition as witness its 'growing concern to submit evidence to official enquiries'. Throughout the 1960s, reports were compiled on a range of diverse issues such as broadcasting, defence, science and transport.[107] But parliamentary reformist parties had this ground cornered. The CPGB had to come up with something highly imaginative to trigger the same kind of response as had the anti-fascism of the 1930s and in the 1960s unilateralism.[108] The commitment of the Tory Government of 1970 to rolling back the frontiers of the state and the fundamental reform of industrial relations was to provide that spark and turn communist Jimmy Reid from local union activist into a national figure (Figure 7).

---

107 Callaghan, *Cold War*, 291, for a full list.
108 Morgan, Cohen and Flinnet, *Communists*, 20.

4

UCS Work-in

Jimmy Reid owes his fame and his place in the pantheon of Scottish radicalism to one event: the UCS work-in of 1971. Reid was not the only leader of the workforce; others, such as James Airlie, Sammy Gilmore and Sammy Barr, also played important roles as part of a truly collective leadership. But it was Reid's powers of communication and leadership that symbolised the coalition of resistance that developed on the Clyde in response to the Tory government's attempt to close UCS and throw the men on the industrial scrapheap. The decision by the trade union leadership in the yards to stage a work-in rather than go on strike or stage a sit-in caught the imagination of constituencies of people way beyond the geographical parameters of the upper reaches of the River Clyde. The press and public were astounded by the audacity of these young (mainly communist) shop stewards. They led marches to Downing Street, orchestrated mass demonstrations in Glasgow and generated a huge wave of international sympathy and support for their actions. The refusal of the workers to accept the messianic logic of the free market laid the basis of, and inspiration for, a wider struggle against the Heath government and its attempts to reform industrial relations and roll back the frontiers of the state.

Shipbuilding on the Clyde had been in trouble since the end of the Korean War; and since 1953 had been rapidly losing its place as a major producer in world markets. In 1956, Japan deposed the United Kingdom as the leading nation in shipbuilding output, remaining the leading producer of ships for the rest of the century. By 1958, Germany had put the UK into third place, with the latter only commanding 15 per cent of world output.[1]

---

1 A. Slaven and H. Murphy, *Crossing the Bar: An Oral History of the British Shipbuilding, Ship Repairing and Marine Engine Building Industries in the Age of Decline, 1956–1990* (Liverpool, 2013), 231.

Thereafter, the UKs share of world shipbuilding output continued to decline. On the Clyde, there were 28 shipyards in 1950, but by 1968 only nine remained. Many of the Clyde's most iconic yards such as Harland and Wolff, and William Denny had collapsed in the 1960s. The latter was particularly well remembered: the workers left off work on Friday and when they returned on Monday the gates had been padlocked and they were jobless.[2] It was against this backdrop of falling market share due to intense international competition, particularly from Japan, West Germany and Sweden, that the Labour government, between 1966 and 1970 set about reorganising shipbuilding on the River Clyde.[3] Labour merged the five existing shipyards on the Upper Clyde, all of which were in serious financial straits, into one group in February 1968. Originally known as Five Yards Limited, it soon became known as Upper Clyde Shipbuilders (UCS), with Anthony Hepper, who had left the Shipbuilding Industry Board (SIB) in London, as chairman.[4] On the lower Clyde, it took another two years before the Lithgow group of shipyards of Port Glasgow and the world's senior shipyard, Scott of Greenock (established in 1711) officially merged as Scott Lithgow Limited.[5] UCS was formed from the amalgamation of five major firms: Fairfield of Govan, Alexander Stephen and Sons of Linthouse, Charles Connell and Company of Scotstoun, and John Brown and Company of Clydebank, as well as an associate subsidiary, Yarrow

2 R. Hay and J. McLauchlan, 'The Oral History of Upper Clyde Shipbuilders: A Preliminary Report', *Oral History*, 2 (1974), 47.

3 The authors wish to express their gratitude for the following details to Professor Hugh Murphy, University of Glasgow. The process began with the Shipbuilding Inquiry Report of 1965–66 (London, HMSO, 1966) chaired by Reay Geddes, then Chairman of the Dunlop Rubber Company. The inquiry panel did not contain any shipbuilders, and recommended mergers of shipyards on river centres, and the rationalisation of slow speed marine engine building in Great Britain. Because of the Shipbuilding Inquiry Report, a three-man Shipbuilding Industry Board was set up to encourage mergers by grants and loans. For this process, see L. Johnman and H. Murphy, *British Shipbuilding and the State: A Political Economy of Decline* (Liverpool, 2002), chap. 6.

4 Hepper began his varied business career with Courtaulds, then Cape Asbestos. He then joined the Thomas Tilling Group and became chairman of six of their subsidiary companies, before being seconded to George Brown's Department of Economic Affairs, and from there to the SIB, and then to UCS. Hepper later described his tenure as UCS Chairman as 'three and a half years of sheer hell'. See *Financial Times*, 3 January 1972.

5 For this long-drawn-out process, see L. Johnman and H. Murphy, *Scott Lithgow: Déjà Vu All Over Again! The Rise and Fall of a Shipbuilding Company* (Liverpool, 2005), chap. 5.

Shipbuilders Ltd, in which UCS and later, government, held a controlling stake of 51 per cent, although Yarrow severed its connection with the consortium in April 1970. The yards had been effectively taken into public ownership by the end of 1969, when the government took a 51 per cent equity stake in UCS. Indeed, by January 1970, UCS was already in receipt of £20 million of taxpayers' cash in grants and loans. In stark contrast, largely due to the long-drawn-out process of merger, Scott Lithgow on the Lower Clyde had received only £20,000.[6]

However, UCS was a shotgun wedding from inception, where the main parties were looking for a quick divorce; in fact, UCS was to exist 'longer as a company in liquidation than it did as a going concern'.[7] The chairman, Sir Iain Stewart, resigned after only two months in his post over the direction of the new group. Such was the fractious nature of the new Consortium that the Labour minister responsible for setting up it up, Tony Benn, in his diary on 17 March 1969 recalled:

> There are many people who want the whole thing to fail: Sir Charles Connell, the Deputy-Chairman … [who] believes in the old idea of throwing men out of work to discipline them; Yarrow, the other Deputy-Chairman … is longing for the moment when he can pull out Yarrows from UCS and make a profit and join up with his old friends in Lower Clyde; then there is Barry Barker of the Shipbuilding Industry Board who wants it to fail for rigid reasons … There are a lot of enemies of Upper Clyde … so I am to have a job propping it up.[8]

Benn's task proved short-lived. The general election in June 1970 saw the Labour government defeated by the Conservatives, led by Edward Heath. This signalled a new approach to British industry. Following the costly public bail-out of Rolls Royce in early 1971, the Tories proclaimed that there would be no more subsidies for what they dubbed 'lame-duck' industries. The previously protected industries would be opened up to Darwinian market competition in which the efficient companies would survive and the poorly performing would go to the wall. This economic

---

6   Johnman and Murphy, *Scott Lithgow*, 206, 210–15. By this stage, only one independent small shipyard remained on the lower Clyde: James Lamont & Co. Ltd., at Greenock.
7   B.W. Hogwood, *Government and Shipbuilding: The Politics of Industrial Change* (Farnborough, 1979), 114.
8   T. Benn, *Office without Power: Diaries 1968–1972* (London, 1988), 155.

strategy marked the increasing influence of supply side economics within the Tory Party; something which would be more evident during Margaret Thatcher's term as prime minister from 1979 onwards. Indeed, prior to taking office, the Tory shadow spokesperson on technology, Nicholas Ridley, MP for Cirencester and Tewkesbury, and a bellicose advocate of the free market, had met Sir Eric Yarrow in December 1969, and minuted the meeting. His conclusions became known as the 'Ridley Memorandum'. In it he advocated giving no more public money to UCS, selling off in the first instance Yarrow and then letting them join the Lower Clyde yards, appointing a 'Government Butcher' to cut up the remaining four shipyards, and then disposing of whatever was left as cheaply as possible to the privatised firms of the lower Clyde or any other interested party.[9] As far as he was concerned, 'the industry has had its chance'.[10] Thus, even before the Tories had formed a government, plans were firmly in place for a harsh reorganisation of the Upper Clyde. The Memorandum, according to Heath, fell into the hands of Tony Benn, who leaked its contents to the *Guardian*, and, of course, to the shop stewards.[11] Of all the actors in the UCS saga, Sir Eric Yarrow was the only one to come out smelling of roses. Yarrow, the United Kingdom's premier builder of frigates for the Royal Navy, which had already left UCS, did so with the substantial bonus of a loan of up to £4.5 million as working capital advanced by the Ministry of Defence, and inherited a construction hall built at a cost of £1.5 million, one of the few items of capital expenditure by UCS.[12]

Part of the industrial strategy of the Tories involved an attack on the trade union movement in Britain. Politicians both left and right had been alarmed by the level of rank-and-file challenges to anti-inflationary incomes policies in the mid- to late 1960s. Reforms of labour relations were first introduced by Barbara Castle, Secretary of State for Employment, on

---

9   L. Johnman and H. Murphy, *British Shipbuilding and the State: A Political Economy of Decline* (Liverpool, 2002), 184–6; J. McGill, *Crisis on the Clyde: The Story of Upper Clyde Shipbuilders* (London, 1973), 71; R. Wishart 'An Introduction to the UCS Crisis', in Reid, *Reflections*, 78.
10 *Guardian*, 17 June 1971; Johnman and Murphy, *Scott Lithgow*, 210–15 highlight the negotiations between Sir Eric Yarrow and Michael Scott and Sir William Lithgow of Scott Lithgow.
11 E. Heath, *The Course of My Life* (London, 2012), 338.
12 H. Murphy, 'Labour in the British Shipbuilding and Ship Repairing Industries in the Twentieth Century', in R. Varela, H. Murphy and M. Van der Linden (eds), *Shipbuilding and Ship Repair Workers around the World: Case Studies, 1950–2010* (Amsterdam and Chicago, 2017), 87–88.

behalf of the Labour government, designed to shackle protest through anti-union legislation. However, in 1969 a co-ordinated series of one-day national stoppages led the Wilson government to abandon its plans to reform industrial relations as encompassed in the policy document 'In Place of Strife' (1968). Edward Heath's plans to do the same through the Industrial Relations Bill would also lead to mass industrial action in the period 1970–1. It was against this backdrop of rising unemployment and perceived economic and industrial instability by the governing classes that the UCS work-in took place.

UCS was financially weak from the start. The fledgling company was saddled with pre-merger losses and those incurred from early UCS contracts, which had not hedged against rising inflationary costs, and took contracts just to stay in business. Even worse, the initial estimate of such losses was £3.5 million which soon proved to be more like £12 million. New fixed-price contracts struck in 1968 were expected to lose £4.8 million, but the actual losses were £9.8 million. Financial weaknesses were compounded by decades of underinvestment in plant, methods and management.[13] Reorganisation of the yards had failed to provide a lasting solution to the problems of the industry of which liquidity was perhaps the most pressing. A few years after it had been formed, UCS was plunged into chaos after the announcement by the Tory Secretary of State for Trade and Industry, John Davies, that the government was refusing a request for further state support: a declaration which led to a crisis of confidence amongst UCS's reputedly 2,000 creditors, and resulted in severe cash flow problems for the company. Davies made the lethal statement in the Commons to the resounding cheers of Tory backbenchers that 'that nobody's interest will be served by making the injection of funds into the company as it now stands'.[14]

The effect of his statement triggered something akin to a run on a bank: UCS creditors battered at the door and refused to grant further credit. By late June, UCS management submitted a request to the government for a further loan.[15] The call for a £6 million working capital loan to the government as a lender of last resort was rejected by Davies; it was a decision that forced the consortium to enter liquidation, despite the yards having a full order book worth £87 million and a forecasted profit for 1972. There is

---

13 DTI, 'Report of the Advisory Board on Shipbuilding on the Upper Clyde', 29 July 1971.
14 Hansard, HC vol. 819, col. 32 (14 June 1971).
15 Wishart 'An Introduction to the UCS Crisis', 78.

no doubt that this was a politically engineered crisis. The Heath government, which concluded a forensic accounting report prepared by Professor David Flint of Glasgow University at the behest of the liquidator to determine the circumstances in which the directors could carry on the business in the lead-up to liquidation, knowingly permitted UCS to continue trading while insolvent. The government held a 51 per cent stake in UCS and knew that the firm could only survive if it kept its implicit promise to fund working capital. This was a promise that the Heath government broke.[16]

Robert Courtney Smith, an experienced partner in a Glasgow accounting firm, was appointed liquidator by the government which assumed that he would quickly sell the remaining four yards: two or perhaps three yards as viable concerns, with the fourth, the Clydebank yard, for break-up value only.[17] Smith had previously liquidated one Clyde shipbuilding business – William Denny – in 1963 and the marine engineering firm of Fairfield Rowan in 1965. However, the legal position of the liquidator rendered the government's assumption invalid almost immediately. To act as the UCS liquidator, Smith had to behave independently, not as a partner in his firm; he was effectively an officer of the court whose only responsibility was to secure the best value for the creditors, not to realise whatever value he could as quickly as possible. Smith never regarded his task as UCS liquidator as anything other than 'just a commercial job'. As liquidator, he assumed personal liability if he failed to realise best value for the creditors. Indeed, he had to use his house as collateral for an insurance policy against future claims by creditors that he had failed in his fiduciary duty. Initially, the banks pressured Smith to maximise cash in hand and then close UCS. Acting as the UCS liquidator was for Smith a highly personal responsibility: 'I could have been bankrupted by UCS. I got some government grants and government loans. If I had not been able to repay those loans, then I would have been bankrupted. … My lawyer kept reminding me that this could bankrupt me'.[18]

A fortnight of due diligence established that UCS debt was around £32 million, and that £8.2 million was owed to preferential creditors, notably the four major Scottish banks.[19] Ordinary creditors were owed around £16 million and, Smith concluded, had little chance of any return. A crucial

16 Robert Courtney Smith, Lecture to the Adam Smith Club, 21 May 1988, Glasgow University Archives, ACCN3613/1/5.
17 A. Gilchrist, interview with McKinlay (2014).
18 Smith, interview with McKinlay (2011).
19 *Scotsman*, 16 June 1971.

step was to take out short-term loans against fixed assets to restart supply lines. The banks had to be persuaded that these secured loans would not erode their position and that 'any loss on trading should fall on the Second Secure Creditors – S(hipbuilding) I(ndustry) B(oard)'.[20] Smith established that UCS had a full order book with significant steel stocks which the liquidated company effectively had as a free resource, and that there were several ships nearing points in construction when the owners had to make significant stage payments or take final delivery of a completed vessel. All revenues from contracts in hand accrued to the liquidated company.

Smith proved to be a shrewd businessman and negotiated hard with shipowners. One New Zealand firm was desperate for a ship for which 98 per cent of the steelwork was complete. Such was their desperation that Smith persuaded the client to waive penalties on two other ships that would be delayed.[21] Other buyers were reluctant to write off their investments in part-completed ships and Smith exploited their weak bargaining position. 'If you can tow it away, you can have it', Smith told one shipping line. Unsurprisingly, 'three-quarters of a ship wasn't much good to them'. In some cases, Smith was able to accelerate stage payments for vessels on the stocks so that the liquidated UCS could buy materials and finish other ships. Smith continued to build even loss-making ships to receive stage payments that he could then use to continue other, profitable contracts.[22] Before liquidation, around a thousand suppliers had sustained the ailing UCS for months through trade credit. Smith froze these debts and now paid cash for any supplies beyond those already inside the UCS yards. By September, the government relented on their pressure to wind-up UCS quickly. Indeed, so anxious was the Department of Trade and Industry (DTI) to avoid *any* liability for triggering an immediate winding-up of the liquidated UCS that it guaranteed £4 million of loans as working capital to allow the company to meet the contractual requirements of four ships and so trigger stage payments from clients. Smith's astute bargaining with shipowners, suppliers and the government had placed him in a much stronger financial position, although the DTI support was conditional upon him doing nothing to compromise the possibility of UCS being broken up into its constituent yards as separate firms.[23]

---

20 Smith, Diary, 23 August 1971, Glasgow University Archives, ACCN3613/1/1-4.
21 Smith, Diary, 23 June 1971.
22 Smith, Diary, 24 June, 17 August, 8 October 1971; Smith, interview with McKinlay.
23 Smith, Diary, 29 June, 20 September, 9, 24 November 1971.

The liquidator used the first formal meeting with the shop stewards' committee to explain his independence as a 'company doctor' and that his first responsibility was to the court and to the creditors. Smith's stressed that his professional independence meant that he had to secure the best return possible for creditors, especially the four Scottish banks who were secured creditors. His professional role defined him as indifferent to any pressure from the government to break up UCS quickly *and* that he had no wider social responsibility for sustaining employment on Clydeside. Privately, Smith saw off government pressure to remove Ken Douglas, the Managing Director of UCS and the architect of the company's strategy to introduce a standard ship design for bulk carriers and radically to improve productivity. Douglas was the focus of hostility of conservative shipbuilders, especially those on the lower Clyde who bitterly resented the higher wage rates of UCS. Again, Smith was shrewd and pragmatic: Douglas was vital not just for his deep experience but also, as he confided to his diary, 'to maintain control over (the) labour situation'.[24]

Instead of acceding to UCS's request for an immediate injection of working capital, the government commissioned a report on the future of UCS from three prominent Scottish businessmen: Alexander MacDonald, chairman of Distillers, Sir Alexander Glen from the shipping industry, and David MacDonald, a director of Hill Samuel.[25] Popularly known as the 'Three Wise Men', they became four when former Labour MP Alfred Robens, chairman of the National Coal Board, who had overseen the loss of 300,000 jobs in the coal industry and the closure of over 400 pits in the 1960s, joined them; they were dubbed by the Clydeside men as 'a renegade socialist and three plastic macs'.[26] The outcome of their deliberations was fairly predictable. The 'wise men' concluded in a report only three pages long that UCS was unviable, without a future, and that to continue to inject public funds into such a business was financially irresponsible. Their recommendation was for a slimmer, more efficient company; a proposal that in practice meant the loss of seven out ten jobs in a climate of increasing unemployment. The former Labour Scottish Secretary, Willie Ross, asked Davies in the Commons whether he understood 'that this is one of the blackest days in the history of Scottish industry? Does he realise that in the area concerned there are already nearly 30,000 men unemployed and that the male unemployment rate is 9.6 per cent?' – the highest since the

---

24 Smith, Diary, 19 August 1971.
25 Hogwood, *Government and Shipbuilding*, 155.
26 *The Times*, 31 January 1972.

1930s.[27] Government plans would have reduced the number of employed in the yards from 8,500 to 2,500. As one worker said: shipbuilding may be a dirty, dangerous, cold and wet occupation, 'but it was a job', and in that part of Scotland there was little else, except, perhaps, the armed forces.[28] The solution to the crisis as far as the government was concerned was the official receiver and the dole queue. The workers had other ideas. As Jimmy Airlie, chairman of the Joint Shop Stewards Coordinating Committee (JSSCC), put it: 'This is a group of workers who are not going to grovel, tugging their forelocks, to the labour exchange'.[29]

Arguably, the shop stewards in the Clydeside yards were among the most experienced in British industry and, perhaps, the best prepared to take action to defend jobs. In the past, shipbuilding had been notable for the degree of division among the various trades that made up the workforce. Demarcation disputes were frequent as trade fought trade for the right to exercise control of different processes and tools. The traditional belief among the labour force that once work was lost it would be lost forever made for internecine warfare. During the 1950s and 1960s, platers and burners fought with each other to control flame-cutting machinery. Welders restricted entry to the trade and refused to allow unemployed workers of other shipbuilding trades to operate welding equipment. Boilermakers used apprenticeship and separate agreements covering their terms of employment to maintain differentials with other trades.[30] Workplace solidarity was a concept barely understood among shipbuilding workers.

But, prior to the work-in, experience gained of inter-trade co-operation in the so-called 'Fairfield experiment' was beginning to turn things around. In 1965, the Fairfield yard had to be rescued from bankruptcy by the Bank of England. One of the conditions of the rescue package was the establishment of a new tripartite management structure that included workers, government and private capital.[31] A new company, Fairfield (Glasgow) Ltd., was formed in January 1966, but its former

27 Hansard, HC vol. 819, col. 38 (14 June 1971).
28 From *Class Struggle: Film from the Clyde*. Cinema Action documentary (1977).
29 *Class Struggle*.
30 J. McGoldrick, 'Industrial relations and the Division of Labour in the Shipbuilding Industry since the War', *British Journal of Industrial Relations*, 21 (1983), 201–2, 207.
31 P. Payne, 'The Decline of Scottish Heavy Industries, 1945–1983', in R. Saville (ed.), *The Economic Development of Modern Scotland, 1950–1980* (Edinburgh, 1985), 105–7.

engineering arm, Fairfield Rowan, was closed. Under the chairmanship of Ian Stewart (who the other shipyard owners detested), and with government support and encouragement, Fairfield became a 'proving ground' for a new type of industrial relations. The 'Experiment' promised 'high and stable earnings, management and union co-operation through a yard council, flexibility within the workforce, increased productivity and no strikes'.[32] However, as Alexander and Jenkins noted, the aims of the 'experiment' were never clearly or comprehensively set out, 'so that the criteria against which success or failure are to be judged are themselves in doubt and may be disputed'.[33] Stable employment saw improvements in industrial relations and better productivity, but over capacity in world markets meant that government subsidies were needed for survival. Subsidies, of course, were removed in June 1971. But, although it proved incapable of solving the deep-seated international problems faced by the industry, in terms of building understanding and solidarity among the workers, the 'Experiment' was an invaluable experience. As Davie Torrance, draughtsman, and one of the UCS shop stewards, pointed out, the workers' representatives were drawn from a cross section of trades and included skilled, unskilled and white collar workers, such as himself. Workplace hierarchies were dissolved within a structure that allowed all an equal say. One of the outcomes of greater democracy was the emergence of meaningful inter-trade co-operation: evident when a six-week national lockout of draughtsmen was ended by the intervention of the manual workers.[34] There was also the fact that all the men were in a trade union (closed shop) and there operated in the yards a disciplined and organised cadre of highly politicised stewards in the Communist and Labour parties.

Indeed, communists had secured the convenerships of the five UCS yards by 1968 after a decade-long campaign. The key figures in the Party's Shipbuilding Branch, established in 1961, were Sammy Barr from Connell, Finlay Hart, a sophisticated advocate of shipyard modernisation, from Stephens, Jimmy Airlie from Fairfield, and Stewart Crawford from Yarrow. Its focus was yard-level industrial relations. Thus, the agenda was defined by events, not by any party line. Decisions were pragmatic,

---

32 Murphy, 'Labour in Shipbuilding and Ship Repairing', 80–1, Johnman and Murphy, *Scott Lithgow*, 152–6.
33 K.J.W. Alexander and C.L. Jenkins, *Fairfields: A Study in Institutional Change* (London, 1970), 209.
34 Torrance, interview with Knox (2015).

rather than ideological. It was a relatively free space and discussions rarely ventured into questions of political theory or inner-party democracy. UCS apprentices also had a YCL group of around 30 members at its peak, which was well connected with key members on the Scottish and British national YCL executives.[35]

In response to government plans for closures, the idea of a work-in in preference to a strike or a sit-in 'evolved' during the discussions among the shop stewards over coffee, rolls and sausages in a fog of smoke in the living room of Bob Dickie's council flat. The idea for a work-in was almost a process of elimination. To go on strike would be to hand victory to the government: they would 'have cheered us out of the yards'. 'Wait a minute. If we go out on strike, once we're out on the street, they'll padlock the gates. We'll have done their job for them. So, we couldn't go on strike'.[36] An occupation was too negative, too passive. Finally, given that there were 14 ships on the stocks at various stages of construction and all the material needed to complete the contracts, the idea of the work-in took shape.[37] Reid explained the logic behind that decision:

> [I]t was the only logical effective form of opposition to closure. Strike action was unthinkable, we would have left the factory, the yards and that would have delighted the government because they would have put padlocks on the gates. So that was out. We did consider a second strike but I reckon it was far too negative that, and we had an enormous order book, plenty of work and the logical thing was, why don't we work-in, refuse to accept redundancy and work.[38]

This was a master stroke, as the novelty of the term 'work-in', as Chik Collins explains, countered the 'main lines of attack likely to be used by the government and media' which would have emphasised the 'then-prevalent stereotypes of strike happy workers … and allowed the stewards to take the initiative in constructing their own positive case. This was that the work-in was not just a defence of particular jobs, but a principled assertion of a

---

35 A. Mills, 'Worker Occupations, 1971–1975: A Socio-Historical Analysis of the Development and Spread of Sit-ins, Work-ins and Worker Co-Operatives in Britain' (unpublished PhD thesis, University of Durham, 1982), 411.
36 *Strike – Jimmy Reid*, BBC Radio Scotland.
37 *Morning Star*, 29 June 1981.
38 BBC Transcript, 'Jimmy Reid – The Campaign Leader', 1 January 2002, Glasgow University Archives, ACCN3717/16/5, 8.

right to work which had much broader relevance'.[39] There was no question of doing nothing and simply accepting mass redundancies. But while 'Big Reid crystallised it as "work-in", the stewards then had to think what that might mean in practice'.[40]

There was, thus, no blueprint for the UCS work-in. However, one thing the communist stewards knew: the work-in was almost certain to be a long haul, quite unlike the timescale of conventional industrial disputes. Certainly, a work-in immediately eliminated any suggestion that the workers were in any way damaging the industry. Quite the opposite: the UCS workers were, through their 'impudence and originality', demonstrating their willingness to work, and that the yards were viable. For Reid, 'There was no "Eureka moment". The work-in was the stage on which we could argue for the right to work'. A work-in 'bought us time' to make – and win – the argument about the right to work. The work-in concept demanded that the stewards always put their case in a wider political context, to ensure that 'our arguments overflowed, they spilled out of the yards and onto the public stage'.[41] After all, there had never been in the history of industrial relations a work-in. The shop stewards were well aware of the audacity of their choice but also the unknowns they would confront: if this was a plan, then it had a starting-point and a destination but at this point little else. This was an unequal struggle that could only be won with imagination, ingenuity and wit, not by conventional forms of industrial militancy. The very novelty of the work-in as a concept provided the stewards with room to manoeuvre tactically, to respond to events, but always turn the issue back to their positive, responsible action and the destructive irresponsibility of the Heath government.[42]

Unlike a strike, the stewards understood that the work-in would be a struggle where the opposition was the government, not management; and one that would be won and lost in public. They did, however, establish three fundamental, inviolable principles of their campaign. First, the UCS stewards had to remain in charge, rather than trade union officials. And,

---

39 C. Collins, 'Developing the Linguistic Turn in Urban Studies: Language, Context and Political Economy', *Urban Studies*, 37 (2000), 233.
40 J. Cloughley, interview with McKinlay (2013).
41 Jimmy Reid, interview with Woolfson (1979), Glasgow University Archives, DC 65/146/14.
42 J. Phillips, *The Industrial Politics of Devolution: Scotland in the 1960s and 1970s* (Manchester, 2008), 101.

in turn, the stewards' authority had to come from the workforces of all four yards. Secondly, workforce solidarity required that there was no horse-trading for this or that concession: only securing the future of all four yards could sustain the workforce's solidarity and so the broader public support they needed. Thirdly, this solidarity *could* gain a moral force that would in itself be a major political asset that the Tory government could not possibly ignore or match.

The stewards' notion of the work-in tuned into the workforce's affinity to some sort of work sharing. As one anonymous boilermaker steward put it to a mass meeting on 21 June 1971: "'We don't want charity. We don't want to be paid for doing nothing. If we are getting wages, then we will work for them, even if it means doubling up on jobs'".[43] Equally, the stewards' immediately dismissed the liquidator's offer of paid leave as contrary to the political purpose of the work-in. In late August and early September, Smith agreed to provide essential administrative mechanisms for the work-in: the work-in levy was collected through the payroll and all workers were covered by employers' liability insurance.[44] Most importantly, Smith accepted the shop stewards' committee as a legitimate player inside UCS, while downgrading the importance of union officials. For Smith:

> [W]e began with significant mutual distrust: more they of me than me of them. But that distrust broke down quite quickly. They realised that I had no interest in having all the yards closed down. ... When they got the message that I was doing my damnedest to get these contracts built and to continue building ships, they began to trust me: we were *almost* on the same side. I think they appreciated quite early on that I was not a creature of the government ... that I was not 'Heath's man'. Over a few weeks I was able to prise money out of the government that the previous management had failed to get.[45]

Tony Benn noted in his diary that the UCS workforce had 'theoretically' taken over the yards. 'Seen from the outside this looks like a revolutionary act. But when you get through the barricades and ask, as a friend, "Well, what are you going to do?", they haven't a strategy, they haven't a plan, they haven't got anything at all'.[46]

---

43 *Glasgow Herald*, 21 June 1971.
44 Smith, Diary, 26 August, 2 September 1971.
45 Smith, interview with McKinlay.
46 Benn, *Diaries 1968–1972*, 350.

From the moment that the management informed the JSSCC of the impending closure of the yards, preparations were put in place to challenge the government's decision. First, and almost immediately, on 15 June, a trainload of 400 UCS workers, paid for by subventions from the Clydebank Common Good Fund, went to London to lobby parliament and meet the Prime Minister, Edward Heath, to discuss the crisis. Ian Jack, journalist, then at the *Sunday Times*, recalled that on the southbound train he was trying to persuade an apprentice that 'not all newspapers were unsympathetic and right wing. My own was "quite left wing"… at which point the apprentice laughed and called to a figure standing at the compartment door: "Hey, Jimmy, here's a fella who thinks the *Sunday Times* is a socialist paper". Reid turned and gave me a pitying smile'.[47] It was not only journalists who were on the train, accompanying the UCS workers were delegations from the Scottish Trades Union Council and the civic authorities, but to no avail. Reid remarked: 'I got the impression that we were talking to men who didn't care, who didn't know what it means to stand in a dole queue, and worse, who didn't seem to care'. They were given tea and sympathy and a 'polite hearing' by Heath that lasted 45 minutes, but little else.[48] One thing the lobby meeting proved, according to shop steward Bob Dickie, was that Secretary of State John Davies 'was shocked that he had met his match in Jimmy Reid … an engineer from the Clyde; but Reid was an intellectual who could hold his own in any company'.[49] Some twenty years later, Jimmy Airlie said: we 'ran rings round them [the government] for fifteen months',[50] a view echoed by Reid who said in a discussion with the historian John Foster: 'we were way ahead of the government' in the 'battle for minds'.[51] But Davies's shock did not shift the Heath government's underestimation of the UCS leadership. 'It soon became obvious', concluded Airlie, 'that the Tories hadn't really thought through their strategy. They were taken aback at the span of the struggle; the ability of the workers to mount what was essentially a political struggle'.[52] The Tories had assumed that any resistance would be short-lived

---

47 *Guardian*, 1 January 2011.
48 Wishart 'An Introduction to the UCS Crisis', 79.
49 Dickie, interview with David Chidlow (2012).
50 Interview with James Airlie, British Shipbuilding History Project, 11 February 1992 (Centre for Business History in Scotland, University of Glasgow). See also Slaven and Murphy, *Crossing the Bar*, 153–7.
51 Discussion between John Foster and Jimmy Reid, n.d. (1986); information passed to us by C. Collins.
52 D. Bain, 'Interview with J. Airlie', *Marxism Today*, October 1979, 17.

as workers scrambled over each other to defend their *own* yard even as others were closed. The UCS campaign turned the tables: they were solid, never reactive, and raised wider questions about the right to work that went far beyond the four Clyde yards. So astute and convincing were Airlie and Reid that they were able, as we will see, to create a compelling, uplifting, but fictional, narrative of the work-in.

From the outset it was the aim of the stewards to build an unbreakable solidarity among the UCS workers. Even before the work-in began, preparations were put in place in order to achieve the maximum effectiveness of the agreed strategy. First, a levy was imposed on all personnel a fortnight before the decision was taken to occupy the yards in order to pay the wages of any worker made redundant in the short term. Secondly, they had to convince the workers being made unemployed not to accept redundancy payments, although some did. Reid eloquently made the case that 'these jobs are social jobs, they don't belong to individuals. And if you sell them these jobs for more money in the short term, the probability is that you are selling the jobs of the next generation and the communities that depend on their work'.[53] Thirdly, communication with the workers was made a vital priority to be built up through a number of channels: mass meetings, smaller departmental meetings and the issuing of a weekly news sheet which would communicate the decisions taken by the JSSCC to the rank-and-file. It was also important that the stewards were not seen as an elite cadre within the yards enjoying special privileges. Equality was maintained in little but important ways such as lunchtime. Reid and the other members of the JSSCC would queue up for their lunch like any other worker, eating their meal among the general mass of bodies.[54] However, the stewards realised that outflanking management and the government involved more than just in-house action and daily demonstrations of egalitarianism. If they were to be successful in their campaign to save their livelihoods and communities then the fight had to involve a wider constituency; indeed, the Scottish people. As Reid put it: 'We could not afford to become embattled within the yards ... [so] we started a programme of meetings all over the country'.[55] Posters bearing the slogan 'Save UCS, Save Scotland' effectively nationalised the campaign. From that point on an attack on UCS became an attack on Scotland. Daily press briefings ensured that their voices reached a

---

53 Jimmy Reid, interview with Kenneth Roy (2003).
54 R. McNicol, interview with Knox (2015).
55 Wishart 'An Introduction to the UCS Crisis', 80.

national audience.[56] The strategy bore immediate fruit: on 24 June 1971, and to the 'amazement' of the JSSCC, over 100,000 workers stopped work for the day in sympathy with the UCS workforce and half of them marched from Glasgow city centre to a meeting held on Glasgow Green.[57] Reid was fond of saying that he had 'more followers in Scotland than Bonnie Prince Charlie had'.[58]

The success in spreading the struggle to keep the yards open lay in the ability of the leading stewards to communicate with the public in clear and uncompromising language. In Jimmy Reid and James Airlie, the UCS workers had two outstanding leaders who complemented each other. Reid was the master orator, a quixotic figure; Airlie the master organiser, a realist. Reid was able to convince people they could move mountains, Airlie made sure they had the means to do so. As Jack Ashton, one-time secretary of the Scottish CPGB, put it, Reid 'wisnae an organiser … [he] could nae pull two bits of string together':[59] a verdict shared by the UCS liquidator, Robert Courtney Smith, who said that Airlie was the 'more business-like of the two' men.[60] Both were engineers, members of the CPGB's influential Scottish district committee, and both had done their national service in the RAF; Reid in a jazz band in England and Airlie in a military policeman's uniform in Libya, where he honed a capacity to project 'an air of general menace … barely suppressed fury'.[61] Airlie was a *physical* presence, rarely domineering, but a presence that could never be ignored. He was not a tall man, but was powerfully built:

> Jimmy learnt certain tricks from his time as a military policeman. Whenever he spoke to management, for instance, he *never* spoke from an inferior position, but always spoke from above; he always spoke with clarity, with authority in *any* setting. He took command of every room he was in: he *occupied* the space. He could size up a crowd or a meeting at a glance; he instinctively knew if trouble was going to start or who would argue against him. This was a kind of genius.[62]

56 Wishart 'An Introduction to the UCS Crisis', 80.
57 Dickie, interview with Chidlow.
58 *The Times*, 19 November 1971.
59 Ashton, interview with Campbell and McIlroy (BL 1049/03).
60 J. Lloyd, 'When the Eyes of the World Were on the Clyde', BBC Radio 4, *Archive on Four*, 2011.
61 K. Aitken, 'Airlie Obituary', *Scotsman* 11 March 1997.
62 J. Quigley, interview with McKinlay (2017).

Similarly, another UCS steward remarked upon Airlie's 'presence' as something that complemented his organisational abilities: 'he was an intimidating physical presence at all times, on every occasion, without exception. He could pin people to the wall with a look. Airlie was *the* presence that kept all the UCS stewards together day-to-day'.[63]

Reid and Airlie were never elected to their key roles in the UCS stewards' leadership: 'there was never an election, never a vote, but that was never an issue. There were no egos involved. Reid and Airlie were leaders because they *were* leaders'.[64] Both men were heavy smokers, although Airlie preferred roll-ups, and enjoyed a flutter on the horses. The comradeship extended to friendship: they drank together, sang together, uproariously altering Frank Sinatra's song *My Way* to 'Their Way'.[65] The two Jimmies could tell each other's jokes, finish each other's sentences. They were relentless critics of sectionalism. Airlie, although the son of a boilermaker, often mocked the alleged superiority of the boilermakers in the most caustic of tones.[66] Reid may have adopted a less confrontational tone when ruing the boilermakers' sense of their exalted status, but he did not hide his sense that the UCS campaign could ill-afford any sectionalism. During a wearisome train journey to London, Reid mulled over the mysteries of shipyard trade unionism. 'Now,' he told his engineer companions,

> 'I'm a well-read man. Sir Isaac Newton's theory of gravity: *that* I understand. I have a working knowledge of Einstein's theory of relativity. And the philosophical meaning of the Sermon on the Mount is clear to me. Now, I've never met any of these scientists, philosophers and theologians but I understand *how* they think. But boilermakers are an enigma that would stump the finest minds. I have worked with boilermakers for thirty-five years and I still cannot fathom their thinking. Boilermakers are an enigma that would confound the combined wisdom of Newton, Einstein and the disciples.'[67]

The men's complementary traits were strengthened by the feeling of complete trust between them. During the work-in, Reid and Airlie's

---

63 G. Tasker, interview with McKinlay (2016).
64 Dickie, interview with Chidlow.
65 Dickie, interview with McKinlay (2016).
66 J. Kemp (ed.), *Confusion to Our Enemies: Selected Journalism of Arnold Kemp* (London, 2012), 139.
67 J. Quigley, interview with McKinlay.

names were often run together; they worked so closely together that they developed if not a political telepathy then something very close to it. Bob Dickie put it most strongly: 'UCS always comes down to those two men: we were fortunate to have them. There wouldn't have been a work-in without Reid and Airlie. Airlie *organised* people; Reid *inspired* people'.[68] Reid often said: 'If you wanted someone behind you it would be Jimmy Airlie'.[69] Reid's warm obituary of Airlie concluded with the remark that 'a bit of me died with him'.[70] One of the UCS workers, Bob Starrett, a painter to trade, who worked in Yarrow, was a talented amateur artist who became the work-in's official cartoonist, providing drawings and sketches for their pamphlets and publicity material. After attending Glasgow School of Art, he headed south, finding work as a scenic painter in the movie industry. He said of them: 'I've spent a good part of my post-UCS life in a job surrounded by charismatic film stars. But the most charismatic duo I ever ran into was Jimmy Reid and Jimmy Airlie. They were from real life and doing something on behalf of others rather than what those movie stars do which is for their own ego'.[71] Bob Dickie, one of the UCS shop stewards, underscored this when he said that Reid had a way of talking that personalised his speeches as if addressed to the individual rather than the assembled mass audience; indeed, he made the 'hairs at the back of your head stand up', such was the emotional electricity he generated.[72] This was echoed in the verses of the poet George McEwan, who saw Airlie and Reid as part of the pantheon of iconic Scottish figures dating back to Wallace and Bruce:

> An so the fecht went oan they days, remember them wi' pride,
> The workin' men an' weeman whae strove tae rescue Upper Clyde,
> Nae slackin', naw nae bevvyin'! Reid's challenge it was clear,
> An' tae a man they laugh alood an' rally when they hear,
> Wi' baith Jimmys, Reid and Airlie, an support roon the Worls,
> At the bosses feet in prood defiance the Gauntlet it was hurled
> ...
> The gallant few who Alba's freedom socht an' fearless took the lead,
> The Wallace, the Bruce and unsung folk we never read.
> Noo tae that list o' fechting men whae strove baith lang an' fairly,

---

68 Dickie, interview with McKinlay.
69 Joan Reid, interview with David Chidlow (2012).
70 Jimmy Reid, Airlie Obituary, *Scotsman*, 11 March 1997.
71 *Herald*, 8 October 2002.
72 *Scottish Legends*, Scottish Television (2003).

Carve wi' respect an' honest pride the names,
Of Jimmy Reid an' Airlie.[73]

But they also had a sense of humour; indeed, even one of their key political opponents, Sir John Eden, industry minister, spoke – with only a hint of condescension – of their 'delightful sense of humour' and that Reid was a 'charming Robin Hood' figure.[74] Reid and Airlie, sitting side-by-side getting ready for a television appearance, an amused watching steward quipped to the make-up artist working on Reid that if she could do anything with '*that* face' she should win an Oscar. Reid pointed at Airlie: 'And if you can do anything with *that* face, you'll get a Nobel Prize'.[75] Of course, humour, occasionally cruel, often surreal, almost always personal was an art form in the yards. In UCS, humour was also employed as a tool both defensively and motivationally. One returning emissary from a tour of supporting miners' lodges in Wales commented on his exhaustion due to late nights and the burden of expectations. Airlie replied, deadpan: 'Aye well, very good brother … it must have been really hard for you; sounds terrible, all that adulation. I don't know how you bore it'.[76] At a tense crucial mass meeting on the future of the work-in towards the end of September (see below), they asked an overweight boilermaker, affectionately known by his workmates as 'The Pig', to sing a sentimental song, do an impression of Louis Armstrong and tell a joke about a man who joined the Foreign Legion because he hated Arabs; he got a 'storming ovation from the 7,000-strong crowd'.[77]

The very visible presence of communists among the UCS leadership was a risk. A founding principle for Reid and the others was not only that the Party had to be kept at arm's length from their campaign, but also that they retained a truly collective leadership. Moreover, the work-in leadership's decisions had to be ratified by the four yards' workforce. The leadership could never allow itself to be seen as anything other than inseparable from the workforce. The communists in the UCS leadership never met as a separate caucus and were careful to avoid using the term 'comrades' at any meeting. Nevertheless, the Communist Party was acutely aware that its credibility, especially in industry, was at risk. 'The Party was

---

73 G. McEwan, 'Ballad of the Upper Clyde', in D. Betteridge, *A Rose Loupt Oot: Poetry and Song Celebrating the UCS Work-in* (Middlesbrough, 2011), 131.
74 Lloyd, 'Eyes of the World'.
75 Dickie, interview with Chidlow.
76 Jenny Buchan, UCS witness Seminar, 2001, Glasgow Caledonian University.
77 *Sunday Times*, 26 September 1971.

not involved', insisted Jimmy Reid some 40 years later, 'because the Party could *not* be involved. The Party was *confronted* by UCS'.[78]

Quite apart from any wider political considerations, there was the sheer impracticality of checking decisions with the Party, given the fluidity of the work-in and the intensity of media scrutiny. The Communist Party was 'worried'. The work-in was seen as adventurous, dangerous – and damaging – '*if* it turned to dust'.[79] Airlie was asked several times by Communist Party leaders if he understood that the Party's reputation was a stake. In reply to Gordon McLennan, the Party's General Secretary, Airlie looked him in the eye, paused, and growled, 'I know. We'll take it as far as we can go'. In August 1971, the Party's Industrial Organiser, Bert Ramelson, convened a meeting of UCS Party members to say that the risks were too great and that they had to find some alternative to the work-in. 'Ramelson told the meeting that the Political Committee had wanted the work-in over because it anticipated attrition, isolation then humiliation: "better to get it over quickly, one way or another", seemed to be their attitude'. We had to explain to him that the workers had rejected this option at a mass meeting that very morning by something like 8,000 votes to 6. I was very angry with Bert, we had an argument with him and finally said, 'Look Bert, we'll take you for a pint and put you on the train back to London. Imagine the arrogance: 500 miles away, no real experience of the struggle, telling us what we should have done'.[80] Far from being a mentor or strategic advisor, Ramelson was kept at arm's length by Reid and the other communists in the work-in leadership.[81] Davy Cooper, a key communist steward on the UCS leadership, expressed this moment vividly: 'Ramelson arrived from London to take control. He arrived at Central Station to be met by Jimmy Reid who spoke to him firmly and put Bert back on the train south. And that was it for the Party: they kept away more or less'.[82]

However, there was good reason for Ramelson to be anxious about the work-in. He represented the careful, calibrated deployment of communist influence through a delicate web of personal and political allegiances

---

78 Jimmy Reid, interview with McIlroy and Campbell.
79 G. Kerr, interview with McKinlay (2013).
80 *Moscow Gold*, final draft (1992), Glasgow University Archives, ACCN3717/16/8; Reid discussion with J. Foster, n.d. (1986).
81 R. Seifert and T. Sibley, *Revolutionary Communist at Work: A Political Biography of Bert Ramelson* (London, 2012), 189.
82 D. Cooper, interview with McKinlay (2016).

8 The Right to Work march, Glasgow 1971 (courtesy of Scran)

that connected the broad left across the labour movement. Many years of patient revolutionary pragmatism would be jeopardised if the work-in failed.

The JSSCC was a *strategic* space. Solidarity was an ideal, a practical aspiration, an asset to be sustained, and the source of Reid and the others' authority and legitimacy. The stewards' leadership capacity to act; indeed, the very fact of its leadership, was based on the projection of solidarity. Solidarity, however, was far from a given, never taken for granted. The stewards' leadership spent enormous energy thinking about solidarity: what it meant, how to portray it in the public domain and how it could be kept intact. Solidarity – as a political objective – provided the stewards with a clear, consistent focus irrespective of the ebb and flow of events. The stewards developed a common language that allowed them to think collectively and to convey a consistent image of the UCS work-in across the four yards as well as to the wider public. The UCS leadership understood themselves as embodying a defensive struggle for the right to work, the right to dignity: these were rights that mattered far beyond Clydeside (Figures 8–9). In an important sense, then, the JSSCC was also a place where language, especially metaphors, were developed and rehearsed.

9 Reid addressing a mass meeting of UCS workers (courtesy of Scran)

However, in spite of the mass wave of public sympathy, on 29 July, in the Commons, Davies recommended the report of the so-called 'Three Wise Men' regarding redundancies. The occupation of the yards by the workers began the next day and Upper Clyde Shipbuilders Unlimited, as Reid christened it, was launched. When asked to distinguish the work-in from an occupation of the yards, Airlie replied: 'We are not a foreign power, we were born in that area and we will work-in. The right to work is our birthright and we won't give it up for any hatchetmen'. The *potential* symbolic value of the work-in was recognised from the first: 'We only want tae work; we are available for work, it's the system, the society, that's denying us the right to work. That's what was symbolic'. Also, to occupy

UCS Work-in

the yards would have placed an impossible financial burden on the UCS workers.[83]

However, by taking the yards into the hands of the workforce the shop stewards had to emphasise that work would go on as usual. Slackers, the workshy and those looking for an easy time, were reminded by Reid, surrounded by thousands of workers on a rare beautiful summer's day, in his now 'off the cuff' famous address to the workforce,[84] that:

> The world is witnessing the first of a new tactic on behalf of workers. We're not going on strike. We're not even having a sit-in strike. We're taking over the yards because we refuse to accept that faceless men, or any group of men in Whitehall or anyone else can devastate our livelihoods with impunity. There's a basic elementary right invoked here – that's our right to work. We're no strikers. We are responsible people and we will conduct ourselves with the dignity and discipline that we have all the time expressed over the last few weeks. And there will be no hooliganism. There will be no vandalism. There will be no bevvying (drinking), because the world is watching us, and it is our responsibility to conduct ourselves responsibly and with dignity and with maturity. We are not going to strike. We are not even having a sit-in strike. Nobody and nothing will come in and nothing will go out without our permission. The shipyard men at UCS are not wildcats. The real wildcats were in 10 Downing Street. The biggest mistake the men could make would be to lie down, capitulate and grovel. We don't only build ships on the Clyde. We build men.[85]

The impact of the speech was electric: even more so that Reid had spoken without notes; indeed, as he says, 'I hardly needed a note during that period'. It was almost a spiritual transcendental experience for him as if he was simply a vessel for other men's hopes and dreams:

> In my experience, a funny thing happens, a peculiar thing, when you are speaking on behalf of a movement, of a cause or a struggle … something happens that you become almost sublimely, sublimely confident of the message and the words come and there's a chemistry. It's going back and forth and you don't think

---

83 Airlie, Linthouse Mass Meeting, 8 October 1971, Glasgow University Archives, UGD181/1/1.
84 Dickie, interview with McKinlay.
85 Woolfson, 'Working-Class Culture', 116–17.

of yourself … you are oblivious, at that moment, of self. You're acting as a catalyst between what happened here and the people.[86]

Reid reflected that this was 'an important speech: it underscored that we were the focus of the debate about the right to work. We had that responsibility, a heavy responsibility, to represent more than ourselves'.[87] However, to understand Reid's oratory as a gift from the Gods is to neglect his long experience as a communist cadre. Reid was schooled to think through the role of the state and of shipyard management as strategic issues. Reid's capacity to connect with the shipyard workforce – and far beyond – was political and strategic. After all, Reid was drawing upon British communism as a deep reservoir of Marxist theory and practical experience.

More specifically, of course, Reid did prepare for major speeches: 'Don't think that Reid didnae prepare because he didnae have notes. Once he knew the issue, that percolated away inside that big heid of his until it came out fully prepared'.[88] For another UCS steward: 'He had this wonderful ability to talk to you as if he was talking to you personally. His mother said to me, "I used to think there were people in the bedroom with Jimmy, but it wasn't that: it was Jimmy doing his writing and preparing his speeches. He worked at it; he had learnt his trade"'.[89] But despite the inspirational impact his oratory had on listeners, Reid always maintained a humble and modest view of himself and his powers, saying, 'When you're speaking, they're speaking through you. And this is a modest feeling because you have to speak for many'.[90]

Combating the drink culture of the yards was an important factor in maintaining the image of respectability, particularly as far as the media were concerned. The no-drinking rule also extended to train journeys to London. Reid and Airlie knew that the press would be waiting to take pictures and it would have been a major blow to the public image of the work-in if workers arrived in the capital the worse for wear. Retired journalist Ian Sharp, at his funeral in 2010, said that Reid loved to relate the story of the work-in committee travelling to No. 10 to meet then Prime Minister Edward Heath. They were lined up in a room opposite a large selection of malt whiskies, but refused Mr Heath's offer of a drink. Jimmy was asked afterwards by the media if it was true the men had turned down

---

86 *Maritime History*, BBC Scotland.
87 Reid, interview with Woolfson.
88 G. Kerr, interview with McKinlay.
89 J. Cloughley, interview with McKinlay.
90 *A Place in My Mind*, BBC Radio Scotland.

a free drink. He replied: 'Yes, it's true. And it will go down as one of the greatest sacrifices made by the working classes'.[91] However, coming back was different![92]

Another shrewd decision was to build on the links with the wider fight against unemployment established early in the campaign. At a huge demonstration in Glasgow on 18 August, said to be the biggest since the 1840s, which involved around 80,000 supporters, including Vic Feather, general secretary of the TUC, Labour shadow minister Tony Benn, and Hugh Scanlon, president of the Amalgamated Union of Engineering Workers (AUEW), Reid declared:

> We started fighting for jobs, and in a matter of days we knew we were fighting for Scotland, and for the British working-class movement. The real power of this country has been forged today in Clydeside, and will be forged now in the pits, the factories, the yards and the offices. Once that force is given proper leadership – is disciplined and determined – there is no force in Britain, or indeed the world, that can stand against it.[93]

The work-in was beginning to receive wide support, both financial and emotional, from a cross-section of society. From 'school children holding sales at street corners, from old age pensioners, people in the arts, people in entertainment',[94] as well as sections of the Scottish business community. The former Beatle John Lennon and his wife Yoko Ono sent a donation of £5,000 and a wheel of roses, which were donated to St Margaret's Hospice in Clydebank. Reid tells of the amusement that this created in the following anecdote:

> Hey Jimmy you've got a big wagon wheel out there of roses for you. I'd never received flowers from anybody, not the done thing in Clydeside for a man to get flowers and so I said: Who's it from? He says: I don't know but there's a cheque here, and he looked and all he could see was Lennon, L-e-n-n-o-n. He said: Lennon, some guy called Lennon. One of the old communist shop stewards from Dumbarton, says, it cannae be Lenin, he's deid.[95]

---

91   *Herald*, 20 August 2010.
92   Reid, interview with Roy.
93   Wishart 'An Introduction to the UCS Crisis', 81.
94   Reid, *Reflections*, 93.
95   BBC Transcripts, 'Jimmy Reid – The Campaign Leader', 1 January 2002.

While some of the donations may have provided an opportunity for humour, others were heart-rending. Even the most hardbitten cynical politico might have been moved by the following:

> 'Dear Shop Stewards, Please find enclosed £2.00 (postal order) my school pals and I raised at a street jumble sale in aid of the UCS workers. This was a hurried jumble sale because we felt you would need the money to fight that bad man Mr Heath who is taking your jobs away.
> We wish you well from Aberdeen'.
> John McConnachie (13),
> Ronald Belsham (14),
> Elaine McConnachie (10)[96]

However, most of the donations came from ordinary workers and fellow trade unionists the length and breadth of the UK, and from overseas. As journalist and playwright Brian McGeachan put it: 'everyone wanted to identify with a dignified stand against the destruction of people who'd built up a tolerance for body blows'.[97] The miners in South Wales donated a £1 a week for months on end because, as Reid says, 'they realised that the stand of the UCS workers was so important. They knew that if they (UCS) won it, they would have recorded a unique and historic victory for the workers against redundancies and closures'.[98] The total amount raised was £485,721 of which £174,814 came from collections in factories, £142,907 came from trade unionists, £127,486 was raised through the 10s. (50p) levy, £32,968 came from donations from the general public and £6,895 came from political parties.[99] In total, this was the equivalent to around £3 million today. The fund was administered with tremendous efficiency and fairness, with every penny accounted for, by Roddy MacKenzie, aka 'the fox', who, prior to the work-in, had a sideline in money-lending in the yards.[100]

The extent of public support also offered the work-in a degree of legitimacy for what was a legally questionable take-over of the four yards. The workers were fortunate that the yards in Clydebank came under the jurisdiction of the Chief Constable of Dunbartonshire, Adam McKinlay.

---

96 Quoted in Betteridge, *Rose Loupt Oot*, 112.
97 McGeachan, *Jimmy Reid: from Govan to Gettysburg*.
98 Reid, *Reflections*, 93.
99 *Guardian*, 23 December 1972.
100 Joan Reid, interview with McKinlay; Dickie, interview with McKinlay.

He was described by Reid as a 'smashing fellow', clearly sympathetic to the position of the men. Reid met him in Clydebank Town Council and offered to 'guarantee' the conduct of the men: that they would act responsibly, that there would be 'no pilfering', and that they would keep the police fully informed of any developments. According to Reid, such were the good relations between police and workers that developed during the lifetime of the work-in that there was less strife between them and the people of Clydebank afterwards than there was before it. There was only ever one policeman at the gates of the Clydebank yard, and he had to be instructed not to wear a badge supporting the work-in on his uniform.[101] In any case, should things have taken a more confrontational turn the police would have found it both morally and politically difficult to eject 'honest' men from the yards for simply working to feed their families.[102]

The tremendous support of the public and the media for the work-in forced the government back to the negotiating table. Understanding the problematic nature of solidarity among shipbuilding trades the government pushed a strategy of dividing the workforce. This involved saving some of UCS and discarding the rest. The initial offer was to keep one yard open; then under pressure from the media and the public it was two. What it boiled down to was retaining the Govan and Linthouse yards with a reduced workforce and closing the other two. The two-yard offer was arrived at after a special meeting of the TUC's Economic Committee in Glasgow on 17 August at which Vic Feather and Dan McGarvey, secretary of the Confederation of Shipbuilding and Engineering Unions (CSEU), president of the Boilermakers Society, a devout Roman Catholic and anti-communist, put forward a proposal to establish a Clydeside Development Agency with the remit of finding employment for those workers made redundant. Discussions at the highest level of government followed in September between McGarvey and John Davies and there were calls in the Scottish popular press for the former to take control of negotiations.[103] As a result, Govan Shipbuilders Limited was established with a board of directors including Sir Hugh Stenhouse, an insurance broker and treasurer of the Scottish Tory Party, Archibald Gilchrist, managing director of the Edinburgh engineering firm Brown Bothers, Angus Grossart, merchant banker, and Robert MacLellan, president of

---

101 Joan Reid, interview with Chidlow.
102 *Strike – Jimmy Reid*, BBC Radio Scotland.
103 J. Foster, 'The 1971–72 Work-in Revisited: How Clydeside Workers Defeated a Tory Government', *Our History*, New Series, Pamphlet No. 9 (London, 2013), 10.

the Glasgow Chamber of Commerce. Significantly, none of the new board of directors had any experience of the industry. The one man who did, Kenneth Douglas, former head of the UCS, and sympathetic to the aims of the work-in, was originally excluded, but later under pressure from the stewards was made deputy chairman. Reid said of the newly appointed board, it was 'more reminiscent of Monty Python's Flying Circus' than a 'serious shipbuilding proposal'.[104] The set-up had more than a whiff of suspicion about it and the immediate response of the JSSCC was to refuse to co-operate with the government-appointed board. When Stenhouse and Gilchrist tried to enter the Linthouse yard they were refused entry. James Airlie said to them: 'Our position is that we are in charge of the gates and we are not co-operating with any Government body'. When Gilchrist introduced himself by remarking that he had served his apprenticeship in the yard, back came the reply from Airlie, 'You will never be managing director here'.[105]

This development presented the most serious challenge to the solidarity of the work-in as the prospect of a split in the ranks between those workers in the 'saved' yards and those deemed surplus to requirements was very real. There was a concerted effort by the media and government to convince the workers that they were in the 'last chance saloon' and that there were no alternatives to the two-yard deal. The *Scotsman* accused the stewards of 'throwing away jobs ... by their pig-headed approach ... The hungry man grabs half a loaf, and hopes it will give him the strength to win the whole one. So let it be with Govan'.[106] However, the offer was completely thrown out by the shop stewards, whose watchword from the outset had been 'no redundancies, no closures'. Although agreeable to negotiations around working conditions, the basic principles that had given rise to the work-in were considered non-negotiable by the shop stewards.[107] A telling factor in the favour of the shop stewards was the fact that the deal to save the two yards involved workers accepting pay cuts and anti-social hours. Reid, in an important speech to the workers on 24 September argued:

> Don't let there be divisions in our ranks ... If the Government succeeded in the butchery of our industry I'd rather be on the dole than among the two and half thousand that would be left to grovel, accept wage reductions and all sorts of other things ...

104 UCS scrapbook 2 (courtesy of Robert Courtney Smith).
105 *Glasgow Evening Times*, 22 September 1971.
106 UCS scrapbook 1 (courtesy of A. Gilchrist).
107 Reid, *Reflections*, 80, 91.

and I'm telling you it would be a short-term solution … it's like a murderer who wants to murder us, we've found out, we've defended ourselves against the murderer and people say 'Please negotiate with the murderer, you might stop him piercing your heart but he can cut your legs and arms and there's a sensible compromise'. And when you're lying bleeding they will tell you in a year or two, wi' you minus the legs, why aren't you standing on your own two feet? And brothers our proposals therefore spring from a sense of responsibility to ourselves, our families and to our community and in the last resort to the British working class.[108]

According to John Fryer of the *Sunday Times*, it was 'the most crucial speech he has made. Crucial because there is a real threat of a split in the ranks with the entry on to the scene of Stenhouse'.[109] However, the speech was also important in regard to the imagery used. The stewards' committee was a rehearsal room for the language of the work-in. An early version of Reid's butchery speech was first aired at a stewards' meeting. In this speech, he switched the government's portrayal of negotiations as reasonable into something much more sinister and visceral. To accept negotiation was not just to undermine the solidarity of the work-in, a priceless asset, but also to accept, in a very real sense, emasculation. After all, this was a leadership that had announced to the world that the Clyde built men as well as ships. To butcher UCS was, quite clearly, to become less of a man. To negotiate on these terms was to accept defeat in principle: all that was left was to become the authors of the fine print of surrender. This was the creativity of Reid's language: to take the languages of the powerful and to transform them into popular languages of resistance.[110]

The co-operation of the JSSCC was agreed when Stenhouse said he would conduct a feasibility study of the Scotstoun yard, and consider the possibility of saving John Brown's on condition that he received: first, the full co-operation of the unions, and, secondly, financial backing from the government.[111] However, when Davies refused to consider the incorporation of the Clydebank division the stewards dug their heels in maintaining that the four-yard package was non-negotiable. On 8 October, before a packed

---

108 Quoted in Foster, 'The 1971–72 Work-in Revisited, 8.
109 *Sunday Times*, 26 September 1971.
110 C. Collins, *Language, Ideology and Social Consciousness: Developing a Sociohistorical Approach* (Aldershot, 1999), 160–2.
111 UCS scrapbook 2.

meeting of the entire workforce, Jimmy Airlie received a standing ovation, when he declared:

> We will not bow before intimidation and blackmail. The Tories cannot allow ordinary people to express their hopes and aspirations. If UCS is defeated then men and women everywhere will be afraid to say 'we have rights'. But we will not fail the Labour movement. We will not fail the working class. Above all we will not fail ourselves. All four yards, the entire labour force, no redundancies.[112]

By the end of 1971, it was becoming clear that the work-in was showing no signs of commitment fatigue: both the workers and the public remained staunchly opposed to the government's plans for the Upper Clyde yards. Little did they know that the government in secret had already thrown in the towel by conceding a few months earlier that it was committed 'to extending Govan Shipbuilders to include a third yard – Scotstoun' and that it had 'no credible social, economic and political alternative';[113] all it had to do was save face. A new feasibility study by Lord Strathalmond, William (aka Billy) Fraser, former managing director of the Kuwait Oil Company, and, later, chairman of Govan Shipbuilders following the death in a car crash of Hugh Stenhouse on 25 November 1971, concluded that something like £35 million would be needed to relaunch UCS in a modified form as a going concern: six times the sum originally requested in June 1971 by the consortium. Bowing to public pressure, the Heath government in February 1972 made a humiliating U-turn, having arrived at a restructuring plan that involved the creation of two new companies: Govan Shipbuilders, formerly Fairfield, along with Scotstoun Marine Limited, formerly Connell, with the Stephens of Linthouse yard closing after the liquidation of UCS. Writing in the *Observer*, the journalist Anthony Bambridge complained that it was throwing good money after bad, saying 'That money will keep 4,300 men in work for three years: £8,000 a man for three years to prop up a bunch of outworn shipyards that are useless now and will be just as useless in 1975'.[114] The final yard, John Brown's, after a great deal of negotiation lasting to September 1972, was sold off to an American company, Marathon Oil, with

---

112 Wishart 'An Introduction to the UCS Crisis', 82.
113 Department of Economic Affairs, 11 October 1971, National Archives, Kew (EW 7/1457).
114 *Observer*, 5 March 1972.

government sweeteners totalling £12 million, as a relatively unsophisticated jack-up oil-rig fabrication yard. But not before Danny McGarvey of the Boilermakers Union and John Service of the CSEU had visited Marathon's headquarters in Houston, Texas and given the company certain assurances involving a much-reduced workforce and changed industrial relations.[115] Earlier, *The Times* remarked that 'rarely can jobs have been secured at such a cash price'.[116] With assurances finally given over employment by Marathon, the work-in was officially brought to an end in October 1972, some 15 months after it had begun.

Politically, the government's position had become untenable, as John Davies made clear in a statement to an Open University forum on the work-in:

> I think that the thing that really developed alongside the problem of militancy ... was the fact that we had unemployment rising rather rapidly at the time ... and, of course, that added fuel to the flames of militancy very much, understandably in some ways. And one had to face the problem that this was not an issue which could be considered on its own industrial merits, that it, in fact, affected more and more the whole attitude of mind of West Central Scotland, with its growing problem of unemployment.[117]

Indeed, as far as Nicholas Ridley, speaking alongside Davies, was concerned, if the plug was pulled on UCS, there was a real fear in government, of 'the spread of terrorism and civil violence', given the number of people with Irish backgrounds in Glasgow and their links to the 'troubles' across the Irish Sea which had emerged at the end of the 1960s.[118]

The government climbdown, for whatever reason, was viewed as a tremendous victory for the workers and their representatives. The mood was captured by the journalist Ruth Wishart when she claimed that 'not a drop of blood was spilled, not an arrest was made, no disturbances took place. The workers of Clydeside had fought for, and won, their right to work, in a bloodless industrial coup'.[119] This view was shared rather surprisingly by R.W. Shakespeare, the northern industrial correspondent of *The Times*, although in more muted tones, who said that 'Mr Jimmy

---

115 Murphy, 'Labour in the British Shipbuilding and Ship Repairing Industries, 88.
116 *The Times*, 29 February 1972.
117 Open University, *Decision-Making in Britain*, BBC television, 11 July 1976.
118 Open University, *Decision-Making in Britain*.
119 Wishart 'An Introduction to the UCS Crisis', 83.

Reid and Mr James Airlie, who led the UCS work-in, can now look back on one of the most successful and possibly one of the most commendable exercises in effective industrial action ever staged'.[120]

However, it was a struggle that took its toll on Reid mentally and physically, not helped by his 60 cigarettes a day habit. The future of a whole community of thousands of families weighed heavily on his mind, desperate as he was not to let them down.[121] On top of this there was the incessant ringing of the telephone which drove him and his long-suffering family to distraction. Then there were the public meetings, the appearances on television, press conferences, the constant explaining and answering questions politely no matter how banal or offensive; everyone at one point seemed to want a piece of Jimmy Reid. Given the sleepless nights, the adrenalin-filled days, it came as no surprise to those close to him that he became so exhausted that he was admitted to Glasgow's Knightswood Hospital. On one occasion at home, his local doctor administered a sedative to help him sleep. A call to meet a prospective buyer for the four yards meant that this had to be counteracted by walking him around the living room, drinking black coffee. He also broke down in London and was taken after his collapse to Charing Cross Hospital, where the medical staff told him if he continued with his schedule he was going to kill himself. As he admitted, 'I was doing all sorts of things: television programmes, meetings ... flying here, flying there and it was taking it out of me'.[122] In such circumstances, family life was out of the question. His eldest daughter Eileen, who was 12 years of age during the work-in, said he was 'public property ... we hardly ever saw him ... our whole lives were taken over ... no normal stuff like going to the [swimming] baths'.[123] Most poignantly of all, his wife Joan spoke of how the family's lives were 'taken over. He always whistled coming up the stairs. And if he wasn't whistling then you knew something was wrong. He never whistled during the work-in'.[124] Reid was also the subject of harassment by the intelligence services: his phone was continually being tapped by MI5. He recalled later, although not at the time, that

> In 1971 ... I had a disturbing visit from a very distressed man. He told me that my phone had been tapped and that he had been

120 *The Times*, 19 September 1972.
121 Joan Reid, interview with McKinlay.
122 *Maritime History*, BBC Scotland.
123 Eileen Reid, interview with Chidlow.
124 Joan Reid, interview with Chidlow.

involved in tapping it. After listening to me he realised the errors of his ways, or those of his bosses, and had come to apologise. I laughed and told him not to worry ... In 1971 I could have told the world about my phone being tapped but I didn't. Other issues seemed more important.[125]

Was it worth it – the stress, the intrusions, the limelight? Is the triumphal tone borne out by history? Indeed, what was achieved by the work-in and what is its legacy? First, the UCS work-in gave workers a novel way of confronting redundancy. Reid explained that before the work-in 'nobody had known how to fight closures, and redundancy ... What do you do? What can you do? Usually after the officials have left, all that's left for you is the question of who goes first. But here was a refusal to accept it, and a lot of workers started to stand a wee bit straighter thanks to UCS'.[126] Indeed, it has been calculated that between 1971 and 1975 there were 200 occupations by workers in Britain inspired by the work-in.[127] Ten years after the UCS work-in women workers at Lee Jeans in Greenock in February 1981 used exactly the same tactics successfully to defend their jobs against a management determined to close their factory down.[128] The influence was also seen in unexpected quarters. On one occasion, when Reid was being interviewed by the BBC regarding the future of UCS in his small flat in Faifley, the local children were parading the streets shouting, 'Bring back Scooby Doo!'[129] Secondly, there is little doubt that by broadening the struggle for jobs into a wider campaign against the Heath government and its industrial policies, the UCS example helped to galvanise the British trade union movement into action and spawned the 'right to work' marches of the 1970s. Thirdly, it undoubtedly turned Jimmy Reid from an obscure local trade union activist into one of the most visible and lauded men in Britain. Reid recalled being at the 1972 TUC

---

125 *Sun*, 31 January 1989.
126 Wishart 'An Introduction to the UCS Crisis', 81.
127 R.K. Brown, 'From Donovan to Where? Interpretations of Industrial Relations in Britain since 1968', *British Journal of Sociology*, 29 (1978), 452; *The Times*, 19 June 1972.
128 N. Lorentzen, '"You Can't Fight for Your Jobs and Just Sit There": The Lee Jeans Sit-in', in H. Levie, D. Gregory and N. Lorentzen (eds), *Fighting Closures: De-Industrialisation and the Trade Unions, 1979–1983* (London, 1984); A. Clark, '"And the Next Thing, the Chairs Barricaded the Doors": The Lee Jeans Factory Occupation, Trade Unionism and Gender in Scotland in the 1980s', *Scottish Labour History*, 48 (2013), 116–35.
129 Joan Reid, interview with McKinlay.

at Brighton where 'he could not get moving for hundreds and hundreds of delegates wanting to come over and shake my hand'.[130] Fourth, UCS and its ramifications, as James Airlie later noted, led the Labour Party, in opposition and in government, from 1974 onwards, to propose nationalising the British shipbuilding industry, which they did in July 1977, by which stage it was arguably far too late.[131] However, Reid's fame extended way beyond the smoke-filled trade union halls. He was elected Rector of Glasgow University in 1971 (see Chapter 5) and there were numerous television appearances on news programmes and light entertainment shows, especially *Parkinson*.

On this basis the triumphalism seems more than justified. However, in arriving at an objective historical interpretation of the UCS work-in and its legacy, and with the benefit of hindsight, the following issues have also to be taken into consideration: first, the role of the liquidator; secondly, the solidarity of the workforce; thirdly, the level of politicisation the action created among the workers inside and outside the yards; and, finally, the extent to which the work-in was responsible for maintaining employment on the Upper Clyde.

The role of the liquidator, Robert Courtney Smith, in sustaining the work-in has to be afforded greater prominence by historians. Aged 43 at the time, he was a highly experienced Glasgow accountant who had handled the liquidation of William Denny and Brothers in the mid-1960s. As the main employer, the closure of Denny was a huge economic blow to the town of Dumbarton, not only to the workers and their families, but also to the local suppliers and small businesses that depended on the spending power of the workforce. Smith was therefore well aware of the social and economic devastation caused by closure before he accepted the role of liquidator. However, his role in UCS was somewhat different from the one he performed at Denny since this was an insolvency case whereas the latter had closed due to falling profit margins and little hope of correcting the decline.[132] He was thus appointed to act on behalf of the creditors rather than the government, which in practice meant that Smith had a vested interest in ensuring that the order books were completed,

---

130 Reid, *Reflections*, 97.
131 Slaven and Murphy, *Crossing the Bar*, 155.
132 Robert Courtney Smith, interview with David Chidlow (2012). Personal communication, Professor Hugh Murphy, University of Glasgow: the Denny family were at odds with each other, naval work was no longer guaranteed, and the yard was spatially constrained in an era when ships were getting larger.

UCS Work-in

as without this the creditors could not be paid. Thus, from the outset there was the potential for collusion between the liquidator and the shop stewards since both had complementary goals: returns for the creditors, jobs and wages for the workers. He was held in the highest regard by the shop stewards. Airlie said of Smith, 'if you must have a liquidator, then you could not have a better liquidator'.[133] So

> We never locked out the management. We never declared a Soviet. We knew it would grind to a halt without the liquidator's co-operation. We saw that his interest in selling the yards as going concerns fitted with our interests. I wouldn't use the term collusion, but we decided on tactics which would not embarrass him.[134]

Indeed, such was the warmth of the relationship between them that Smith and his wife were later invited by the stewards to the celebratory dinner to mark the end of the work-in.

The role of Smith in forging the much vaunted solidarity of the UCS workers was crucial. Solidarity would have crumbled after a short period of time if the weekly wage packet had failed to be delivered. It would have signalled a premature end to what became one of the historic moments in working-class struggle. But Smith's view was all along that the work-in was 'more of a myth than a reality, but a powerful myth',[135] although he readily acknowledged its enormous symbolic power. However, he was adamant that managerial control remained firmly in his hands. As he put it:

> The yards were never taken over. Management absolutely remained in charge. Had the yards been taken over I would have turned off the tap: nobody would have got paid. They couldn't have done my job. They couldn't have paid the men, paid for any materials or equipment. They had a highly successful fighting fund: this raised just short of £500k of which £285k was paid out to men who were involved in the work-in. The £285k represents ten days of the full payroll … The extent to which the stewards … were in charge was negligible. They had the power of negative action; they could stop things, but they couldn't make things happen.[136]

---

133 *Daily Record*, 13 December 1972.
134 *Scotsman*, 27 June 1981.
135 *Glasgow Herald*, 18 November 1972.
136 Smith, interview with McKinlay.

Smith in a radio interview joked that he was even 'paying Jimmy Reid and Jimmy Airlie … they were *my* workers'.[137] Even then, pay differentials between the trades were maintained, with those involved in the work-in being paid based on take-home pay prior to the industrial action.[138]

The other issue of importance in assessing the role of the liquidator was insurance. Employers' liability insurance was necessary for the protection of the workers in an industry with a fair number of accidents and occasional deaths. Insurance companies would only agree to provide cover if they were assured that the liquidator was in control of operations and this also applied to suppliers of materials. If there had been a takeover of the four yards Smith said he would have had no choice but to close them down with immediate effect.[139]

However, it was not just the wage packet that created the basis of solidarity during the work-in, it was the willingness of previously competitive sections of the workforce to work together to save their livelihoods. This unity was at best precarious and it was severely tested in September 1972 when the most powerful group of workers, the boilermakers, at newly created Govan Shipbuilders, were prepared to place the whole venture in jeopardy over the question of a few days' back pay. This was a low point in the work-in. Reid addressed a mass meeting at Clydebank and warned of the crucial weakness of craft sectionalism.

> In my opinion, and it's always been my opinion, sectional differences within the working class, no matter what it's based on, is always eventually self-destruction for the working class. And that goes for colour, for creed, for religion, or for caste. And as workers, we've got to stand together, and look upon each other as brothers, and only recognise one label, and that is 'fellow worker'.[140]

Reid stated that retrospective pay was not an issue. 'But a certain section of the Boilermakers Society are using it as a vehicle which could be self-defeating and suicidal' and their attitude was bringing the 'concept of the rat race into the trade union movement'.[141] There was also an unwillingness to accept into their ranks men who had undergone retraining in

---

137 Lloyd, 'Eyes of the World'.
138 Hay and McLauchlan, 'The Oral History of Upper Clyde Shipbuilders', 57.
139 Smith, interview with McKinlay.
140 Reid, 21 September 1972, in Woolfson, 'Working-Class Culture', 330.
141 *Scottish Daily Express*, 4 September 1972.

new skills. A few days later, the boilermakers showed their recalcitrant side by opposing the reintroduction of the 50p levy to support those continuing the work-in at Clydebank until Marathon could re-employ them after the year's end. Only 600 men supported the work-in, and these were mainly electricians and draughtsmen at Govan, only welders at Linthouse, and no one at Scotstoun, prompting James Airlie to resign as convenor of the JSSCC. Five other stewards followed his example. Airlie declared it was the 'end of the magnificent solidarity and unity shown by the workers in UCS ... which was responsible for saving the four yards', and that he was 'ashamed at the workers at Govan'.[142] At a subsequent meeting a thousand workers in the finishing trades voted to continue the levy, but the boilermakers stubbornly refused to budge.[143] What had triggered the opposition was the fact that those workers at Clydebank had been awarded redundancy payments but not Govan workers. The reason offered was that there was a change of work from ships to oil rigs.[144] Solidarity had given way to unseemly squabbling over money and status. As Maurice Baggott, industrial correspondent of the *Scotsman*, remarked: 'the saga of UCS ends ignominiously'.[145] Sectionalism had restored itself.

On 9 October 1972, the agreement with Marathon that secured the Clydebank yard's future was completed. Reid told the stewards' committee, 'we will not crow today. They told us it could not be done. It could be done because it *has* been done'.[146] The Marathon agreement swept away unnecessary demarcation lines. All trades were paid the same rate; the boilermakers were now deposed as the kings of the Clydebank shipyard trades. The boilermakers did not give up their status easily, however. Reid and Dickie were critical in convincing the workforce of the necessity of changing working practices and attitudes. Sam Purdie, Marathon's personnel manager, was involved in the daily struggle to modernise the former John Brown's yard.

> Those were the guys who had built the QE2. We had to convince these guys that they were no longer building Rolls-Royces, they were building jeeps. The world was only prepared for jeeps. That wasn't easy for them to hear, because they took such a pride in

---

142 *Guardian*, 27 September 1972.
143 *Guardian*, 3 October 1972.
144 UCS scrapbook 2, 27 September 1972.
145 *Scotsman*, 7 September 1972.
146 Joint Shop Stewards Coordinating Committee, Minutes, 9 October 1971, Glasgow University Archives, UGD181/1/1.

their skills. That was a big adjustment for the men. Building a jack hammer rig is entirely different from building a liner.[147]

The return of inter-trade tensions held in check during the work-in also had repercussions inside the Communist Party Shipbuilding Branch. Each Party branch was entitled to send delegates to the Scottish Party conference. Reid and Airlie were the obvious nominees for the Shipbuilding Branch. These nominations became politically and personally highly charged for the communists at the core of the UCS leadership.[148] The core group of around 70 UCS communist shop stewards met on 20 September 1971 to clear the air. In part, this meeting was to challenge any sense that Sammy Barr had devised the work-in strategy on behalf of the Communist Party. Lest there be any doubt, both Airlie and Jimmy Cloughley credited Reid with the innovative concept of the work-in. Only a single voice spoke for Barr. Reid opened the 'comrades meeting' by rounding on the boilermakers for their reversion to sectional bargaining and hostility to the Marathon agreement. This effectively ended the solidarity nurtured and sustained through the 14 long months of the work-in. *Only* this solidarity allowed the communists to maintain their strategy and leadership in the yards.

To criticise the boilermakers' sectionalism was not, insisted Airlie, about being 'Simon pure' politically. This was impossible given 'the manoeuvring around principles' necessary to secure the Marathon deal for Clydebank. Reid was persuaded not to resign from the Communist Party's Scottish leadership, at least not yet. There were also the first hints that Reid and Airlie were angered at what they regarded as personal attacks on them. For Reid, such personal attacks were part of 'a pattern … for years'. 'One sided slander' emanated from the Party hierarchy to cut him and Airlie down to size: 'it's been selective. It's been concerted over the years. It's so foreign to the Party'.[149] A month later, 'roughly fifty' of the Shipbuilding Branch met to elect its nominees for the Scottish Executive. This meeting was a turning-point in Reid's career as a communist. Again, the vexed question of boilermaker sectionalism was central. Unlike before, however, disagreements over bargaining tactics inside the yards surfaced as major differences in political strategy and what it meant to be a communist. Sammy Barr, a boilermaker and the Govan union convener, became the

147 S. Purdie, interview with McKinlay (2012).
148 'Comrades Meeting', 26 September 1972, Willie Thompson Collection, Glasgow Caledonian University Archives.
149 'Discussion: Ashton, Reid, Airlie, Murray', 30 October 1972, uncatalogued item, Glasgow Caledonian University Archives.

focal point of criticism; he was almost the embodiment of the boilermakers' sectionalism. Even Barr's supporters admitted that he sometimes allowed criticism of the Party in order to curry favour with his boilermaker constituents. Reid was 'raging' as he paced up and down the room's central aisle, 'like an evangelical preacher', his cool anger channelled into wounding words.[150] Reid's fury dispensed with comradely etiquette. He insisted that Barr was so compromised that he had to stand down, insisting that the work-in depended upon the Party remaining studiously aloof from the stewards' committee. Reid continued:

> No serious mistakes were made. I can *forgive* mistakes. I can *forgive* lack of ability. I can *forgive* lack of competence. I can even *forgive* cowardice. But I *cannot* forgive a stab in the back. That was Barr's position. I would have been for his expulsion. During the fight (i.e., work-in) S(ammy) B(arr's) limitations were obvious. No control at Scotstoun. Party members were the first to hold Sammy responsible. Had Jimmy Airlie and Jimmy Reid been of the same calibre (as Sammy) then the struggle would have been lost.[151]

These actions could only be understood as 'acts of betrayal', Reid concluded. The debate lasted four hours. 'Jimmy Reid *destroyed* Sammy Barr, he picked him apart. Sammy was crying. The mood in the room was that Jimmy was correct in his analysis but unfair in how he did it'.[152] Barr later explained his emotional response at the prospect of being expelled from the Party: 'I always wanted to *be* a communist. I always wanted to be *part* of the Communist Party'.[153] Barr was devastated: he pleaded, '*dinnae* take my Party card, comrades; *dinnae* take my Party card'.[154]

Reid cared little for the approval of others, comrades or not. Accusations, both petty and personal, could be shrugged off: accusations that threatened Reid's vision of the solidarity of UCS could not. In effect, this was a debate about how UCS was to be remembered. The Communist Party could not claim this legacy without Reid and Airlie: there was no alternative but to back down. There was to be no reconciliation; however, Airlie, who was no less incensed than Reid and more anxious to seek some compromise,

---

150 Kay, interview with McKinlay (2011).
151 Uncatalogued handwritten notes, Scottish Papers, CPGB, Glasgow Caledonian University.
152 Cooper, interview with McKinlay.
153 S. Barr, interview with Campbell and McIlroy (BL 1049/13).
154 D. Chalmers, interview with McKinlay (2017).

accepted their nominations for the Scottish executive. Barr was not expelled; Reid and Airlie were nominated to the Scottish Executive. But this *was* an uneasy peace. The moment of UCS – of an overarching solidarity – was now over. By so fiercely distancing himself from any attempt by the Communist Party to claim anything more than a supporting role in the work-in he served notice that he would not hold with any future attempt to rewrite the history of the work-in. As Alex Murray, the Party's Scottish Secretary and a confidante of Reid, put it in a private meeting, the real danger was 'destroying the myth' of UCS.[155] Equally, he had severed any working relationship with Barr, and, for the first time, strained his relations with Jimmy Airlie and Finlay Hart. The minutes recorded the meeting's extremely tense atmosphere and that Reid's 'prestige sank as a result', especially as Barr recovered his composure. The danger in allowing the bad blood – 'uncomradely action' – to continue was that it would 'harm the Party'. Reid was 'sickened. Didn't think that this happened in the Party. That's what's wrong with the Party'.[156] Again, for Reid, a question of strategy and organisation became fused with personal integrity.

Then there is the question of employment. At the start of the work-in it was only white-collar staff – mainly draughtsmen from the drawing office rather than the hourly paid who were made redundant, as the consortium was not taking on new work. The rest of the men were 'working normally'. The actual numbers made unemployed increased, but were still a fraction of those being paid by the liquidator. At the start it amounted to 1.5 per cent, or 121 workers spread over four yards, climbing to a peak in October 1971 of 5.2 per cent, or 390, before falling back to 177 from February to June 1972.[157] During the 15 months of the work-in the workers and management completed 17 ships and started another two.[158] This was a measured success for the work-in, but the 'no closures, no redundancies' policy of the shop stewards came under severe pressure in September 1972.

The agreement for the Texan company Marathon Oil to take over John Brown's yard was concluded between McGarvey and the firm's

155 J. Ashton, 'Notebook', 30 October 1972, Glasgow Caledonian University Archive.
156 Ashton, Notes, 27 October 1972; Communist Party of Great Britain Scottish Committee, Notes and 'Informal Discussion', 30 October 1972, uncatalogued item, Glasgow Caledonian University Archives.
157 Second Report by the Liquidator to Creditors, Glasgow University Archives, ACCN3613/1/9.
158 Lloyd, 'Eyes of the World'.

owner Wayne Harbin with no stewards' involvement; in any case, as communists, Airlie and Reid would have been denied an entry visa into the USA. Marathon wanted flexible working arrangements and a 'no-strike agreement' lasting four years – something agreed to at a meeting at the Glasgow Airport Hotel on 7 August an hour before the imposed deadline by the firm. The no-stoppages clause in the agreement may have struck at the fundamental right of workers to withdraw their labour, but was traded for guarantees of employment for most of the John Brown's workers. However, Marathon only provided work for 1,900 out of a workforce of 2,500 under UCS, giving only vague promises that in time there would be employment for 3,000. This target was never reached: two years later the total workforce still only numbered 2,000 and even then management felt that the yard was 'overmanned'. By June 1974, the 'no-strike agreement' was in tatters as the workforce struck over bonus payments.[159] However, perhaps looking at the UCS experience from an economistic view is the wrong lens to use: as far as Reid was concerned, the moral aspect was just as important. The transformational power of the work-in to change lives, to allow people schooled in inferiority to take responsibility for themselves and their communities, was the real gain.[160] It was the duty of young workers to aspire, to 'storm the heavens', as Reid so eloquently put it.[161]

The other question to address is whether the work-in held out the promise of a new approach to management in industry in which the workers had an equal say in the day-to-day running of the enterprise? Tony Benn when touring the yard as Labour's shadow spokesperson for industry claimed that UCS had 'given birth to a new concept in industrial democracy'.[162] Perhaps UCS was an influence on Alan Bullock's 1997 report on industrial relations in Britain, which championed the idea of workers' representatives on the board of directors in firms with over 2,000 employees. But in relation to Clydeside, Benn's claims were never vindicated, and Bullock's vision for industry never realised. The stewards after all had been careful to stress that their actions amounted to a 'work-in' and not a 'take over'. They rejected any suggestions that they were establishing a syndicalist style of workers' control. As one reporter observed: 'When the men report at 7.50am each morning it's still the foreman who tells them what work to get on with. He gets his orders from

159 *Observer*, 2 June 1974.
160 Joan Reid, interview with McKinlay.
161 *A Place in My Mind*, BBC Radio Scotland.
162 *Guardian*, 27 June 1981.

the departmental heads ... [they in turn] are briefed by directors. The chain of command reaches up to the liquidator ...'.[163]

The communist stewards decided that the Party leadership had to be kept at arm's length for principled and practical reasons. Indeed, there was little or no possibility of the stewards accepting any directions from the Party's NEC during the work-in. The politics of the work-in, at all levels, was so complex and fast-moving, and as a result constantly undergoing change, that they were impervious to formulaic industrial strategies. That, combined with intense media scrutiny, ensured that Party involvement was marginal. Thus, it became ideologically almost impossible to go beyond the political rhetoric of the Labour left: that is, get the Tories out and nationalise shipbuilding. Moreover, after the work-in was over, labour relations resorted once more to normal patterns of adversarial negotiated dealings between labour and capital. The bosses were still the bosses and the workers still the workers. The moderateness of the so-called revolutionaries amazed Tony Benn, who over a coffee asked a number of the communist shop stewards what they saw as the 'next step'. All they asked for was joint production committees in which decision-making would be shared with management. Incredulous, Benn retorted: 'Surely you want more than this?' They replied, 'No – you must let the workers learn before you give them added responsibilities. You must let them learn ... the most modest demands are being made by these people'.[164] Reid himself considered the idea of workers' control of the shipyards as 'romantic'.[165]

Although the work-in undoubtedly constituted a victory of sorts for the UCS workers the road ahead was to prove a rocky one. It did little to boost membership of the CPGB in the Upper Clyde. Before the UCS work-in the Party's Shipbuilding Branch on Clydeside numbered no more than 60, with a core of around 20; even after the massive success of the UCS campaign the branch only numbered 80, still with a core of around 20 activists.[166] It also failed to provide guarantees for future employment in the shipbuilding industry. By 1977, British shipbuilding had been nationalised by the Labour government as British Shipbuilders

163 *Sunday Post*, 22 August 1971.
164 Benn, *Diaries 1968–1972* (10 March 1972), 413.
165 Jimmy Reid, interview with Gerry Ross (1972).
166 Shipbuilding Branch', membership lists, Glasgow University Archives, DC65/52; G. Kerr, Secretary, Communist Party, Shipbuilding Branch, interview (February 2013); A. Murray, Scottish Secretary, 'Report to Scottish Congress', n.d., 5, Glasgow University Archives, DC65/50; Bain, 'Interview with Jimmy Airlie', 17; *Morning Star*, 29 June 1981.

Plc: an admittance that the industry was unable to survive without state control. In 1980, Marathon pulled out of Clydebank, selling the yard to a French consortium UiE Scotland, which used it to build jack-up and semi-submersible rigs for North Sea oil fields. UiE closed the yard in 2001. The once great symbol of the Clyde's dominance of world shipbuilding, John Brown's, has now been cleared. All that remains is a crane, known as the Titan, in which tourists are taken by a lift 150 feet in the sky from where they can imagine below the organised chaos, the hustle and bustle, hurrying and scurrying, of a myriad of little dots that once made the term 'Clyde-built' mean something; now a barren strip of land peopled by ghosts. The poet Brian Whittingham wrote:

> The Titan Crane sits beside the empty dock
> With only its coat of blue paint to shield it from the
>   Clydeside wind
> That licks the flattened debris that was a yard.[167]

As shop steward Davie Torrance said, they may have won a great victory in 1971–2, but they 'didn't necessarily win the war'.[168] However, a testimony to the case made by the men for keeping the yards open is that shipbuilding still survives to this day on the Clyde, admittedly on a much-reduced basis, but still employing 4,000 workers.

For Reid personally UCS had turned him into a national figure. Handsome, articulate and charismatic, his allure, his appeal made him an iconic political figure. But while undoubtedly hugely popular with a cross section of society, would that charisma be enough to induce his many admirers to support him politically? The 1974 general election would answer that question: an answer that Reid would find uncomfortable and difficult to come to terms with.

---

167 B. Whittingham, 'The Titan Crane', in Betteridge, *Rose Loupt Oot*, 120.
168 Torrance, interview with Knox.

5

Transitions

The UCS work-in turned Reid from a prominent local trade unionist into a national figure whom everyone from television producers, to journalists, to politicians and inevitably hangers-on seemingly wanted a piece of. There was an obvious desire by a wide section of society to bask in the reflected glory of the poster boy communist. The Jimmy Reid who emerged from the work-in was not the same Jimmy Reid who preceded it – how could he be? His entry into the arena of national public affairs, his embedment in the popular consciousness, forced him to come to terms with the trappings of fame: the envy, the jealousy, the pettiness, as well as the adulation. As we have seen, he had already had some experience of envy in the Communist Party leadership's 'One-sided slander', emanating from the desire 'to cut him and Airlie down to size'.[1] But for now the sun shone brightly as the golden boy of the British left dazzled a legion of admirers.

The first indication of his growing popularity occurred in late 1971 when he was asked to stand as Rector of Glasgow University to replace his old friend, the Revd George MacLeod. The position of Rector dates from medieval times, but currently he/she represents the students on the ruling body of the university – the Court – and works closely with the Students' Representative Council, bringing student concerns to the attention of the university's managers. In the past the Rector was generally a politician or a titled gentleman; indeed, three out of the four previous incumbents had been peers of the realm. Things were beginning to change from 1968: students had demanded a greater voice in university affairs and roughly about the same time as Reid's campaign got under way the future prime minister Gordon Brown, then a postgraduate student in Edinburgh University, was

---

1 'Discussion: Ashton, Reid, Airlie, Murray', 30 October 1972, Glasgow Caledonian University Archives.

running for Rector. The student campaign for Reid was broad-based and far from confined to the university's Communist Club. Moreover, it reflected the desire for a working rather than a strictly honorary rector. A committee, which included George Brechin, Martin Caldwell and others, met with Reid in a trade union club by the hospice on the River Clyde to discuss the possibility of him standing. Reid did not take much persuading as he recognised, on the one hand, that if elected it would raise the profile of the work-in; on the other, he empathised with the student fight for recognition as he had fought nearly 20 years ago for apprentices.[2]

A key group in the campaign were young Catholic activists, influenced by the university's Jesuit Chaplain, Gerry Hughes. From his appointment in 1967, Hughes made the Catholic chaplaincy a vibrant open house. Ecumenical in everything, not just theology, Hughes actively promoted dialogue beyond the church. Reid spoke several times at the chaplaincy, including a seminar with Professor William Barclay on the Sermon on the Mount. The Professor explained the meaning of the original Greek text while Reid demonstrated his 'passionate commitment to the Beatitudes': 'he had all good practising Catholics sitting on the edge of their chairs and in some degree of alarm as they heard from the Communist what they were convinced to as Christians'.[3] Reid in fact was becoming more explicit in his use of religious imagery and specific texts as a way of critiquing contemporary life. 'Everything that I fight for', he told the presenter Robin Day in December 1971, everything 'in my philosophy corresponds … to the social teachings of the Sermon on the Mount and I would consider myself … not only a communist, but someone who's living up to the moral code of the Sermon on the Mount'.[4]

The two men, the Marxist and the Jesuit, had, perhaps surprisingly, much in common. At the centre of Hughes's theology was the search for spirituality in everyday life. Both regarded their beliefs as providing an alternative to, and a living condemnation of, capitalist society. For both Reid and Hughes, the relationship between belief and the organisation, always open to private doubt, should be open to public challenge. If there was a clear overlap between Hughes and Reid in terms of their practical politics, then they also shared nagging doubts about the organisations to which they belonged. For Hughes, there was always the danger that the Church would forget 'her meaning, becoming absorbed instead in her own

2   G. Brechin, interview with Knox (2017).
3   G. Hughes, *Walk to Jerusalem: In Search of Peace* (London, 1991), 139.
4   *It's Your Line*, BBC Radio, 3 December 1971.

10 Reid in his rectorial robes (courtesy of Scran)

11 The mature Reid (courtesy of Scran)

survival as an organisation, when maintenance becomes more important than mission'.[5] There were to be clear echoes in Reid's increasing, if private, unease within the Communist Party. The radical Hughes was dismissed from his post in 1972 but his refusal to go quietly stayed his departure until 1975. Hughes refused to accept that his public criticisms of the Church were disloyal. Quite the reverse: he reaffirmed his faith precisely by criticising a Church whose first priority was preserving its organisation, power and authority at the expense of its ministry.

The Reid campaign was for a student voice in university decision-making and also to demonstrate student support for the UCS workers.[6] However, first indications among 356 students polled showed that the television presenter Michael Parkinson was favourite with 53.3 per cent of the vote, Reid 26.2 per cent, Teddy Taylor, Tory MP for Glasgow Cathcart, 11.5 per cent and Peggy Herbison, former Labour MP for North Lanarkshire, 9 per cent. Parkinson was forced to withdraw when his nomination was rejected by the university Court as he had not handed in a signed declaration. The re-run poll without Parkinson showed Reid to be clear favourite with 50.2 per cent of the vote. Behind him came Taylor with 31.4 per cent, and even further behind, Herbison with 18.4 per cent.[7] He became the youngest person ever to hold the office of Rector in the University of Glasgow since it was established in 1648.

Once elected, the Rector is formally installed in a ceremony and gives a speech known as an Address, which on Friday, 28 April 1972 Reid sensationally used to communicate his social and political philosophy as the first communist to hold the office; more precisely, the first working-class communist (Figures 10–11). He took as the theme for his Address the subject of alienation. Typically, the university only received the Address the day before the installation, and then he improvised when a line from Robert Burns came to mind.[8] It may have been last-minute, but the impact was nothing less than electric. It was printed in full in the *New York Times*, which claimed it was the greatest speech since President Lincoln's Gettysburg Address. It contained the memorable lines:

> Reject the values and false morality that underlie these attitudes.
> A rat race is for rats. We're not *rats*. We're human beings. Reject

---

5 G. Hughes, *In Search of a Way: Two Journeys of Spiritual Discovery* (London, 1986), 172.
6 Brechin, interview with Knox.
7 *Glasgow University Guardian*, 22 October 1971.
8 *Guardian*, 9 October 1976.

the insidious pressures in society that would blunt your critical faculties to all that is happening around you, that would caution silence in the face of injustice lest you jeopardise your chances of promotion and self-advancement. This is how it starts and before you know where you are, you're a fully paid-up member of the rat-pack. The price is too high. It entails the loss of your dignity and human spirit. Or as Christ put it, 'What doth it profit a man if he gain the whole world and suffer the loss of his soul?'[9]

There were several strands to Reid's Address. The juxtaposition of a Marxist concept with Christian themes reflected both Reid's own interests and a wider dialogue between the Communist Party and Christianity. This dialogue had flourished through the mid-1960s and established common ground on which philosophical and practical differences could be shared, rather than contested.[10] It was no longer taken for granted that to be Catholic was to be anti-communist or vice versa. For a natural doubter like Reid, to discard either Christianity or Marxism was, as the philosopher Alasdair MacIntyre puts it, 'to discard truths not otherwise available'.[11]

Certainly, Reid's Address draws upon the Marxist concept of alienation in which individuals confronts a bewildering world that they have made but cannot understand. They confront a hostile world over which they have little influence, far less control. This impotence becomes associated with indifference and passivity. Reid followed Marx in his understanding that collective action provided humans with a sense of how the world actually is *and* that it can be remade. James Klugmann's Communist Party pamphlet, *The Future of Man* (1970), spoke of humanist Marxism as a practical and moral alternative to the dehumanising forces of consumer society: 'the drab standardised society, supermarket uniformity that haunts so many nightmares of the future'.[12] It was not, then, Marxists who were economic determinists but capitalist society which squeezed out the morality and autonomy of people, reducing them to consumers and human resources. Overcoming alienation comes through not just an intellectual understanding of its existence but also by practical, collective action. This is what Reid understood as the significance of the UCS work-in. In

---

9   Reid, *Reflections*, 101–2 (see *Reflections*, Appendix 1 for the whole Address).
10 J. Klugmann (ed.), *Dialogue of Christianity and Marxism* (London, 1968).
11 S. MacIntyre, *Marxism and Christianity* (London, 1995).
12 J. Klugmann, *The Future of Man* (London, 1970), 14. See also G. Andrews, 'Culture, Ideology and Strategy of the Communist Party of Great Britain 1964–1979' (unpublished PhD thesis, Kingston University, 2002), 92, 95.

later years he often remarked that his pride in the work-in stemmed from bearing witness to the extraordinary, often undreamt of, skills brought forth in ordinary working people. Reid also spoke of his own experience of communist fraternity: of lives dedicated to a practical idealism, of optimism tempered by trial and failure.

Running through Reid's Address was a powerful moral critique that spoke to the ambitions of idealism. He spoke with clarity, passion and sophistication, but in the voice of working-class Clydeside. This was a self-assured voice, unfazed by the formality of the setting and ready to speak in its own terms rather than defer to custom. Reid's call to graduating students to make their own futures was an echo of the communist call for the working class to remake capitalism, a reminder of agency and the openness of the future. Looking back on the Address one is also struck by the liberal overtones, the assertion of middle-class, even Victorian, values of public service. Again, we hear Reid discussing an abstract philosophical term that addresses the moment in everyday language. Throughout his speech Reid used the inclusive 'we', never offering a personal opinion, but a collective imperative. This admixture of religion, liberal individualism and Marxism was potent, and its complexity allowed it to speak in different registers to different constituencies. To struggle is individual and moral (maybe even religious), rather than an economic contest between the forces of individual self-interest, avarice and greed and those of community. Here is the sense that contemporary society stunts the full potential of the individual and the community. The resolution of this conflict can only be found when we 'gear our society to social need'.[13]

For a communist and a Marxist Reid's failure to emphasise the class basis of society and the role of class struggle in its transformation was surprising. Indeed, he later claimed that when he wrote the Address, he was influenced by some old shipyard workers that he had met in Connolly's bar some months before, 'wiping away their tears' at the news of the sinking of the Queen Elizabeth in Hong Kong harbour. The tears of these hardened shipyard workers gave Reid a glimpse into the intense identification between the men, their skill and the product of their labour. This pride was being eroded by the technologies of modern industry and the cash nexus. The philosophy had derived from his recollections of his 'youthful reading of William Morris'.[14] His was a classic tale of the little people, the majority, against a small minority of powerful and anonymous figures in

---

13 Reid, *Reflections*, 104.
14 *Herald*, 13 August 2010.

business and politics. It was not an attack on capitalist exploitation, which Marx saw as the basis of alienation, rather it was a powerful appeal for the creation of a socially responsible economic system in which 'our wealth-producing resources and potential [are] subject to public control and to social accountability'.[15] This led to a stinging rebuke from his Trotskyist opponents on the left. Regarding the alienation speech, Trotskyist Stephen Johns of the Socialist Labour League said: 'This could be one of these speeches by the Archbishop of Canterbury, the Duke of Edinburgh, or even a Tory. After all we are all against the "rat race", and it would be nice if the ordinary bloke got a bit more say in things – make him feel wanted. It is noticeable that the "communist" Reid censored all mention of capitalism, the working class, revolutionary change and socialism'.[16]

Despite the expected criticism from this quarter, the underlying theme of the Address seemed consistent with the CPGB's critique at the time of monopoly capitalism and the pursuit of left unity as its basis.[17] However, while its links to Marxism might be tenuous there is no denying the Address added to Reid's allure in the media. Part of this lay in overturning the entrenched assumptions among the middle classes concerning the inarticulateness of working people. Reid, who had left school at the age of 14, not only demonstrated the fallacy of this to the students and academics who attended the installation but did so in a wonderfully poetic manner that stunned those present into rapturous applause. It also brought him fulsome praise from the CPGB's Scottish Committee. In a speech to the Party's Scottish Congress, Alex Murray said Reid's election as Rector was emblematic of 'new forces amongst the students and the working class' and that:

> Previous Rectors, among them Gladstone, Disraeli and Sir Robert Peel, must be spinning in their graves. Let them turn. Let them gyrate. Go into orbit if they will. It matters not as they represent the past ... that which he (Reid) represents; those whom he represents – our Party, our ideas and our ideals, the working class, the youth, represent ... Scotland's future.[18]

Reid immediately proved himself to be on the side of the students who had elected him, in the process proving himself to be an innovative Rector.

---

15 Reid, *Reflections*, 103.
16 S. Johns, *Reformism on the Clyde: The Story of UCS* (1973), 94.
17 Andrews, *End Games*, 86.
18 Alex Murray, Speech to the Scottish Congress of the CPGB, 4 November 1972, Glasgow University Archives, DC65750.

Indeed, he had made it clear in a pre-election interview with the university staff magazine that he would advance the interests of students and see that they were properly involved in the running of the institution; he would also campaign for greater student participation in the planning of the curriculum and raise the issue of student grants. Moreover, he promised to be 'a working rector', who would take his responsibilities seriously.[19] When asked by a student reporter if he could combine his duties as Rector with his commitment to the UCS work-in, Reid replied: 'There is not just one person to take my place at UCS, but many. It is the best collective committee I have worked on in my life. I have never taken on a responsibility which I have not fulfilled'.[20]

The first thing he did, and something that his predecessor George MacLeod had failed to do, was to appoint George Brechin as his assessor and he became the first student to sit on the university Court in its 500-year history.[21] Brechin was followed by Bridget Corr, former honorary secretary of the Student Representative Council, who also made history by being the first female to sit on the Court. Reid also ruffled a few feathers by insisting, in the absence of the Vice-Chancellor, who normally chaired the meetings of the Court, that he as rector should occupy the chair;[22] an announcement that particularly irked the Vice-Principal.[23] Gordon Brown had also made the same demand and ran up against university authorities, which suggests that there may have been some collusion between the two men. However, his efficiency and preparedness won over the sceptics on the Court and they gradually recognised that he brought a different dimension to proceedings.[24] More predictably, he won the backing of the students, who when Reid's term of office came to an end in October 1974 expressed the view that both he and his predecessor George MacLeod had enhanced the importance of the position as they were both 'working rectors' rather than just 'figureheads'.[25] Just a few months before his time was up as rector Reid was at the head of a demonstration in February 1974 calling for an increase in student grants.[26] However, any hope of his time in office acting as a catalyst for student radicalisation was dashed as

19 Jimmy Reid, interview with Gerry Ross (1972).
20 *Glasgow University Guardian*, 22 October 1971.
21 *Daily Record*, 14 April 1986.
22 Brechin, interview with Knox.
23 B. Prentice (née Corr), interview with Knox (2017).
24 Prentice, interview with Knox.
25 *Glasgow University Guardian*, 17 October 1974.
26 *Glasgow University Guardian*, 14 February 1974.

he was replaced by Arthur Montford, a football commentator. However, his time as Rector was not simply spent appeasing middle-class sceptics on the Court or leading student demonstrations. As George Brechin astutely recognised, Reid was also honing his skills as a communicator, a manager and a negotiator, particularly among the middle classes; something that was strengthened by his appearances in the media.[27]

Indeed, such was his national persona that he appeared three times on one of the most watched shown on British television –*Parkinson*, but most memorably in 1973 in a debate with the right-wing comic actor Kenneth Williams, famous for his starring roles in the *Carry On* films. The previous week, Williams, pontificating on the failure of the working class to make the most of themselves, had provoked Parkinson into a sharp retort. The deeply insulted Williams demanded a right of reply. Reid was invited as the foil to Williams before an invited studio audience of people who had written to express their horror or support for Williams's politics. To Reid, 'Williams was a bully. Cruel, insensitive and a 22-carat bampot'.[28] The show's host, Michael Parkinson, recalled that during the pre-show sound checks, Williams, who viewed Reid as uneducated and uncivilised, tried to belittle him by directly quoting a passage from a famous poem and asking him if he knew who had written it. Much to Williams's chagrin, Reid answered correctly – W.B. Yeats – then stood up and declaimed an incredibly powerful piece of poetry. When he finished the recitation, Reid asked Williams if he knew who had written it. Williams replied that he didn't – and Reid with a wry smile said: 'I did'. Williams, not Reid, was flustered just as the show opened.[29] 'Game, set and match', noted the watching Parkinson, 'before we went on'. Reid's strategy in the debate was to give Williams enough rope to hang himself and he duly delivered. As the programme proceeded, his 'rantings got wilder, his arguments weirder … he was exposed as a nasty little man, an intellectual pigmy …'[30] Privately, Williams 'seethed' against Reid in his diary and autobiography.[31] Williams's views were those of an incoherent highly individualistic libertarian, based solely on his own life. During the exchanges, Reid was careful not to

27 Brechin, interview with Knox.
28 Reid, *Power without Principles*, 297. 'Bampot' means 'a foolish, annoying, or obnoxious person'.
29 BBC Scotland News, 19 August 2010; M. Parkinson, *Parky: My Autobiography* (London, 2009), 209–10.
30 Reid, *Power without Principles*, 297.
31 C. Stevens, *Born Brilliant: The Life of Kenneth Williams* (London, 2011), 274–5; R. Davies, *The Kenneth Williams Diaries* (London, 1994), 663.

interrupt Williams but to take his arguments seriously. Williams was experienced enough to know that his cynical incoherence was losing the audience, but his misplaced self-mockery only deepened the impression that this was someone who lacked not just a political intelligence but was also bereft of empathy. The pivot in the exchange was Reid's capacity not just to deflate William's self-importance but to turn this into a wider commentary on the nature of class; prime time Marxism:

> You would think that the powerful people are the captains of industry, stockbrokers, bankers, and the sort of people you see at horse shows and Royal Ascot: all the important people. Well, I'm prepared to volunteer the services of the Clyde workers: we'll build boats – luxury yachts – fill them full of food and we'll send these powerful and important people of British society cruising around the world for six or nine months. And do you know something? We wouldn't notice their absence unless some society columnist drew our attention to it, because they don't really *matter*. But let the workers all simultaneously decide to go on holiday and Britain is on the brink of a national disaster. Because it's the dockers, the engineers, the railwaymen who are the really important people in society … Who is the real power in this land? It is the people who produce the wealth. Wealth is not produced in any boardroom: it is produced on the factory floor.[32]

Reid's appearance on *Parkinson* did much to enhance his image as 'everyone's popular Communist … You were looked on as the good-guy red'.[33] Indeed, Jimmy Reid was often described as the best-known and best-loved communist in Europe (Figures 12–14).

By now Reid was the 'golden boy' of the left, the poster boy of the Communist Party. The time seemed right to realise his political ambitions. He was already a town councillor for Clydebank's seventh ward and had stood (unsuccessfully) twice as the CPGB candidate in East Dunbartonshire in the 1964 and 1970 general elections. Despite enthusiastic support from the Jimmy Reid Youth Brigade, who plastered the streets of Clydebank with posters, distributed hundreds of leaflets and chalked the streets white with slogans,[34] Reid polled a derisory total

---

32 *Parkinson* (show).
33 *Sunday Herald*, 27 March 1994.
34 Jimmy Reid Youth Brigade, Newsletter, Willie Thompson Collection, Glasgow Caledonian University Archives.

of 1,171 votes, or 1.98 per cent of total votes cast. Unconsciously anticipating his reaction to the 1974 election result, Reid, in a letter to the editor of the *Clydebank Press*, vehemently attacked the local paper as a 'public relations mag[azine] for a group of Labour councillors', declaring the editor himself to be 'a little tin pot, red baiting McCarthy, spewing out his prejudices week by week ... characterising everyone who opposes the polices of his cronies on the Council as communists'.[35] Making so many enemies, it was not surprising that he didn't do much better in 1970, polling 1,656 votes, or 2.27 per cent of total votes cast.

In 1974, his Labour opponent was Hugh McCartney, the son of a tram driver, and like Reid a time-served engineer. Boundary changes after 1966 created the Central Dunbartonshire constituency: one of three constituencies formed to replace the now defunct constituencies of East Dunbartonshire and West Dunbartonshire and the largest in Scotland with around 100,000 voters. The new parliamentary seat was dominated by Clydebank, making up 60 per cent of the voting population, and offering Reid an excellent prospect of political success against McCartney, considering his track record in the fight to save the old John Brown's yard and the fact that he was still a working shop steward in Marathon. For the CPGB, 1974 was different from previous elections. Electoral outcomes in the past were not a major concern for the Party as it considered itself to be a vanguard organisation ready to provide a lead to the workers during a crisis of capitalism, as the Bolsheviks had done in 1917. Standing in an election was simply a way of creating a political presence and hoping that the campaign would encourage in the aftermath some of the voting public to join the Party. Few communist candidates went into an election with any expectation of winning a seat, but the difference was that in 1974 Jimmy Reid did. This was not a case of self-delusion on his part. In the local authority elections of May 1972 he had been re-elected to Clydebank Town Council (CTC), defeating the Labour candidate by 572 votes; thus, there were grounds for optimism. Moreover, it was a view shared by sections of the media. 'In Clydebank', reported the *Guardian*, 'the Communist candidate is hailed on all sides as he walks along the street. The young, old, and middle-aged come up to shake his hand, wish him well and usually add some encouraging criticism of the opposition. In Clydebank they say: "This is Jimmy's town"'.[36]

35 *Clydebank Press*, 17 September 1965.
36 *Guardian*, 14, 19 February 1974.

12 Addressing the Congress of the Romanian Communist Party (courtesy of Brian McGeachan)

13 Robert Courtney Smith (courtesy of John Hume)

14 The *Ailsa*, the last ship launched by UCS
    (courtesy of John Hume)

The Communist Party in Clydebank was well-established, had a presence on the town council and a membership of around 350. Reid's campaign was chaired by Grant Thomson, a Labour member for some 20 years. The campaign had 'all the panache of a popular carnival', including a folksy theme tune belted out of campaign vans:

> We'll have a man in Parliament,
> To voice our every need;
> His voice is known the world over – Make way for Jimmy Reid,
> They tried to shut the shipyards down,
> And throw us on the dole;
> We took our lead from Jimmy Reid,
> And we just took control.[37]

The influx of supporters weakened the position of the local Communist Party – accustomed to tight control of campaigns – inside the Reid campaign. Throughout the campaign, he refused to follow the schedule devised by the local Communist Party. It was also his personal insistence that he stand as an engineer rather than as a communist, against the wishes of the local Communist Party. Indeed, relations between Reid and the Clydebank Communist Party were strained from the outset. At the last minute, he rushed to the Council Chambers to ensure that his nomination form did describe him as an engineer, and not as a communist. Some of the local communists resented this loss of control and the sense that Reid's highly personal campaign was too remote from *any* identification with the Party. For Arnold Henderson, one of the grand old men of Clydebank communism, Reid's 'tantrums' were those of 'a prima donna' who was beyond the reach of Party discipline: 'uncontrollable'.[38] At one of the branch meetings during the campaign Henderson 'tore right into him', in 'the wee single-end where we held our meetings'.[39]

Reid attempted to mobilise the same broad-based campaign that had brought success in the UCS struggle. A former female Tory from one of the more 'salubrious parts of Glasgow' was his publicity manager and as mentioned above his election agent was a Labour councillor.[40] His campaign

---

37 *Observer*, 17 February 1974.
38 A. Henderson, interview with Charles Woolfson (1979), Glasgow University Archives, DC65/146/27a.
39 V. McGuire, interview with McKinlay (2015); Rafeek, *Communist Women in Scotland*, 176.
40 *Guardian*, 19 February 1974.

message focused on criticising the Tories as out of touch and Labour as corrupt, saying: 'Tory was as alien to the concerns of Clydebank as a Martian; while Labour was tainted by the petty corruptions of Tammany Hall'.[41] But, while his campaign was considered to have been 'excellent', George Tasker, his opponent's election agent, described the campaign as 'irrelevant'. 'I knew Reid could not win'. Two factors ensured his defeat. The first was trade unionism. As Tasker explained: 'Clydebank was regarded as a union constituency'. For years it had been an 'AEU seat'.[42] It was, in his words, 'the local unions doing politics'.[43] This, together with the regularity of council elections, ensured a well-organised electoral machine, with seven branches in Clydebank alone. Labour had deep and up-to-date knowledge of where and how to canvass households to maximum effect. Each branch had an intimate knowledge of their electorate. As Tasker said, 'we knew our people. They were our people'.[44] Reid might have had big turnouts at his meetings, but he had neither the knowledge and organisation nor the support of any trade union, leading Tasker to conclude: 'If he had had political acumen, Jimmy would never have stood in Clydebank ... it was the last place in the world he should have stood'.[45] Moreover, his outbursts in 1965 stacked up against him as suggestions of corruption among the 'socialist cronies' did not play well with those on the Labour left that might have been inclined to support him. The generally warm relations between Labour and Communist councillors were far from universal. Bob Calder, the Labour Provost, 'hated Jimmy Reid: he actually *hated* him. Mind you, he hated *all* communists'.

The second factor was religion. Unfortunately for Reid, Clydebank had proportionately the highest concentration of Catholics in Scotland, with something close to a third of the electorate in the constituency belonging to that faith. Given the Church's implacable opposition to communism, the election became as much a contested terrain of political identity as anything else. Faith versus class became the central issue in this election. The Bishop of Glasgow, Thomas Winning, was the youngest Catholic bishop in Scotland and an arch conservative who was said to be 'utterly devout and certain of his faith, not just in God but in Catholic doctrine. He does not question Rome's certainties and he has difficulty seeing why

---

41 *Guardian*, 19 February 1974.
42 G. Tasker, interview with McKinlay (2017).
43 Tasker, interview with McKinlay.
44 Tasker, interview with McKinlay.
45 Tasker, interview with McKinlay.

anyone else should'.[46] He had trained for the priesthood at the Scots College in Rome and was ordained in St John Lateran's Basilica in 1948. Given his uncritical acceptance of Catholic doctrine, he zealously supported Pius XII's 1949 'Decree against Communism', which excommunicated all Catholics joining, or collaborating with, communist organisations. But opposing communism did not mean unreserved approval of free market capitalism; indeed, Winning was quite left-wing when it came to social and economic affairs. Prior to the 1974 election, the *Scottish Catholic Observer* published the Church's stance on social justice, reminding its readers that 'every working person has a right to a living wage without having to work excessive hours' and that those unfit or too old to work should have 'a right to financial provision that will ensure for them and their dependants reasonable comfort and security'.[47]

Other parishes, notably those with Jesuit priests in 'Little Moscows', such as Renton, simply sidestepped instructions from the Church hierarchy. Encyclicals about not voting Communist were dutifully read out but then neutralised by the priest giving his congregation tacit encouragement to make up their own minds. In February 1974, however, the Church ensured that its priests did not deviate from its instructions: from the pulpits it was made clear that nobody should vote for Reid.

Winning had reluctantly remained silent about the UCS work-in. If his silence could have been interpreted as tacit support for the work-in then there was no mistaking his opposition to Reid as a communist parliamentary candidate. The ambitious auxiliary Bishop of Glasgow convened a war council consisting of himself and 20 priests from the nine parishes in the constituency. They issued a statement condemning communism. Although Reid was not named, Winning's target was clear enough.[48] 'A Catholic must not vote for a Communist', parishioners were instructed from the pulpit on the Sunday before the election. The action of Winning and his priests received the blessing of the *Scottish Catholic Observer*:

> Bishop Thomas Winning and priests whose parishes fall within the Central Dunbartonshire constituency called on Catholics not to vote Communist in yesterday's election … The *Scottish Catholic Observer* applauds the bishop and his priests for doing as they did.

---

46 *Guardian*, 19 August 2000.
47 *Scottish Catholic Observer*, 1 February 1974.
48 S. McGinty, *This Turbulent Priest: A Life of Cardinal Winning* (2003), 149.

> Why? Because you cannot separate Christianity from society. And if politics has nothing to do with society then it has nothing to do with anything.[49]

Reid refused to respond except to say that he did not accept that Christianity and socialism were necessarily opposed.[50]

Strangely, despite the opposition from the Catholic Church in general, and Thomas Winning in particular, Reid did not hold a grudge against the latter. When hearing of his death in June 2001, he said of him:

> We had our differences, but these didn't diminish a friendship that started many years ago in Clydebank. Tom was a progressive man in social and economic matters though deemed a reactionary by liberals within his own church on matters theological. This was between him and his flock. His social politics affected all in Scotland. I cherish the thought that his last public statement before his death was to condemn the racist attacks on asylum seekers in Glasgow when the politicians were running for cover. May his God bless him.[51]

However, to counteract the negative attacks from the Catholic Church and his political opponents he played down his communist membership, projecting himself as the candidate of the labour movement. He ran a highly personalised campaign, including, as we have seen, standing as 'an engineer' not as 'a communist'. *The Times*' correspondent noticed that his election headquarters in Clydebank's Kilbowie Road carried 'no trace of hammer or sickle but concentrated on homely slogans [such as] "Reid for MP", or badges declaring "I'm for Jim"'.[52] Indeed, Reid was de facto an Independent candidate. But, as Tasker points out, 'he could call himself what he liked; as far as Clydebank was concerned, Reid was a communist'.[53] And this was a vital distinction in the polling booths. When the votes were counted, Reid had increased his vote over 1970 to just under 6,000, but it still only amounted to a disappointing 14.6 per cent of the total number cast, while McCartney won 40.4 per cent of the poll, defeating Reid by more than 10,000 votes. At the election count Reid vented his disappointment and bitterness against the local Labour Party

---

49 *Scottish Catholic Observer*, 1 March 1974.
50 *Daily Record*, 25–6 February 1974.
51 *Scotsman*, 18 June 2001.
52 *The Times*, 12 February 1974.
53 Tasker, interview with McKinlay.

activists. He claimed in an ill-advised, angry and highly emotional rant that he was:

> the victim of the most scurrilous, unprincipled attack on any candidate in Britain. I have not reacted, I have turned the other cheek as the good book says because I do not want to create social divisions such as exists in a stretch of water across from this island ... I associate myself with all that is good in the Labour Party and the labour movement but I'm saying now ... there are elements in the Clydebank Labour Party that if they were living in Spain would be supporters of Franco and members of the Falangist Party.[54]

The charge of Falangist brought an audible cry of 'absolute rubbish' from McCartney, but it was clear that Reid viewed himself as the victim of a well-orchestrated campaign of vilification motivated by sectarian religious loyalties. The Falangist Party in Spain had a pronounced Catholic identity and as such was fiercely anti-communist, and this was an apt description applicable to the Clydebank Labour Party.

Undoubtedly, the local Party had manipulated the sectarian loyalties of the people of Clydebank. Personal knowledge meant Labour canvassers and candidates could tailor their message to suit their sectarian audience. In council elections, candidates were selected for certain wards based on their faith: for example, in Ward One a Protestant 'would seldom get elected', whereas in Ward Five, 'if the candidate was a Protestant he would win handsomely'.[55] Thus, Labour accepted sectarianism as a reality that had to be navigated, rather than something that had to be confronted and condemned. In the end, regardless of how justified his charges were, Reid's language only intensified the opposition to him; indeed, it would be a choice of words and a judgement that would come back to haunt him in more ways than one.

Still, he had polled ten times the vote of any other communist candidate. Broadly, the communist vote was a protest vote, except in the new seat of Dunbartonshire Central. Reid's was a personal vote. Of the 44 candidates fielded by the CPGB in February 1974, Reid's was undoubtedly the most successful. Indeed, he was the only one to save his deposit. Reid had polled more than any communist since 1950, but it

---

54 'Election '74: Jimmy Reid Goes Down Fighting'. See www.youtube.com/watch?v=6dHNAE0UTSY.
55 Tasker, interview with McKinlay.

was a result that proved a bitter disappointment to him both personally and politically.[56]

However, despite his resounding defeat, he defiantly declared he would stand again as a candidate for Central Dunbartonshire; an event which came sooner rather than later. The failure of the February election to provide Labour with a working majority led to another general election in October of that year. Reid stood once again against McCartney but this time his share of the vote tumbled from 14.6 per cent to 8.7 per cent of the total, or from 5,928 to 3,417, which lost him his deposit; an outcome that was in line with Party experience. The CPGB had fielded 44 candidates in February, winning a mere 32,743 votes; in October, it fielded 29 candidates, who between them polled a disappointing 17,426 votes. According to a contemporary joke, the CPGB at this time was pursuing the 'British Road to Lost Deposits'. Still, Reid's vote was the highest communist vote since 1959, but second time around it was squeezed between a much stronger Labour campaign in Scotland and an SNP surge.

This was not the only election Reid lost in 1974. Standing as CPGB candidate in the May 1974 district and regional elections for the 46th Ward, known as Clydebank/Kilpatrick North, he came last in a field of three, beaten by Labour and an Independent Progressive, but the level of support was higher than the general election at 22.8 per cent of votes cast, or 2,700 out of a total of 11,822.

The following year Reid compounded his estrangement from the Labour Party in Clydebank, publicly denouncing some of its members on Clydebank Town Council for carrying out a 'vendetta' against him, saying: 'Some people in this town would like to see me crucified'. These claims were supported by SNP councillor John Hamilton, who said that 'a Labour clique were intent on having Councillor Reid sacked'. However, while motivated by his Falangist comments during the '74 election, the attack was masked by a procedural issue much of his own making. It was his failure to attend committee meetings of the Council that allowed his Labour enemies to call for his disqualification. In his apology to the CTC, Reid claimed that he had been unable to attend meetings owing to the fact that he 'was ill for nine weeks, my child was in hospital for five weeks, and I was involved in the General Election'. Bob Calder justified the group's position by pointing out that Reid had never once asked for leave of absence. In the end, no action was taken against Reid over attendance;

---

56 D. Butler and D. Kavanagh, *The British General Election of February 1974* (London, 1975), 336–7.

indeed, it was to all appearances rather pointless since the old CTC was being wound up and ceased to exist from April 1975. However, it was far from meaningless gestures on the part of the Labour group on the CTC. In the light of the allegations, a clear political rupture had occurred between Reid and the Clydebank labour movement; politically, he was becoming *persona non grata* in certain Labour circles.

There was much for Reid to reconcile in his mind. He was a recognisable national figure, appearing in the media and on prime-time television, and yet he was rejected twice in the space of eight months by the electorate of Clydebank. It was clear that he had no political future as a communist candidate. The election results had shown that the Party was moribund – a political irrelevancy. During the campaign he had also been accused by senior members of individualism, of self-aggrandisement, of developing a personality cult. Behind the pettiness of these charges was a scarcely concealed desire to cut down to size someone who had got above himself. For Reid it was becoming obvious that either the Party had to change, or he had to find a new political home. As he put it: 'On the face of it, this [UCS] was my moment of triumph but instead I was deeply troubled. My people were identifying with me as a communist at a time when my doubts about communism were hardening into disbelief'. But for the moment he turned his energies away from the political field to the industrial, but that shift in direction only produced more frustration and bitterness, emotions which would play an important part in his break with the Party.

6

Leaving

The years 1975 to 1976 were to prove momentous for Jimmy Reid. It was during this brief period that he re-evaluated where he stood politically. The general elections of 1974 had not only proved a disappointment for him personally, but also were embarrassing to the Party as the derisory vote it received in October that year proved, if it needed proving, that it was as an organisation politically irrelevant. However, the Party remained an important presence on the industrial front in the 1970s. Despite predictions from some influential social critics that class struggle was a thing of the past, between 1970 and 1972, over 47 million days were lost in Britain due to strikes. The two main events, the UCS work-in and the miners' strike of 1972, saw Party activists, such Reid and Airlie, Arthur Scargill and Mick McGahey, play major roles in both disputes. However, as the 1970s wore on, these disputes were increasingly being viewed by the Eurocommunist section of the Party as 'economistic and centred on maintaining the privileges of male, white, skilled workers'; something that became very explicit during the 1984 miners' strike.[1] Reid had experienced at first hand the Party's impotency in the political arena, he was now to experience it in the industrial field too.

Feeling that he enjoyed an enormous reservoir of goodwill among engineering workers throughout Britain, Reid decided to run for office as AUEW divisional officer – Division 1 (Scotland) – describing himself on the candidate's list as 'a reasonable and in the proper sense of the word a moderate person'.[2] The position had become vacant due to the election of the right-wing and anti-communist John McFarlane Boyd as general secretary in 1975. Reid faced a straight fight against ex-communist Gavin Laird (later Sir Gavin Laird), who had left the Party over Hungary in 1956,

1 Eaden and Renton, *Communist Party*, 165.
2 *Glasgow Herald*, 6 March 1976.

and who had defeated James Airlie earlier in 1972 for a regional officer's post by 17,500 votes to 10,000.[3] Laird was also a part-time director of the Highlands and Islands Development Board, enjoying a salary of £1,800 per annum on top of his full-time union salary of £4,500.[4] The two opponents had a common history stretching back to their childhoods in Glasgow. Reid at 43 was the elder of the two by one year but they both had served apprenticeships in engineering, and both had received their first blooding in industrial conflict in the 1952 apprentices' strike. They qualified as fitters and graduated to become full-time convenors of shop stewards in their respective places of employment.

Laird was a formidable opponent: already embedded within the officialdom of the AUEW, he had far more experience than Reid in building support networks across the shop stewards and full-time officers. He also had strong links to Clydebank, having served as chairman of the constituency Labour Party, and had the support of sections of the media. As Laird put it: 'Jimmy Reid is campaigning in a political bandwagon style. We are campaigning inside the union'.[5] Indeed, Reid launched a barnstorming campaign, drawing at one meeting in Glasgow 1,400 engineering workers and receiving a standing ovation from those present.[6] He also had the support of the AUEW's president, Hugh Scanlon, who declared: 'It would be a tragedy if you don't allow men like Jimmy Reid to be the next representative for Scotland on the Executive Committee of the AUEW to maintain the fight against (the Labour government's) statutory wages policy'.[7] The contest was a political one rather than simply an election to decide the best person to represent the membership in regard to wages and conditions. Both candidates recognised this.

Reid was standing as a candidate of the 'Broad left', a loose coalition of different political factions within the AUEW opposed to the incomes policies introduced by the Labour government in its fight to bring down high levels of inflation, running at 23.7 per cent in 1975, but whose impact was to reduce the real earnings of most workers. In some families, this meant a loss of 20 per cent of disposable income.[8] If Reid had been

3 *Glasgow Herald*, 18 October 1975.
4 *Observer*, 12 October 1975.
5 *Glasgow Herald*, 8 September 1975.
6 *Glasgow Herald*, 18 October 1975.
7 *Glasgow Herald*, 8 September 1975.
8 See N. Bosanquet and P. Townsend (eds), *Labour and Inequality: A Fabian Study of Labour in Power, 1974–79* (London, 1980).

successful then it would have altered the balance of power within the AUEW in favour of the left and signalled an all-out fight against the government's policy of wage restraint; something that Boyd and others on the right did their best to ensure didn't happen. As it turned out, Laird won easily by 24,838 votes to Reid's 12,115 on a turnout of 37.4 per cent of Scottish members.[9] Asked if being a communist had acted as a deterrent to members voting for him, Reid replied: 'I am not going to pander to people's prejudices. I will stay in the Communist Party unless I can see in the British context, a more tenable alternative Party which will bring Socialism and all it involves in an ethical sense'.[10]

Being a communist was not such a drawback within a European perspective, as the French and Italian parties were hugely influential in their respective countries. In the late spring of 1975, Reid was at an AUEW meeting in Blackpool where he was approached, in spite of his opposition to Britain joining the European Economic Community (EEC), by two bureaucrats from the Commission of the EEC to become a member of a study group charged with producing proposals on what was termed 'new characteristics of socio-economic development'. At first Reid declined, as most of the left in Britain were opposed to joining. However, when the British people voted overwhelmingly in the referendum to join the EEC that year, he changed his mind and accepted the offer. Members of the study group met regularly in Brussels and included, as Reid put it: 'Europe's most outstanding academics, economists, industrialists, bankers and a number of trade unionists. Across the table from me sat a young professor from the Université Paris-Dauphine. His name was Jacques Delors. The report was published in 1977, entitled 'A Blueprint for Europe: A Discussion Document'.[11] This document was crucial to the later formulation of the European Union's Charter of Fundamental Human Rights, which originally sought to guarantee the legal right of workers to organise in trade unions, to negotiate with employers and to withdraw their labour when deemed by them justified. It also included the legal right of employees to be consulted by employers on all matters affecting their interests as employees; in Britain it was opposed by both the Tories and Labour.[12]

Reid's prestige could not have been higher, but despite this he received another blow to his self-esteem, which came in a subsequent election for

---

9   *Glasgow Herald*, 19 November 1975.
10 *Glasgow Herald*, 19 November 1975.
11 *Glasgow Herald*, 27 July 1993; Reid, *Power without Principles*, 11–12.
12 *Guardian*, 27 November 2000.

a full-time officer's post in the AUEW. This time he faced an inexperienced nonentity Tom Dougan, an engineering shop steward in the American-owned Honeywell factory on the periphery of Glasgow, and another candidate who dropped out after the first ballot. On the first ballot Reid was comfortably ahead of his rivals, polling 13,389 votes compared with the other two candidates' votes of 9,662 and 5,704 respectively. However, when it came to the second ballot, Reid lost by the narrowest of margins: 81 votes.[13] He immediately took legal advice claiming that the AUEW executive had conducted a flawed election. His main complaint was:

> 48,674 members (35 per cent of the membership) were not registered for voting by the union ... many others who ... received ballot papers in the first election ... [and] have declared that they voted for me did not receive papers for the second ballot ... I asked the union executive committee to declare the total election a nullity and to hold another based on an updated ... register the request was turned down.

Gavin Laird, AUEW Scottish National Executive member, said dismissively that Reid's claim that as 'many as 1000 of his supporters did not get voting papers' was the result of his own 'appalling ignorance of the rules of the ... union ... Mr Reid ought to know that under the union's rules members could inspect a register of names for a total ballot at their branches. If a name was missing, it could be easily rectified'.[14]

The campaign to overturn the election as null and void due to faulty registration procedures was a costly one. Reid, writing in *Tribune*, declared:

> the (legal) costs involved ... have been substantial and this is why I cannot proceed any further ... Even so I have incurred what is for me a considerable debt ... a debt which quite frankly I find difficult to meet ... I feel justified in asking for assistance from people on the democratic left. If the amounts raised exceeds the costs the surplus will go to *Tribune* ... Please send any contributions to me at 47 Melbourne Avenue, Mount Blow, Clydebank.[15]

From this point on Reid campaigned for more democracy and transparency in union affairs, later saying: 'Unless you democratise the

---

13 *Tribune*, 14 January 1977.
14 *Glasgow Herald*, 4 November 1976.
15 *Tribune*, 14 January 1977.

unions you cannot have a truly democratic Labour Party. The block votes of the unions are decisive. How those who fought … for the mandatory reselection of MPs can support the appointment for life of a trade union leader is a perverse contradiction beyond my comprehension'.[16]

In losing to his anonymous rival Reid could not by then say that being a communist was a deterrent as he had faced that 'heart-wrenching' moment and made the decision after an apparently 'sleepless night' to send in his resignation letter on the evening of 9 February 1976. Three days later it appeared on the front page of the *Daily Worker*. 'To leave the Party was to leave behind not just a politics but a way of life for the individual and their family'.[17] His wife Joan recalled her husband's anguish at leaving: 'a huge thing for him. He was absolutely broken-hearted. Jimmy cried the day he left, *not* for leaving the Party, but for leaving the people he knew. He had loved those people'. His daughter Eileen underscored this, saying: 'The day he left the Communist Party was a terrible day. I only knew the day before. I understood the enormity of it: it was almost frightening. The Communist Party was the backdrop to our family's life. We were severing something from our family. He was cutting himself off … from twenty-five years of his life'.[18] Peter Kerrigan, who he loved 'like a father', was consulted, but was unable to dissuade Reid.[19] Similarly, Jock Smith, one of the Clydebank veterans, spent all night trying to keep Reid in the Party, walking up and down Bowling beach.[20] This was, then, a deep regret, a sense of *personal* loss, akin to a bereavement, that echoed his feelings at the death of Harry Pollitt. Reid's sadness was a kind of grief, a parting from individuals, a political choice but also a rejection of a way of life. According to him, the main reason for leaving was the dogmatic position of the Party 'that it was right and everyone else wrong'. He expressed genuine regret for leaving some of the 'finest people', but no regret in leaving behind what he termed the 'closed brethren'. He claimed that the build up to the resignation was 'gradual … a reaction to a style of work, the challenging of the treatment of a comrade, condemnation of a sectarian approach'. He continued that 'doubts, confirmed over and over again by experience, arose about the

---

16   *Glasgow Herald*, 13 September 1982.
17   See Jackie Kay on how political differences destroyed one of her communist father's dearest friendships. J. Kay, 'Non-Stop Party', in P. Cohen (ed.), *Children of the Revolution* (London, 1977), 36.
18   *Daddy's Girl*, BBC Radio Scotland, 2008; Eileen Reid, interview with McKinlay (2017).
19   Joan Reid, interview with McKinlay.
20   D. Cooper, interview with McKinlay.

ability of the leadership to effect changes necessary to open up the Party. To turn it outwards to the people'.[21]

As evidence of his growing estrangement from the CPGB, Reid pointed to the fact that he had not attended a Party congress in Scotland between 1970 and 1976 – 'a deliberate act of disassociation' – and had resigned from the Scottish Committee in 1972. Although he had originally declined to accept nomination to the Party's National Executive in 1973, he eventually was persuaded, or 'brow beaten', as he had it, by members and reluctantly took his place out of respect for John Gollan: to Reid 'the finest creative political brain in the leadership'. Perhaps, suggests Kevin Morgan and his colleagues, John Gollan's resignation due to poor health released Reid from his strongest ties of personal loyalty to the Party's leadership: 'I was most reluctant to [resign] while Johnnie was there, because such was my affection for him'. Again, the ties that bound were personal more than political: the severing of the personal ties to Gollan left only the political, and that was no longer enough for Reid.[22] Gollan died in September 1977 after a long illness. However, the process of disassociation, according to Reid, went as far back as 1967. Davy Cooper, one of the leading communist stewards in UCS, was certain that Reid was 'uneasy' about the Party for several years before his resignation: 'faithfully following the Party line never suited Jimmy'.[23]

His original intention was to follow the pattern of many others: to leave the Party gradually. As he put it: 'I had all my class feelings; I had all my socialist convictions. I went about my council work; my trade union work *quietly*. I thought, I'll drift out of the Communist Party on my tiptoes'.[24]

The UCS work-in and his role in it made this impossible. Reid, the recanting communist, disavowing a Party that he had been a member of since he was 16, was always bound to be front page news. Answering the charge that it was an opportunistic career move, he later said: 'In a sense it is the most courageous thing you can ever do – admit you are wrong. I could have gone on trading on being a character communist, a popular communist liberal and not a Stalinist. It would have been a nice cushy wee role in society'.[25] Over the coming years, he offered

---

21 Reid, *Reflections*, 156.
22 Morgan, Cohen and Flinnet, *Communists*, 142; Reid, *Reflections*, 164.
23 Cooper, interview with McKinlay.
24 Jimmy Reid, interview with Campbell and McIlroy.
25 M. Ritchie, 'The Road from UCS to the Sun', *Glasgow Herald*, 15 June 1987.

two further reasons for his resignation: first, a growing distaste for the conformity of opinion imposed by democratic centralism; and, secondly, the debates which led to departures from the Party reinforced the hold of outdated dogma, a process which reduced still further the chance for organic change from within. He said: 'Basically I came to the conclusion that the changes needed in the Party would not materialise. People who were responsive to new ideas and new attitudes were voting with their feet and relinquishing responsibility. Their replacements were more in the bureaucratic mould'.[26]

To the end, Reid insisted that there were no personal animosities behind his exit from the Party. Quite the opposite: he spoke of grassroots communists in the warmest terms, of their nobility and their selflessness. Nearer home, his wife Joan, who remained in the Party (although not for long), as did his mother-in-law Emily, was rather sanguine, saying, 'There is no basic disagreement about politics in our house. Indeed, our thinking is very similar'.[27] Some Party members saw his resignation as a positive event. London member Bob Cole spoke for reformers in the Party when he said that this was an opportunity for renewal, for more openness and a politics focused on community. John Moore, member from Coventry, said that Reid's 'imaginative expression of socialism in terms of moral values struck a chord in many people inside the Communist Party and for those outside its ranks'.[28] But not everyone in the CPGB was of the same opinion regarding his decision or the alleged motives behind it. While local reaction towards the news of his resignation may have been mixed nationally, it was met by widespread surprise and disappointment by the ordinary members.[29] His close ally James Airlie publicly said of his resignation: 'It is Jimmy's decision. I personally feel he is making a mistake but nevertheless I still hold Jimmy Reid in the highest regard'.[30] Although the journalist David Scott claims that privately Airlie took it personally, remarking that he 'was pissed off by the manner of his leaving' and deeply 'saddened'.[31] Finlay Hart, former Chairman of the Scottish Committee of the CPGB, and a hugely influential figure in the west of Scotland, who

---

26 Reid, *Reflections*, 165.
27 *Glasgow Herald*, 7 October 1976.
28 *Morning Star*, 26 February 1976.
29 *Morning Star*, 12, 17, 23, 26, February 1976; minutes and correspondence of Communist Party of Great Britain Executive Committee, 13–14 March 1976, Peoples' History Museum, Salford, CP/CENT/EC/15/08.
30 *Glasgow Herald*, 13 February 1976.
31 D. Scott, interview with McKinlay (2015).

rarely if ever used an expletive, on hearing the news of Reid's resignation simply said, 'that bastard'.[32] Miners' leader Mick McGahey and the Communist Party historian Robin Page Arnot were both of the opinion that the main sources of corruption – 'money and ego' – had turned Reid's head. Jack Ashton, Scottish industrial organiser, compared Reid's resignation unfavourably to that of John Reid's, saying that the former 'invented a load of political excuses', while the latter had resigned at a meeting of the Scottish Executive of the Party simply because he felt 'it [CPGB] wasn't getting anywhere'.[33] His English comrades were rather bewildered by his resignation; some were also angry. The Liverpool Press Branch of the Party wrote to the Executive Committee saying that while they held Reid 'in the highest regard', the manner in which he resigned and the way he used the media and the press 'to publicise his attack on the Party has certainly earned him our contempt'.[34] They also stated that he had never:

> at any meeting of the EC expressed 'disenchantment' with the Party, nor were any members of the EC aware of its existence. He certainly never expressed any such view when accepting nomination for the EC, and on 9 January when telephoning his apology for not being able to attend the EC that week-end, expressed his full support for the positions taken up by the Party.[35]

Finally, Davie Todd, a close friend and confidante, recalled attending a social at King Street with Reid shortly after his resignation from the Party. As soon as they entered the premises Reid was verbally abused by five female members who, according to Todd, were 'ready to scratch his eyes out'.[36]

Thus, we have two competing narratives of the events and motives behind Reid's resignation. The authorial version is one in which thoughts of resignation gestate over a fairly long period of time, but beginning roughly in 1967. From that point onwards, he undergoes a daily process of questioning his conscience and beliefs, eventually reaching the conclusion

---

32 Barr, interview with Campbell and McIlroy.
33 Ashton, interview with Campbell and McIlroy.
34 Letter from Gordon Bell, secretary of the Liverpool Press Branch, to the Executive Committee of the Communist Party of Great Britain, *Morning Star*, 3 March 1976.
35 Letter from Gordon Bell to the Executive Committee of the Communist Party of Great Britain, *Morning Star*, 17 March 1976.
36 D. Todd, interview with Knox (2016).

that what he had held to be self-evidently true was now a fiction: indeed, a delusion, which denied the realities of the undemocratic nature of the Soviet Union and the CPGB itself. Membership of, and commitment to, the Party was only made possible through the twin ties of loyalty to family and comrades. The other narrative depicts him as an opportunist in thrall to the sins of vanity and venality. Finding the truth among partisan and polarised positions is an almost hopeless task for the historian. Undoubtedly the attempt by Reid to construct a narrative of a man acting on the highest moral and political principles involved him in the selection of events and memories to provide the motive for, and justification of, his actions, while airbrushing out the uncomfortable reminders of his past commitment to international communism. His critics within the Party viewed Reid as a traitor betraying the principles and comradeship that had sustained them, and him, over the years, especially during the difficult period of the Cold War, and as such they understandably felt incredibly bitter and biased towards him. Thus, each narrative was dependent on a selective reading of the past and of individual intentions and only by examining the evidence objectively can we get close to resolving the obvious tensions that exist in the competing accounts.

If we take Reid's narrative that real doubts about the Party and its direction set in around 1967 then we must take the following into account. First, in that year he was selected to present the updated version of the *British Road to Socialism* to the 30th Congress of the CPGB which would suggest that he was being groomed as a future general secretary of the Party. Therefore, it is worth examining the policy document in some detail for any light it sheds on where Reid stood politically at the late end of the 1960s. The main theme of the *British Road to Socialism* was the call for the formation of an alliance of the British people against the big monopolistic firms that had come to dominate the economy and government. This alliance included workers, small shopkeepers and farmers, professional groups such as students, housewives, teachers, doctors and nurses, and even 'small capitalists'. As it said: 'The programme which we put forward unites the interests of the working class with those of virtually all sections of the people outside of big business'.[37] Or, as Reid put in his speech: 'The essence of the real political struggle in Britain today, as distinct from the verbal fisticuffs between the [Labour] Government and the Tory Front Bench, is the people versus the monopolies'.[38] However, the success of the alliance in

---

37 Communist Party of Great Britain, *British Road to Socialism* (London, 1968), 16.
38 Jimmy Reid Collection, Glasgow University Archives, DC455/3/1/1, 9.

combating the malign influence of monopoly capital was dependent on the unity of the CPGB with the left wing of the Labour Party', a unity which would achieve a peaceful transition to socialism through constitutional means.[39] Thus, the advance to socialism, argued Reid, would be the work of 'all left, progressive and socialist forces'.[40]

The *British Road to Socialism*, with its emphasis on building alliances between groups that in the past had shown antipathy towards each other, was a poorly constructed document full of contradictions as well as top heavy with wishful thinking. Veteran Party member Idris Cox said that it was 'most unsatisfactory', 'repetitive', 'long winded', 'and most unlikely to make any significant positive impact upon Communist Party members, let alone the labour movement as a whole'.[41] There is no good set of reasons to think that the growth of powerful business conglomerates would be sufficient reason on its own to unite such widely disparate social groups in Britain or elsewhere for that matter. It also deluded itself in thinking that an organic political unity could be created between the CPGB and the left wing of the Labour Party. Many of the latter were opposed to the affiliation of the former to Labour, although there existed co-operation on some issues, such as nuclear disarmament and industrial relations reform. However, what is important is that the construction of alliances, of a broad left, was fundamental to Reid's political philosophy both pre- and post-UCS. There was little in the *British Road to Socialism* that he could or would find politically disagreeable; after all, he was one of the authors. In an article published in *The Times* seven days after he resigned from the Party, his analysis of the condition of Britain, its economy and social and political structures could have been lifted wholesale from the *British Road to Socialism* as he continued to speak of the threat big business posed to 'democracy, to democratic institutions' and of the need for an anti-monopoly alliance, saying:

> I believe that the true leadership will come from the left in British politics, but I reject the naïve concept of instant Socialism. What I want is the start of a process of renewal in British life, democratic, human and compassionate. This must involve fracturing the grip over our economy and our lives of a tiny handful of large combines. The small and medium-sized businessmen, small farmers and

39 B. Warren, 'The British Road to Socialism', *New Left Review*, 63 (1970), 27–41.
40 Jimmy Reid Collection, Glasgow University Archives, DC455/3/1/1, 15.
41 G. Andrews, *End Games and New Times: The Final Years of British Communism, 1964–1991* (London, 2004), 90.

shopkeepers, intellectuals and genuine Christians have so much to gain from such a process as any industrial worker.[42]

Secondly, as we have seen, Reid was prepared to leave the CPGB if the leadership had not condemned the Moscow Pact's invasion of Czechoslovakia in 1968. But the criticism of the Party could at best be described as mild, or at worst as toadying, preferring the term 'intervention' to that of invasion. Only three days after the invasion, Reid's mentor, John Gollan, said, 'we completely understand the concern of the Soviet Union about the security of the socialist camp … we speak as true friends of the Soviet Union'.[43] During the UCS work-in in an interview for the University of Glasgow's staff magazine, he was asked if he was a Marxist. To which he replied that he was 'proud to consider himself a Marxist'. When further asked why he was in such a dogmatic Party, given that he argued that Marxism was a science and therefore the 'enemy of dogma', he replied that that was 'an unfair characterisation of the Communist Party … which does not spring from an understanding of the Party I am a member of today'.[44]

Moreover, despite his disenchantment with the Soviet Union, and his criticism of the invasion of Czechoslovakia, he was still quite prepared to accept the hospitality of the Russian labour movement: 'It was in the aftermath of the UCS work-in and my health was not good. I needed to go somewhere where I could relax and unwind. The Soviet trade unions offered me anywhere I wanted so I chose a resort on the Black Sea' – Sochi.[45] The resort, a favourite of Stalin, was described by his daughter as 'paradise'. The accommodation was 'a magnificent neo-classical villa on the breast of a hill which ran down to the beaches and the then, crystal clear waters of the Black Sea', where they stayed for three weeks.[46] Before Sochi, the exhausted Reid and his family had spent two days in Moscow, staying in the Sputnik Hotel, where he was checked by 'the very best' Soviet doctors. The Reids were treated as communist royalty (Figure 15). They were driven everywhere in special lanes free of traffic normally reserved for Party officials, known as the 'Zil' or 'Chaika' lanes.[47] Jimmy

---

42 *The Times*, 16 February 1976.
43 Andrews, *End Games*, 93–4.
44 Jimmy Reid, interview with Gerry Ross (1972).
45 *Scotsman*, 23 May 1988.
46 E. Reid, 'To Russia with my Dad, Jimmy Reid', *Scottish Review* (June/July, 2014), 4.
47 Reid, 'To Russia with my Dad', 2.

15 Moscow, 1971

was unimpressed, feeling that such privileges were 'just not right'. His unease at what he saw was to surface in nightly discussions at Sochi with two other families sharing the accommodation – one German, the other Greek – and their interpreters. Eileen, although only 12, heard them from her bedroom 'talk long into the night … the tone was passionate, agitated and I heard enough to know that all was not well in the Soviet Union and much disagreements among the comrades'.[48] This view is somewhat tempered by that of Igor Yurgens, today an influential figure who straddles industrial and political worlds in post-Soviet Russia, and was the young interpreter who accompanied the Reid family in the summer of 1972. In Sochi, the Reids relaxed, swam and took short boat trips. Other Western guests of the Soviets stayed in the same compound as the Reids, and Yurgens says that several evenings were dominated by political discussions. Reid, he recalled, was 'a good drinker', and a straight-faced 'joke-teller of the highest calibre', who mixed easily with the other guests. He expressed his unease about the Soviet system, which was nothing exceptional as it was apparently common among Western visitors after 1968. However, Reid did not, he claims, lead these conversations, nor did he give any sense of a more profound disillusionment with the USSR – at least, not in front of his hosts, although this may have been out of politeness to his hosts.[49]

While it is hard to accept that his resignation was influenced by ego and money as, unlike some of his contemporaries in the labour movement, there was to be no future Sir Jimmy or Lord Reid, or that it was simply opportunistic as evidence of his questioning of his beliefs, his time at Sochi shows he was in a certain amount of ideological turmoil, but the authorial narrative is open to question regarding timing. As such there appears a much more compelling case to argue, as has the journalist Neil Ascherson, who had interviewed Reid in his home the morning after his resignation while his daughter served him his breakfast on his knee, and that the triggers for resignation were of a more recent, local and political nature:

> Somewhere in this area, in the maze where union and local politics are subtly entwined with half-admitted religious sectarianism, some Communist officials – it's a fair guess – behaved towards Jimmy Reid in a way which deeply affronted his sense of right and

---

48 Reid, 'To Russia with my Dad', 5.
49 I. Yurgens, interview with McKinlay (2018).

wrong. And this affront apparently catalysed long-held anxieties and doubts about the Party's practice of internal democracy. For whatever reason, the Communist Party has now lost its most popular and celebrated member.[50]

What constituted these recent, local and political triggers? Reid refused to make his reasons public – 'unless provoked' – since this 'could be hurtful to thousands of good men and women in the Communist Party'.[51] His silence means that much of what follows can be dismissed as speculation, but it has arguably more than a ring of truth to it. First, his defeat in the first general election of 1974 made Reid realise that the CPGB was a political irrelevancy as far as the Scottish working class was concerned. In an interview with the *Guardian*, he said: 'People had the Party wrong when they said it was a menace to capitalism ... it was precisely because it isn't that he made the break. If it had made itself relevant as the Italian Party had done, he might have felt different'.[52] The CPGB had for some time relinquished its revolutionary role and there was little after that to distinguish it politically from the left wing of the Labour Party. The only differences lay in support for the Soviet Union, which was fast disappearing, and the transformational role of the Party, practically rejected by the Eurocommunist wing of the Party as utopian. Therefore, the political leap for Reid was not that great once the ties of loyalty to friends and comrades were broken.

The local was personal and just as important. Shortly after the end of the UCS work-in, Reid was one of 13 Clydebank councillors who refused to sanction record rent increases introduced by the Conservative Government's Housing Finance Act of 1972. He swore that rents would only go up 'over my dead body'. For several months, the mainly Labour controlled council stubbornly maintained its stance on opposing rent increases; an action which resulted in the imposition of a substantial fine of £40,000. Although this was part of a national campaign, it was clear that the Clydebank councillors stood virtually alone in Scotland. Despite this, the Communist Party's British leadership insisted that they continue their campaign and seek support from the trade union movement. Reid, the other councillors, and key members of the Party's Scottish executive warned that this was an impractical and doomed strategy.[53] Reid was

50 *Scotsman*, 12 and 13 February 1976.
51 *The Times*, 16 February 1976.
52 *Guardian*, 9 October 1976.
53 Woolfson, 'Working-Class Culture, 372.

clear: there was no mass support for a rent strike in Clydebank, adding that it was the 'The responsibility of leadership', faced with the prospect of isolation, to decide 'how best to retreat'.[54] The arguments over strategy within the local Party were 'vicious', something that rankled with Reid and something that he remained 'bitter about'.[55] Clydebank's opposition to the legislation crumbled when resistance of other Labour councils collapsed, and Reid was given the task of trying to strike a deal with George Younger, a junior minister in the Scottish Office in the Heath government:

> It was decided that I should meet George Younger to try to reach an understanding. We met at the old Glasgow airport before his departure to London. He agreed that the Government would take no further action if we implemented the [housing] policy. We shook hands on it and afterwards a colleague asked: 'Will he honour the handshake?' To which there was only one reply: 'George Younger might be a Tory but he is a gentleman'.[56]

However, the failure of the Party's national leadership fully to understand the situation or to take seriously the local councillors' assessment, together with an executive prepared to pull rank, disheartened Reid, who was 'very bitter' as he was 'getting terrible abuse' to the point that he 'was absolutely demoralised'. 'I went home and wasn't well'.[57] Alex Murray, the Party's Scottish secretary, and a very close friend and ally of his, was criticised by the Scottish Committee for not pulling out 'all the stops' to win union support for a wider industrial strike in support of the Clydebank rent strike.[58] Murray accepted responsibility for what he tactfully described as communication breakdowns in order to force the national leadership to reflect on its shortcomings. His attempt to open debate about internal Party democracy focusing on local autonomy for decision-making failed: the national executive refused to discuss any wider flaws in Party organisation or decision-making. In part, what was an impossible strategic dilemma was for Murray complicated further by the way that Gordon McLennan, who was to become the Party's General Secretary in 1975, made the vote to censure Murray a test of

---

54 Reid, interview with Woolfson.
55 Reid, interview with Woolfson.
56 *Sun*, 1 August 1988.
57 Jimmy Reid, interview with Margot Heinemann (1988).
58 Alex Murray, 'Notes' (Spring 1973), Communist Party of Great Britain. Our thanks to John Foster for access to this material.

his personal authority.[59] Political tensions were overlaid by personal differences: Murray's rise through the Party hierarchy had been halted by McLennan's personal intervention.[60] Murray immediately resigned as Scottish secretary, although he remained in the Party. This did not sit well with Reid, who also criticised the National Executive's decision to proceed with the rent strike as 'adventurous, divisive' and one which left 'an infinitely worse situation for our Party, our Councillors and the Left, than that which exists'.[61] It seems highly likely that this incident was crucial in influencing Reid's growing disaffection with the Party leadership, in both the short term and the long term.

From this it would appear that Reid's break with the CPGB was less about its overall philosophical and political direction, and more to do with its seemingly unbreakable attachment to democratic centralism: an organisational practice that stifled debate and reinforced dogma as handed down by the National Executive. Party members, like the so-called 'high priest of communism' Palme Dutt, who stated that 'A communist's duty is to believe' was anathema to Reid. For him, a communist's duty was 'to disobey'.[62] However, a revealing discussion later with Neil Kinnock put a different spin on his decision to resign from the Party. Over steak and kidney pie, Kinnock recalled him saying:

> Nobody knows *the* moment or the person or persons that threw the switch. So, I always settled from the view – and he was never clear about it: he used to say things like, 'it's part of evolution'. I doubt anybody could identify who or why *specifically*. There was no material change or influence that could be identified as to why he came out of the Communist Party or why – essentially – he joined the Labour Party. Actually, the second part is relatively straightforward since he couldn't stay alone with his personal standing and his commitment to collective action. You *can* be politically independent on the right, but *not* on the left because you're just marginal. So, he was going to join the Labour Party at some stage. His reason for joining Labour was that he came to be acquainted with lots of good socialists in the Labour Party: and it was part of being what mattered, what counted.[63]

59 Alex Murray, 'Notes'.
60 W. Thompson, interview with McKinlay.
61 Alex Murray, 'Notes'.
62 Jimmy Reid, interview with Campbell and McIlroy.
63 N. Kinnock, interview with McKinlay (2015).

In a couple of lengthy *Tribune* articles that followed his resignation he was scathing in his assessment of the CPGB, its strategy, and claustrophobic internal disciplines. Ironically, this was at the very moment when such historical constraints were collapsing.[64] The domination of the Party's leadership by the Eurocommunists witnessed an attempt to abandon the class approach to politics, and make the Party more open to embracing gay and women's issues.[65] In this context, Reid could have been the perfect Gramscian 'organic intellectual'. Instinctively, he was someone who could take demanding abstract ideas and translate them into everyday language. But he was indifferent to the 'cultural turn' in communist politics. To take the 'cultural turn' would have required him to question, if not reject, his vision of political leadership, a vision drawn from the experiences of interwar communists like Harry Pollitt and Peter Kerrigan. To engage with the cultural turn was to accept that the classic working class by itself was no longer necessarily crucial to political change. Again, Reid's capacity to create and lead political alliances should have made him receptive to this type of politics. Thus, for the first time, Reid faced the prospect of being a conservative: if not resistant to then certainly sceptical about fresh ideas and new strategies of political mobilisation. More than this, ironically, he would now risk being regarded as a defender of vanguardism or, at the very least, a marginal figure in these key Party debates. Alternatively, Reid simply anticipated an exhausting stalemate between Party traditionalists, on the one hand, and pluralists, on the other. There was little appeal for him at the prospect of brokering ever-more unsatisfactory compromises to keep the Party intact, even as it faded into irrelevance.

Within the Party, the 1970s threw up loud and acrimonious debates. The economics committee 'was a virtual battleground between younger academic economists and trade union figures marshalled by [Bert] Ramelson'; trade unionists laid into academics 'on the grounds they were middle class'.[66] The division boiled down to those members grouped around the *Morning Star* – traditionalists – and those in the Party leadership – Eurocommunists. The struggle to break the hold of democratic centralism was being waged within the Party and Reid could have been part of it but he chose resignation instead. This decision left him unclear about where his future lay, about how he would earn a living – he was still employed in the Marathon yard, Clydebank – and whether he would have a political life of

64 *Tribune*, 22, 29 April 1977.
65 Laybourn and Murphy, *Under the Red Flag*, 167.
66 Morgan, Cohen and Flinnet, *Communists*, 95.

any kind. In a revealing discussion he had with Stephen Kelly, a political journalist on *Tribune*, at the 1977 Labour Party conference in Brighton, Reid revealed the inner turmoil he was going through at the thought of leaving the CPGB:

> We sat up to two or three in the morning persuading Jimmy that he should join the Labour Party. He wasn't against this in principle but felt that he would lose a lot of friends, a lot of old allies in the CP. This was a big step as he would be regarded as a traitor.[67]

Out of the CPGB Reid might have been tempted to join the newly formed Scottish Labour Party (SLP). This breakaway from the British Labour Party was led by Jim Sillars, MP for South Ayrshire, whose motivation was the failure of the Wilson government to deliver a Scottish Assembly. Although never at this point a separatist, Reid was sympathetic to the idea of home rule for Scotland. Indeed, he wrote that on his return to Scotland after some ten years in London he was 'convinced that the main task for the Scottish Left was to win the Scottish Labour Movement for a policy of Home Rule in the form of a Devolved or Independent parliament in Edinburgh'.[68] This he felt could be better achieved through the labour movement than either through the SNP or through Sillars's new organisation. Reid calculated that the SLP would be just another fringe organisation, quite impotent to influence the course of Scottish politics. Contrastingly, Sillars saw in Reid a potential rival to his leadership who was even more charismatic than he was. Thus, he was probably a relieved man not to receive an application for membership from the man from Clydebank. In any case the SLP from the outset was a divided party and collapsed soon after the 1979 general election.[69] Having had his fill of impotent politics, Reid took the obvious and predictable step of applying to join the Labour Party in October or November 1977. For several years Labour had courted him; indeed, Reid had been a regular speaker at the Party's Annual Conference's fringe events of which the *Tribune* rally was one of the highlights. In 1976, Neil Kinnock and Dick Clements, editor of *Tribune*, organised 'a glorious piece of political theatre', with Reid as the star, unveiling him as a prospective Labour Party member:

---

67   S. Kelly, interview with McKinlay (2013).
68   J. Reid, 'Not Scared to Be Ourselves', *Scottish Left Review* (November/December 2007), 6–7.
69   See H.M. Drucker, *Breakaway: The Scottish Labour Party* (Edinburgh 1978).

We came up with the wheeze that we would make the announcement from the platform. 'Comrades, before I ask for your money, I want you to understand that *Tribune* is at the centre, is the very *soul* of democratic socialism in this country. The are many reasons I could give you to prove that, but *nothing* could prove it better than what I'm about to tell you. Tonight, we have two new comrades who will join us on this platform. One has come from a lifetime in the Communist Party: the *absolutely* unparalleled Jimmy Reid'. Jimmy strides onto the stage. *Wild* delight: clapping and cheering. It was a triumphant moment: it was a sense of *wonder* that he had joined us, he was one of us.[70]

However, while a great piece of 'political theatre', Reid joining the Labour Party was to prove not as straightforward a process as he or Kinnock thought it would be, although his application was not as controversial as Peter Hain's which was subjected to a barrage of criticism due to the fact that he was formerly the poster boy of the Young Liberals.[71] The Falangist jibe still rankled with Labour members in the Central Dunbartonshire constituency and they were not inclined to accommodate a recanting communist. If they were seen by Reid as comparable to the Spanish Falangists in 1974 then what specifically had changed in three years? What made Reid wish to join a political party made up of such a reactionary bunch of Labour activists? With these considerations in mind his application to join his local branch of the Labour Party – Dalmuir – was turned down by six votes to five, although the general management committee of Central Dunbartonshire was in favour.[72] His rejection created a storm of protest on the left of the Party. *Tribune* called on Labour supporters to write to the secretary of the constituency in support of Reid; an attempt condemned by the Party's Scottish organiser, Jimmy Allison, as blatant interference.[73] Local opposition, however, was overruled and at a meeting of the Central Dunbartonshire Constituency Labour Party Reid was accepted into the Party by a vote of 27 to 7.[74]

Once in the Labour Party Reid associated himself with a loose coalition of political interests known as the Broad Left, and spoke on its platforms on many occasions as well as contributing articles to its

70 Kinnock, interview with McKinlay.
71 *Tribune*, 23 September 1977.
72 *Tribune*, 4 November 1977.
73 *Glasgow Herald*, 5 November 1977.
74 *Glasgow Herald*, 12 November 1977.

mouthpiece *Tribune*. The Tribune group emerged in the early 1960s to challenge the Labour leadership on several important issues, such as nuclear disarmament and Clause Four of the constitution, which committed the Party to the socialisation of the means of production and distribution of wealth. Prior to its emergence, the Labour leadership between 1948 and 1960 'suffered only one defeat at Party conference'.[75] However, in less deferential times, left-wing MPs harried the Wilson governments of the 1960s over Vietnam, welfare cuts, incomes policies and so on. Most of these MPs were grouped around the journal *Tribune*, which had been founded in 1937 by Sir Stafford Cripps MP and George Strauss MP, but reached its peak of influence in the 1970s, when it commanded the support of about a third of the Parliamentary Labour Party (PLP). Although it tried to articulate the views of a newer generation of left trade union leaders as well as criticise the Labour government within parliament, *Tribune* was never able to mobilise Party members in campaigns as its membership was limited to MPs only. Its limitations were summed up by Stephen Kelly who said that it had 'a very loose agenda … very informal … deliberately informal to avoid any accusation of being a Party within a Party'.[76]

The other important left-wing group to appear in the 1970s was the Campaign for Labour Party Democracy (CLPD). It was founded by Party activists in 1973 with support from about ten Labour MPs. The main motivation for the Campaign was the record of the Labour governments in the 1960s and the way that Annual Conference decisions were continually ignored on key domestic and international issues. Thus, the Campaign was to bring about important and far-reaching changes to the constitution of the Party to ensure that Labour MPs and Labour governments enacted policies which had the support of the membership. The most important changes desired by the CLPD were, first, the mandatory reselection of MPs; secondly, for the Party leader to be elected on a wider franchise to include trade unions and Constituency Labour Party members (CLPs) rather than simply MPs; and, thirdly, for the Party manifesto to be drafted by the National Executive. The foremost advocate of the CLPD demands was Tony Benn MP. By 1974, the CLPD had secured ascendency in the constituencies but they had less than 10 per cent of votes cast at annual conference. Initially, the demands had little support among the trade unions – in 1974, only 39 union branches were affiliates. However,

---

75 S. Fielding, *Labour: Decline and Renewal* (Tisbury, 1999), 51.
76 Kelly, interview with McKinlay.

reflecting the leftward turn in the Labour Party, the number increased to 161 in 1980.[77]

The growth of the CLPD was down to several factors. The mass industrial struggles over trade union reforms radicalised rank-and-file trade unionists at a time when union influence in the Party was growing. The proportion of union-sponsored MPs began to rise – from 120 out of 317, or 38 per cent, in 1964, to 127 out of 301, or 42 per cent, in 1974.[78] It led to most union votes on the NEC and Party conferences going against the leadership. Moreover, the social profile of the Party was changing: becoming increasingly dominated by middle-class activists whose radicalism was the outcome of their participation in student protests in the sixties. At the 1978 Labour Party Conference half the delegates were middle class and a quarter were university graduates, politically to the left of the leadership. There was also penetration of the Party from far-left Trotskyist groups such as Militant Tendency.[79] Under the weight of these forces the Party pulled heavily towards the left. Stuart Holland's book *The Socialist Challenge* (1975) influenced the leftward move of the Party towards advocating greater public ownership and state influence over the economy. This became known as the Alternative Economic Strategy (AES), which essentially sought to extend the democratic principle beyond the sphere of politics in the belief that sovereignty over the direction of the economy should rest with the elected government rather than with global markets, and that the balance of power within the workplace should be adjusted in favour of the shop floor. Specifically, in the context of economic crisis, it meant reflation, price and import controls to protect nascent and struggling British industries, public ownership of major financial institutions, and the tackling of systemic inequalities through progressive taxation and social spending. These proposals were welcomed by the CPGB as they were very close to the programme laid out in the *British Road to Socialism* and they 'increased the feeling amongst the Party leadership that it was having an impact on mainstream Labour opinion'.[80]

Despite the 1976 conference voting overwhelmingly for the radical *Labour's Programme 1976* and the AES also endorsing the nationalisation

---

77 D. Kogan and M. Kogan, *The Battle for the Labour Party* (London, 1982), 31–2.
78 A.J. Reid, *United We Stand: A History of Britain's Trade Unions* (London, 2004), 385.
79 Fielding, *Labour*, 54.
80 Andrews, *End Games*, 127.

of the clearing banks,[81] Prime Minister Harold Wilson and his allies in the Cabinet, James Callaghan and Denis Healey, were able to block the proposals without ever seriously considering them. Indeed, when given the paper drafted by Tony Benn, then Minister for Industry, Wilson wrote a short note in red ink for his Cabinet office across the cover saying: 'I haven't read it, don't propose to, but I disagree with it'.[82] Through the simple but devious cover of a strategic reshuffle of his government, Wilson was able to neutralise the influence of Benn by moving him from Industry to Energy. The defeat of the Labour government in 1979 furthered the process of deradicalisation in the Party, symbolised as it was by Benn's defeat in the Deputy Leader contest of 1981. He had epitomised the leftward shift of the Party, and although he only lost out to his rival Denis Healey by less than 1 per cent of the vote, when the demographics are examined, they show that he won 75 per cent of the votes cast by the CLPs, but only a third of the PLP was prepared to back him, and 60 per cent of the trade union vote went against him. Although barely perceived at the time, the contest for the deputy leadership marked the high-water mark of the Broad Left's influence on the Labour Party, as well as that of the CPGB.[83] The 1981 NEC election results saw important successes for the trade union right. By 1982, they had removed all their target left-wingers on the Party's Executive. The repercussions of these developments and electoral setbacks saw the union left, like the PLP Tribune group, fracturing into 'hard' and 'soft' wings.[84] However, it would take the catastrophic defeat of the Party in 1983 to extinguish the dying embers of the AES completely and move Labour towards a more neo-liberal economic strategy.

Where did Reid stand in all of this? As we can see from the brief discussion of the politics of the Labour left in the 1970s, there was little to distinguish the AES from the *British Road to Socialism* in terms of economic strategy and the long-term goal of transferring power and wealth from the haves to the have-nots. But it was the question of internal Party democracy, of democratic centralism, that was perhaps the main reason for Reid's resignation from the CPGB.

81 L. Baston, 'The Age of Wilson, 1955–79', in B. Bravati and R. Heffernan (eds), *The Labour Party: A Centenary History* (Basingstoke, 2000), 103. See also J. Medhurst, *That Option No Longer Exists: Britain 1974–1976* (London, 2014) for a detailed analysis.
82 Medhurst, *Option*, 103.
83 Fielding, *Labour*, 56–7.
84 S. Ludham, 'Norms and Blocks: Trade Unions and the Labour Party since 1964', in Bravati and Heffernan, *The Labour Party: A Centenary History*, 230.

At his first Labour Party conference, in October 1978, according to Geoffrey Parkhouse of the *Glasgow Herald*, what he found most impressive about the proceedings was the Party's ability to conduct its internal strife on the floor of the hall. 'It is all out there', he said. 'That is the overwhelming impression one gets. The public ventilation of differences. That is the immense strength of the British Labour Party'. Asked if he found it different from his days in the Communist Party, he replied: 'Those are real issues we are debating in there. The people taking the decisions could actually influence the course of events in Britain. It is all out in the open'.[85] Perhaps in the Labour Party fewer decisions were taken behind closed doors, but an end to factionalism and internal strife? The 1980s would prove that there was as little harmony and openness in the Labour Party as he had found in the CPGB. Moreover, Reid argued that there was a fundamental contradiction in the CLPD's campaign in as much as the same trade union leaders that had voted for mandatory reselection of MPs did not put themselves through the same democratic process. As he put it: 'a few years ago I was involved with a campaign to strengthen Labour Party democracy' but he was 'appalled … [that] they were not prepared to submit themselves to mandatory re-election by their members … It is intolerable, an affront to the democracy of the Labour movement'.[86]

In the maelstrom of political debate regarding the political direction of Labour it was clear that Reid was more comfortable associated with the soft or social democratic centre than the hard left. In a number of articles in *Tribune* in the early 1980s he attacked the far left in the trade unions and the Labour Party and wrote: 'The political orientation of the Broad Left in the trade unions is the natural ally of the mainstream democratic left of the Labour Party. Together these two elements should constitute the real left in the British labour movement'.[87] This was a coded attack on CPGB membership of the Broad Left and the entryist elements of the Trotskyist left. However, as a born again social democrat, Reid's position was viewed as unprincipled by several people on the left, while on the right he was never able to shake off the communist tag. Indeed, his past activism proved more of a handicap to him than to many others in the Labour Party, such as his namesake John Reid and Alastair Darling, both of whom had begun their political lives on the far left. This past was put up for public examination in the 1979 general election.

85 *Glasgow Herald*, 7 October 1978.
86 *Daily Record*, 16 June 1986.
87 *Tribune*, 23 March 1980.

Reid had been looking for a parliamentary seat in Scotland and was 'strongly tipped' by Colin Bell of the *Glasgow Herald* as one of four possible Labour candidates to fight Garscadden, Glasgow, in the by-election of February 1978.[88] The Garscadden bid came to nothing, but hot on its heels came an offer to stand as Labour candidate for Dundee East, a constituency that had been created in 1950 and had been solidly Labour until 1974 when it was won for the first time by the SNP. Reid was not the original choice to fight the seat. That opportunity had in the first instance been offered to Janey Buchan, but when she showed little interest in standing, David Whittock, a former Dundee United footballer, and a Roman Catholic, was selected. Unfortunately, he died in a tragic car accident earlier in 1978, which created an unplanned-for vacancy in Dundee East. A three-man delegation, including the former chairman of the Dundee Labour Party, John McAuley, visited Reid in his home in Clydebank where they invited him to stand for selection as Prospective Parliamentary Candidate (PPC).[89] Reid was not unknown in Dundee; in fact, he was quite popular, having spoken at various rallies in the city, and had links with the trade unions, so the decision to approach him was not as surprising as it first seemed. His opponents for the candidacy were Charlotte Haddow, ex-chair of the Scottish Council of the Labour Party, Daniel Chisholm, liaison officer of the Forth Ports Authority, and Robert Cairns, Edinburgh town councillor. But he 'had such a large majority in the first ballot that no further voting was necessary'.[90]

However, while popular with the membership, Reid was not the favoured candidate of some of the younger activists grouped around the politically eclectic North East Debating Society (NEDS), whose leading lights were George Galloway and Willie McKelvey, both future Labour MPs, but also included ex-members of the Dundee Communist Party.[91] While numerically and politically insignificant in Dundee, communists were the educators of the labour movement there as elsewhere. All the leading shop stewards in NCR, Timex and the Robb Caledon shipyard were Party members and, as such, they wielded a great deal of influence on Labour Party activists through their discussion groups and summer schools.[92] This was evident in the activities of NEDS, which, despite

---

88 *Glasgow Herald*, 10 February 1978.
89 J. McAuley, interview with Knox (2015).
90 *Glasgow Herald*, 26 June 1978. The actual result was 38 to 20 in favour of Reid.
91 R. Mennie, interview with Knox (2016).
92 Mennie, interview with Knox.

its rather insipid designation, was hardly a simple talking shop. Its political aim was to wrest control of the Party in the mid-1970s away from the more right-wing older city councillors, some of whom had been excoriated in the media for alleged corrupt practices, leading to the incarceration of the Lord Provost, Tom Moore, before his and two other councillors had their convictions quashed in 1980.[93] Their strategy came to fruition in what McKelvey called the 'night of the long knives', when six senior members of Dundee District Council resigned the Labour whip in protest at the 'Party's NEC's ... refusal to investigate the activities of an illegal left-wing cell operating in the city'.[94] The city's Labour Party was thus riven by factional infighting not just between left and right but also between the left, as those who questioned and challenged the political philosophy and tactics of the Galloway/McKelvey faction were deemed to be 'anti-socialist'.[95] Thus, Reid was entering a viper's nest of intrigue.

The NEDS favoured the candidacy of Chisholm, who was sponsored by the Transport and General Workers' Union (TGWU), because, according to Galloway, they 'thought that we would be tagged with the ex-Communist Party label' and this would bring 'unwelcome attention' to Reid, thus, damaging the chances of victory.[96] But in pursuit of their 'stop Reid campaign' they adopted a questionable strategy. McKelvey, as nominated by the Dundee East Young Socialists, decided to put himself forward as a candidate in Dundee East, the constituency where he had held office as Secretary-Organiser (which was against Party rules, as he was well aware). Knowing that his application would be scrutinised by the National Executive he privately hoped they would also extend their inquiry into Reid's candidacy, as it too broke Party rules, since he had only been a member for eight months while the rule stipulated two years, although this condition could be waved 'in special circumstances'.[97] It was noted in the local press that McKelvey's gambit 'brought to a head the split in the Left-Wing faction of the Dundee city Labour Party ... There are two voices of opinion in the left ... some members saying Mr Reid is the ideal candidate others regarding him as unsuitable'.[98]

93 *Scotsman*, 25 September 2004.
94 W. McKelvey, interview with Knox (2016); *Guardian*, 22 June 1977.
95 McAuley, interview with Knox.
96 G. Galloway, interview with Knox (2016).
97 McAuley, interview with Knox, *Guardian*, 28 June 1978.
98 *Dundee Courier and Advertiser*, 30 May 1978.

McAuley, who with others had, as we have seen, convinced Reid to stand, put forward a different explanation to that offered by Galloway for the left opposition: one based on simple economics. As a member of the TGWU, Chisholm would have been better financed than Reid, who had less generous backing from the Engineering Union, and the Galloway/McKelvey faction was dazzled by union gold,[99] an explanation contemptuously dismissed by Galloway.[100] But in faction-ridden Dundee there exist other competing accounts to that offered by Galloway and McAuley. Party activist Ian Leggatt claimed that the opposition stemmed from the fact that Reid was perceived as having moved to the right of the Labour Party and as such the left distrusted him, in spite of the fact that he identified with the left-leaning Tribune group and the CLPD.[101] In a letter to *The Times*, leading Fabian and former Labour MP for Bedford Tom Skeffington-Lodge spoke scornfully of the 'strong local left-wing opposition expressed at his selection and since'.[102] Indeed, most of Reid's support in the selection process came from the centre-right with only a 'handful of Left-wingers' on his side.[103] Thus, the selection process produced a number of contested narratives that were consistent with the divisions in the Dundee Labour Party which had surfaced in the turbulent years of the mid-1970s. Ever since, each grouping has jostled with one another to control and determine the political story of this period. But the truth, if there is one to be found, lies somewhere in the middle of this twisted tale: finance and politics (past and present) each had a part to play in galvanising the left opposition to Reid's selection.

But Reid not only suffered attacks from the Dundee hard left, his candidacy was also opposed by the right-wing Manifesto group in the Labour Party, which expressed dissatisfaction over his selection and called on the National Executive not to ratify his adoption as PPC for Dundee East. In a letter to the Party's general secretary, Ron Hayward, Ian Wrigglesworth, MP for Thornaby on Teesside, claimed that 'Mr Reid's selection would be offensive to the vast majority of Labour Party members'. His argument was that it breached the two-year rule, as Reid had only been a member of the Party for eight months.[104] This was also the view taken

---

99 McAuley, interview with Knox.
100 Galloway, interview with Knox.
101 I. Leggat, interview with Knox (2016).
102 *The Times*, 3 July 1978.
103 *Guardian*, 28 June 1978.
104 *Glasgow Herald*, 25 July 1978.

by the equally right-wing Social Democratic Alliance, which had been set up in 1975 by Labour councillors to expose Labour MPs with links to communist organisations. In a letter to *The Times*, the honorary secretary, Douglas Eden, not only reasserted the breach of Party rules but also argued that this was another example of entryism from the Marxist left, writing:

> Mr Reid joined the Labour Party only eight months ago after many years in the Communist Party and having fought against Labour candidates in the last three general elections. The reasons he gave for his resignation from the Communist Party were not ideological but were tactical. He said the Communist Party was too sectarian and inflexible ... In applying to join the Labour Party he did not express any conversion from his Marxist-Leninist and pro-Soviet views. We believe that if the NEC now waives the rules, makes a special exception for Mr Reid, it will confirm the existing suspicions that our Party is being manipulated by its Left-wing into an International Front with communism.[105]

However, after some debate, the National Executive of the Labour Party endorsed his selection as candidate by 14 votes to 6. Shirley Williams 'expressed pleasure that Mr Reid had joined the Party. However, she also felt that the two-year rule should have been observed'.[106] The Tories also used his selection to argue it was an indication how far Labour had moved to the left. Teddy Taylor, the Tory Shadow Secretary of State for Scotland, challenged the prime minister to say if he agreed with the Labour Party Organising Committee's decision to endorse Reid as PPC for East Dundee: 'The fact that an exception has been made for a prominent ex-Communist who has never renounced his views is a clear sign of the extent to which the extreme Left is taking over the power points of the Labour Party'.[107]

There was little doubt that Jimmy Reid was the best and ablest candidate, and for that reason most Labour members were prepared to back him based on his impressive showing in the February 1974 election. However, while Reid did not face the kind of interference from the Catholic Church that had badly damaged his chances of election in 1974, Dundee East was a difficult seat for Labour to win, for although it included council estates such as Douglas and Whitfield within its boundaries it also contained the middle-class burgh of Broughty Ferry as well as the affluent

---

105 *The Times*, 3 July 1978.
106 *Glasgow Herald*, 27 July 1978.
107 *Glasgow Herald*, 12 July 1978.

suburb of Monifieth. Thus, unlike Dundee West, which was predominately working class and 60 per cent to 65 per cent Catholic, the East constituency had a solid core of Tory voters.[108] It was represented by Gordon Wilson of the SNP, a graduate in law from the University of Edinburgh, who was employed by T.F. Reid Solicitors in Paisley from 1963 until his election as an MP. He won the seat for the SNP from Labour in the February 1974 general election with a majority of 3,000 votes; by October of that year he had increased his majority to 7,000. Arguably, Wilson was a more formidable opponent for Reid than Hugh McCartney had been in the last general election. Politically, he was on the centre right and also a committed Christian; indeed, in 2010, he co-founded and became Chairman of Solas (Centre for Public Christianity), a Christian body dedicated to the revival of the faith. He was one of the 11 SNP MPs who had voted along with the Tories in favour of a no-confidence motion against the Labour government; an action that triggered the general election of 3 May 1979. As the Prime Minister at the time, James Callaghan remarked in the case of the SNP that: 'it is the first time in recorded history that turkeys have been known to vote for an early Christmas'.[109]

Wilson was also a genuinely popular MP: hard-working and conscientious. And with his moderate political views he was able to draw support from a cross section of Dundee society. Compared with Reid, Tories saw him as preferable parliamentary material. Indeed, some local employers appealed to Alastair McAlpine, the Scottish Conservative Party's Honorary Treasurer, to encourage Tories to vote tactically to keep Reid out. The following extract from a letter written by W. Rennie Stewart of William R. Stewart & Sons (Hacklemakers), Dundee to McAlpine is representative of Tory attitudes to Reid. He writes:

> Incidentally, I am naturally concerned at the candidature of Jimmy Reid for Dundee East and think that all possible steps should be taken to avoid him succeeding; I understand from a friend of mine that a number of local conservatives decided to support Gordon Wilson at the last election, because they felt (correctly as it turned out) Gordon Wilson had a better chance of gaining the seat from Labour than their own candidate. I wonder whether the Conservative Party have thought of this aspect and

108 D. Morley, *Gorgeous George: The Life and Adventures of George Galloway* (London, 2007), 50.
109 Hansard, HC vol. 965, col. 471 (28 March 1979).

whether it might be in the best interests of the constituency to allow Mr Wilson a free run against Mr Reid by withdrawing the Conservative candidate altogether. I realise this may well be political anathema but I do know that all the local people I have spoken to think Gordon Wilson is an able and pleasant young man of moderate outlook who has represented the constituency very well since his election. As my factory is in his constituency I feel very strongly that I would very much prefer Gordon Wilson as a representative, especially compared with the likely alternative of Jimmy Reid.[110]

Reid not only faced opposition from a Tory/Nationalist bloc, he also bore the brunt of an onslaught from the local press. Although predominately a working-class city, Dundee had a right-wing, anti-union press owned by the D.C. Thompson family. The main conduit of local news and opinion was their newspaper – the *Courier and Advertiser*. On every occasion the paper mentioned Reid's name it was always prefixed with the label 'ex-Communist': a ploy designed to play on Catholic antipathy to communism.

However, despite the degree of opposition Reid faced in Dundee East there were high hopes of Labour winning the seat. This was a view shared by the *Glasgow Herald*, whose correspondent, in a rather unreliable and selective piece of analysis, pointed out that the SNP had failed to win through 'in the local elections during the five years in power' (which is difficult to comprehend as they did not contest council seats until the late 1970s) and that Tayside had voted 'No' in the recent referendum on devolution, although clearly the city of Dundee had voted 'Yes'.[111] While the journalism was untrustworthy, there may have been an element of propaganda in its construction. However, there was no doubting the evidence from the polls that the SNP bandwagon, which had made spectacular electoral ground in 1974, was becoming derailed, if not grinding to a complete halt. Moreover, a survey carried out by the SNP itself in the spring of that year had predicted 'the loss of the constituency'.[112] Reid himself sounded confident of victory, saying:

> The seat is certainly winnable. I believe the loss to the SNP was, let's say, an aberration. No, wait, delete aberration and put in

110 Gordon Wilson Papers, University of Dundee, MS 315/3/3.
111 *Glasgow Herald*, 14 April 1979.
112 G. Wilson, *SNP: The Turbulent Years, 1960–1990* (Stirling, 2009), 198.

anachronism ... Say that the SNP in Dundee are an anachronism, only transient. A majority of almost 7000 might look formidable but it can be quickly overcome.[113]

During his election campaign Reid relentlessly attacked the SNP's policy of independence. In a speech at Douglas Primary School he said: 'The Nationalists claim Scottish ills have been caused by an English conspiracy ... Based on this infantile analysis, not surprisingly, they draw an infantile conclusion – separate Scotland from England ... When the diagnosis is wrong the medicine prescribed can be fatal'.[114] In his election leaflet, he went further, calling the SNP 'petty and superficial ... and irrelevant'.[115] But while viewing separatism as 'infantile', he maintained support for a 'system of government for Scotland, not as a region of Britain but as a nation in its own right'.[116] Throughout most of its history the CPGB had supported home rule for Scotland but always stopped short of advocating separation. Their thinking on the subject was influenced by Stalin's pamphlet, *Marxism and the National Question* (1913), which was compulsory reading for cadre. As a means to resolve the nationalist pretensions of minorities such as the Georgians and Poles in Russia, Stalin advocated 'regional autonomy', or home rule, as the only solution to maintaining the integrity of Russia since 'it does not divide people according to nations, it does not strengthen national barriers; on the contrary, it breaks down these barriers and unites the population in such a manner as to open the way for division of a different kind, division according to classes'.[117] Reid in his campaign delivered a modified version of Stalin's thesis, recognising the right of Scotland to self-determination, but only within the framework of a federal UK. Put another way, he was in favour of nationhood but not statehood for Scotland.

He was no less critical of the Tories bemoaning the collapse of one-nation Conservatism and its replacement with the new neo-liberal, market-based philosophy of Thatcherism. Speaking to an audience of NCR and Veeder-Root workers on 20 April, he contrasted the crassness of the new Toryism with the compassion of Labour, saying: 'Mrs Thatcher's shadow cabinet represents a brand of Tory extremism that Iain Macleod, Rab Butler

113 *Glasgow Herald*, 27 June 1978.
114 *Courier and Advertiser*, 18 April 1979.
115 Election Leaflet, Lamb Collection, Dundee Central Library (441(9)).
116 *Courier and Advertiser*, 17 April 1979.
117 Stalin, *Marxism and the National Question*. See https://www.marxists.org/reference/archive/stalin/works/1913/03.htm.

and Harold Macmillan would have dismissed with disdain. The choice is stark. Either a Labour Government, stable and compassionate or a Thatcher government, inexperienced, immature and strident'.[118]

After weeks of campaigning, the contest essentially, as the *Glasgow Herald* argued, boiled down to one between the 'charismatic appeal' of Jimmy Reid versus the 'proven local record' of the sitting MP Gordon Wilson,[119] and when the votes were counted the sitting MP won. Wilson held his seat, but with a reduced majority, down from 15.07 per cent (6,938) in October 1974 to 5.04 per cent (2,519) in 1979. Reid increased the Labour vote from 15,137 (32.7 per cent) to 17,978 (36 per cent) over these elections, although it could be argued that it was only in line with the 4 per cent increase in the turnout over 1974. It was a credible performance, but it remained a disappointing night for Reid, as his defeat contrasted rather badly with Labour's Ernie Ross winning Dundee West with a massive majority of more than 10,000 votes over Jim Fairlie of the SNP. Nationally, the results bore out Callaghan's prediction: the SNP lost nine of the 11 seats won in October 1974, only holding on to Dundee East and the Western Isles.[120] In the case of Dundee East there was a suggestion of tactical voting by Conservatives and this was the view of the Labour Party in explaining the failure to capture the seat.[121] But the problem with this analysis is that the Tory vote actually went up from 7,784 (or 16.8 per cent of votes cast) in October 1974 to 9,072 (or 18.2 per cent of votes cast) in 1979. In the end, local loyalties had trumped Reid, but it was also clear that the *Courier* had done its work effectively. Drunken SNP supporters in the city square on election day hurled abuse at Reid, shouting 'Commie': a rather strange thing to do considering that Reid was carrying with him a gold medal awarded in the previous year for 'Services to Scotland' by Wendy Wood, one of leading voices for Scottish independence.[122]

However, in the end, his history was his undoing.[123] A hugely selective leaflet put out by the SNP highlighting Reid's communist past badly damaged his appeal to the middle classes and among the upwardly mobile section of the working class. It said:

118 *Courier and Advertiser*, 21 April 1979.
119 *Glasgow Herald*, 14 April 1979.
120 *Courier and Advertiser*, 4 May 1979.
121 McAuley, interview with Knox.
122 McAuley, interview with Knox; Wilson, *SNP: The Turbulent Years*, 198.
123 'Comments re National Party at All Levels', Wilson Papers, MS 315/3/3.

> What about the Labour Candidate? Mr Reid has been a Communist for 25 years. As a Communist candidate for Central Dunbartonshire, his home area, he polled only 3,417 votes, a lost deposit – Rejection by the electorate. When leaving the Communist Party, he restated his beliefs ... 'I am still a Marxist Socialist ... I want to say this without qualification I don't want anyone to vote for me today who would not vote for me last week. For I have not changed my views, my beliefs, my ultimate aims in any way'.[124]

Thus, not only was Reid depicted as an unreconstructed Marxist, with the reference to his 'home area' he also was portrayed as an interloper and opportunist. Reid himself confessed to friend and journalist Brian McGeachan that 'he was carrying baggage from his communist Party days ... the fixed image of him was still as a communist, and certainly this was the key factor ... behind his inability to be elected'.[125]

Inside the Dundee Labour Party Reid had found himself isolated. On the one hand, he insisted on his independence from the activists who had been crucial to his selection.[126] Equally, Reid did not have the support of older Labour members in Dundee, especially from influential councillors resentful of their loss of authority to the hard left. In his biography of George Galloway, David Morley claims that even his supporters in the Labour group 'thought he had let them down'. As one of them put it: 'We had trouble fighting the election with him because he had a different strategy over meetings and was not always able to turn up'.[127] Indeed, his choice of election agent, Ian Borthwick, a former deputy Lord Provost, who was considered locally as a 'bit of a maverick', raised a few eyebrows, but he found Reid unconvincing as a candidate. While recognising him as an outstanding public speaker, able to pack halls to the rafters, Borthwick felt that he had little stomach for the daily slog of canvassing, shaking hands, and building a rapport with the electorate, all the things that his SNP opponent Wilson revelled in.[128] But it may have simply been a clash of styles: Borthwick concerned with the minutiae of electioneering and Reid

---

124 Election Leaflet, Lamb Collection, Dundee Central Library (441(9)); *Daily Record*, 13 February 1976.
125 Information from Brian McGeachan, 22 June 2016.
126 Morley, *Gorgeous George*, 52.
127 Morley, *Gorgeous George*, 52.
128 McAuley, interview with Knox; I. Borthwick, interview with Knox (2017). The latter left the Labour Party a few years later to stand as an Independent.

adopting his well-worn holistic approach in which context was prioritised over content. But whatever the reason, the mix was not complementary, more conflictual.

In the run-up to the election, the *Glasgow Herald* saw two possible outcomes for Reid: 'if he wins, a long parliamentary career would be confidently expected; alternatively, he could soon be dumped back into limbo'.[129] Unfortunately for him it was to be limbo. Despite his undeniable inspirational presence and his unmatched qualities of oratory Reid never stood for parliament again. There was no safe seat found for him. In Scotland, he was never accepted. Scottish Labour officials remained distrustful of Reid's motivations.[130] Jimmy Allison, Scottish organiser, publicly stated that he had 'deserted the CP in a blatant bid to get into parliament'.[131] A view shared by leading left-winger Eric Heffer, MP for Liverpool Walton, who disparagingly said of him that: 'Many years earlier Reid had come to Merseyside seeking support from fellow shipyard apprentices for the apprentice's strike. He was a very different man then from the poacher-turned gamekeeper he has become'.[132] During the 1979 election, the press officer at Keir Hardie House, Glasgow, Harry Conroy, a financial journalist seconded from the *Daily Record*, on receiving press releases and speeches from the Dundee East campaign trail allegedly 'threw them in the bin'. His justification was that Reid's language was 'too over-blown and went over the heads of the punters'.[133]

Whether any of this materially affected his chances of winning Dundee East is difficult to say but it is evidence of the contempt and hostility Reid was held in by Labour Party officials in Scotland. Tam Dalyell MP was of the opinion that it was due to the negative influence of Donald Dewar and the fact that he was closely associated with Tony Benn.[134] For Reid it was more straightforward. He was about to embark on a new career: 'people might find it strange to leave a job without another to go to … [but] My diary is full of engagements and I have my book to work on … Joan and I can go on a really quiet holiday … I want to emphasise how cordial this parting is and how much warmth has been shown to me personally'.[135]

---

129 *Glasgow Herald*, 27 June 1978.
130 J. Allison, *Guilty by Suspicion: A Life and Labour* (Glendaruel, 1995), 106.
131 Allison, *Guilty*, 106.
132 Quoted in Allison, *Guilty*, 144–5.
133 Information from Brian McGeachan, 22 June 2016.
134 T. Dalyell, interview with Knox (2015).
135 *Glasgow Herald*, 22 October 1979.

This was not the end of his participation in public debate, but it would be as a commentator, a journalist and a pundit that his engagement with the political system would continue and, as we will see, be no less divisive or controversial.

7

Strike

After his defeat in the 1979 election Reid embarked on a new career in the media in the 1980s. As we will see, in many ways this was an accidental development, something he almost drifted into. A growing reputation in journalism, however, saw other work in the media open up for him in television and he became a prolific presenter of programmes covering everything from the topography of Scotland to the Russian Revolution. This coincided with the election of the Thatcher government in 1979, which triggered a series of heroic and sometimes futile struggles by the labour movement over industrial relations reform, the Poll Tax, poverty and unemployment, symbolised in the miners' strike of 1984. From the peripheral contours of British society there also came challenges in the form of riots in inner cities from young men and women alienated from parliamentary democracy. Over the Irish Sea, the 'Troubles' were not only tearing Northern Ireland apart, but leading to a wave of bombing attacks on the British mainland: most spectacularly, the attempt to blow up the Tory front bench in the Grand Hotel, Brighton, in October 1984. Beforehand, there was also war to contend with. In 1982, Britain sent a task force to retake the Falkland Islands from invasion by Argentina; after a ten-week conflict, British forces prevailed.

Reid was forced to comment on all these events; indeed, it was an extremely challenging news environment. However, his new career in journalism began rather sedately. He was initially asked to write a column for the *Scottish Daily Express*, but this was blocked by the National Union of Journalists as he did not hold a union card. After this setback, he slipped in through the back door, writing a weekend guest column for the *Glasgow Herald* reviewing television programmes. His stint was only expected to last a few issues but instead it grew from television reviews into a weekly current affairs column, so much so that he could proclaim: 'I've become a scribbler. A fully paid-up card-carrying scribbler … About four years ago someone asked me to write a television column ... for two or three weeks ... It lasted two years'.[1] The column in the *Herald* provides a unique insight into Reid's views on domestic and international affairs in the earlier part of this turbulent decade.

His role in the weekly column was essentially to puncture the pomposity and pretentions of the cultural and political elite. He wrote from the perspective of the working man who could only laugh at their foolishness, aloofness and pretend superiority; and this is the approach that characterised his later writings in the tabloid press. One example out of many concerned the Edinburgh Festival, which Reid saw as elitist and therefore phoney:

> I remember being at ... a reception a few years ago. It had something to do with the Edinburgh Festival. ... The place was crammed with ... wall-to-wall phoneys. I got out quickly, had a quick pint in a pub to re-establish contact with the real world, and then caught the first train home. Apart from going to a few jazz concerts and to see Nureyev dance, I haven't been to the Festival. I much prefer the company of the punters I was with on Saturday. They are also better singers.[2]

Under the cover of the faux everyman persona, Reid was given free rein by his editors to articulate his highly personal take on the events of the day. However, the consistency in political analysis he had displayed as a communist was absent, and his opinions became riddled with contradictions and some rather surprising volte-faces. He still supported the limited empowerment of the working class and the shift in resources from the haves to the have-nots, but it was more an emotional rather than theoretical position he assumed. Indeed, his socialism was more in keeping with neo-liberalism than with Marxism. As far as he was concerned, 'The communist system isn't just flawed but fundamentally wrong'.[3] Alternatively: 'Market forces are a vital mechanism without which industry and commerce will eventually grind to a halt'.[4] If you 'totally subjugate the market ... the true value of commodities is lost, the economic system collapses and you get Stalinism. A balance must be found'.[5] Thus, in

1   J. Reid, *As I Please* (Edinburgh, 1984), 9; *Journalist*, October 1983.
2   *Daily Record*, 23 June 1986.
3   *Sun*, 6 June 1989.
4   *Sun*, 4 April 1989.
5   *Sun*, 11 April 1989.

essence, what Reid was looking for was a third way between communism and capitalism, one which would combine the perceived efficiencies of the market with social justice and rights for individuals. However, whichever way you run a market economy it involves the acceptance of inequality; the question is how wide the gap between the rich and poor can become before action is taken to ameliorate the disparities in income and wealth? In short, what is an acceptable level of inequality?

For an ex-communist, his views on the royal wedding of Prince Charles and Lady Diana Spencer must have raised a few eyebrows among former comrades when he proclaimed that: 'Charles seems a personable young man, genuinely interested in others. His bride is a lovely young lass'.[6] But as he later explained, he was pretty relaxed about the monarchy, saying: 'If people want a monarchy it is all right by me, providing its powers are strictly limited. In a democracy real power must always be accountable to the people through the ballot box'.[7] Another example was his attitude to the 1981 London Riots. Referring to the Scarman Report on these events, and sounding like a *Daily Mail* journalist, he said: 'No matter what your views are on how anti-social behaviour emerges, and for me environment is a major factor, it has to be combated by force … You stop the attack by whatever means are necessary and available'.[8] Lastly, regarding the Falklands War, although he was opposed to the jingoism of the British press and the triumphalism of Thatcher in the moment of victory, he nevertheless supported the war, saying: 'Britain had really no alternative but to send a task force to the South Atlantic'.[9]

These views seem to suggest that Reid was becoming deeply embedded within the social democratic centre of British politics. This was made clear in his attitude towards the 'Troubles' in Northern Ireland. The position of the CPGB and the left generally in Britain on Ireland was that it was a colony, part of the dying imperial project. The partition treaty of 1921 had left unresolved questions regarding unification, which were reignited in the 1970s as Catholics fought Protestants and bombings and shootings became part of the fabric of everyday life in the streets of Belfast and Londonderry. To calm the situation, British troops were sent in, but while initially welcomed by both sides of the religious divide, very shortly they lost the confidence of the Catholic community after the shooting of

---

6   *Glasgow Herald*, 1 August 1981.
7   *Daily Record*, 30 June 1986.
8   *Glasgow Herald*, 28 November 1981.
9   *Glasgow Herald*, 26 July 1982.

unarmed civilians on 30 January 1972 in what became known as 'Bloody Sunday'. The left favoured the unification of Ireland as an independent sovereign state and part of this process involved the removal of British troops. The present leader of the Labour Party, Jeremy Corbyn, regularly addressed meetings of the Troops Out Movement, urging the withdrawal of British troops from the north, and caused controversy by inviting Sinn Fein's Gerry Adams to Westminster in 1984, just weeks after the Brighton bombing.

Reid had for some time argued that far-reaching change in the spheres of politics, social and economic life could only be achieved by peaceful democratic means, thus he was highly critical of the Irish Republican Army's (IRA) attempt to bomb its way to a united Ireland. Indeed, he argued that such tactics could only put back the cause of a unified Ireland, saying, in reference to the Hunger Strikers, like Bobby Sands:

> The art of leadership is not to lead those who trust you to certain death ... Surely now is an opportune time for the IRA to call a ceasefire ... I think the British people should tell the participants two things – first no one will or can bomb their way to a united Ireland ... The British people ... couldn't and wouldn't permit the Protestant majority in Northern Ireland to be dragged screaming against their will into an all-Ireland republic.[10]

He followed this with another piece in the *Glasgow Herald* the following year using the same condemnatory tone:

> In years past the Irish nationalist movement enjoyed fairly widespread support of sympathy among liberal minded people in the country and elsewhere. Today this situation is profoundly different. The Irish republican cause has been besmirched. Its banner has been trampled in the dirt by those who ironically claim to be the heirs of Robert Emmett and James Connolly ... there is no possibility of a United Ireland ... The credit for this should go to the provisional IRA. The Provos and their blood brothers – the Protestant extremists – also destroyed the Civil Rights movement.[11]

Reid had experienced sectarian hatreds growing up in Glasgow in the 1930s and 1940s and still in later age, given his love of football, witnessed

---

10 *Glasgow Herald*, 10 November 1981.
11 *Glasgow Herald*, 26 July 1982.

the tribalism among Celtic and Rangers supporters, but the situation in Northern Ireland was different from that in Glasgow. On the British mainland, the state was even-handed in its dealings with members of both faiths. The problem in Northern Ireland lay in the existence of an authoritarian sectarian state in which the monopoly of coercion was held by one section of the community to subjugate the other. Reid was right to point to the need for a political solution, but somewhat naive in his belief that without the armed struggle there would have been a movement towards negotiation for a peace settlement that would bring full civil and political rights for the Catholic community in Northern Ireland. Indeed, contrast this with his position on apartheid in South Africa, where he felt that in the context of that undemocratic system the armed struggle was permissible: 'The white Afrikaners denied blacks the peaceful means of change through the ballot box. So the blacks sought the changes which would give them elementary freedoms through the use of force … Who can say they are wrong?'[12] Irish Catholics may have had the vote in principle, but in practice the Protestant ascendancy rendered the casting of that vote futile. The parallels were obvious, as was the dilemma of how to secure the rights of minorities in the face of determined opposition by the majority.

His naivety was also shown in his opinions on nuclear warfare. Reid consistently championed unilateral nuclear disarmament since his conversion in the 1960s, saying that if Britain acted in this way it 'would free our country to play a role in developing initiatives for world-wide multilateral disarmament'. However, while abandoning nuclear weapons Britain was to remain in NATO – a nuclear club for Western powers formed in 1948 to contain the spread of communism. He vigorously attacked the 'sectarian left' who had persuaded delegates at the 1983 CND conference that it should campaign round the slogan 'Britain out of NATO and NATO out of Britain'. By adopting this policy, he argued, would exclude those members of a more moderate persuasion and enforce a 'political outlook' on the organisation which was of the left.[13] Reid could not have it both ways: favouring democratically taken decisions by conference and then when the result proved uncomfortable arguing that it was forced on the delegates by the left. To say that in some way they were manipulated into voting for a sectarian policy was patronising, and in many ways insulting, to the membership of CND. After all, some of

---

12 *Daily Record*, 15 December 1986.
13 *Glasgow Herald*, 28 December 1982.

the finest minds in Britain were members, including scientists, religious leaders, academics, journalists, writers, actors and musicians, such as the composer Benjamin Britten, the novelists Doris Lessing and E.M. Forster, the politician Michael Foot, the historian E.P. Thompson, the scientist Julian Huxley and the philosopher Bertrand Russell, to name but a few. Moreover, the Labour Party had adopted a unilateral disarmament position during most of the 1980s until the 1989 conference rejected it for multilateralism. This change of mind was largely the work of the Party's leader, Neil Kinnock, of whom Reid was a trusted ally and friend. Indeed, according to the *Guardian*, 'the voice of Reid is regarded by well-placed observers as the voice of Kinnock'.[14] These episodes are illustrative of the political direction Reid was heading in; a journey into the social democratic centre of British politics. But although his position on various events reveal an inconsistency, some woolly thinking and a little bit of hypocrisy, they did not create the level of outrage on the left that his views on the miners' strike of 1984 did.

In many ways Reid's attitude to the miners' strike might have been predicted by the stance he took on the Polish Solidarity movement. The struggle for democracy in Poland was mainly a working-class movement of factory and shipyard workers. There was mounting discontent in the 1970s with the economy as prices increased and wages fell. Strikes and factory occupations had been crushed by the Polish government, but in August 1980 at the Lenin shipyard in Gdansk a strike led by a former electrician Lech Walesa put in motion a movement that was in the end to prove unstoppable. Within a week, most of Poland was engulfed in strikes and the government had in the end to recognise the demands of the workers for free independent trade unions, a relaxation of censorship, and new rights for the Catholic Church, among others. By September, a nationwide labour union had been formed known as Solidarity. The government's reaction was to suppress Solidarity through censorship, and through violence, as soldiers opened fire on striking workers. On 8 October 1982, Solidarity was banned. In a memorable phrase, Reid said that Poland had become a 'penitentiary for the proletariat'.[15]

Reid was one among many critics from all sides of the political spectrum of the Polish authorities' handling of Solidarity, including Ronald Reagan, Margaret Thatcher, Pope John Paul, Enrico Berlinguer (National Secretary of the Italian Communist Party), to name but a few.

---

14 *Guardian*, 15 October 1984.
15 *Reid about Poland*, Scottish Television.

Through his column in the *Glasgow Herald* he called on the British labour movement to 'Break off all relations with the puppet trade unions in Soviet Russia and Eastern Europe. All delegates to and from these countries already planned should be cancelled. Holidays in these countries organised through the union should be cancelled. The British Government should be urged to take all possible measures against the Polish Junta economic as well as diplomatic'.[16] To Reid, what was at stake here was not just the rights of Polish workers but the future of socialism. Socialism to him meant 'the extension of freedom, not its curtailment or denial … Those who remain silent … act as apologists for these indefensible regimes'.[17] Thus, socialism was a democratic movement of the people to transform society by peaceful and constitutional means, something which could not be imposed on people against their wishes by cadres or vanguards, or through violence. Something that in his television programme – *Reid about Poland* – he reminded Solidarity leader Lech Walesa about. Indeed, he viewed Walesa as somewhat autocratic and dictatorial, and was critical of the way the movement under his leadership dealt with dissidents in its own ranks.[18] Given these views, it was predictable that Reid would seriously question any attempt to bypass these avenues of political action in favour of unconstitutional and undemocratic challenges to the status quo. The miners' strike of 1984–5 was to provide the severest test for his principles.

The miners' strike had its origins in the attempts of miners to defend jobs against a backdrop of mass unemployment which saw two million manufacturing jobs lost in Britain between 1979 and 1981. Their communities were dependent on these jobs for their continued survival: no jobs, no communities. The struggle that ensued in many ways mirrored the UCS demand for the 'Right to Work' and as such it might have been expected that Reid would have been in the forefront of the campaign, shoulder to shoulder with the miners and their leaders. He had written a very favourable profile in the *Glasgow Herald* two years before the strike of the miners' leader Arthur Scargill saying:

> We've been friends for 25 years … He is [a] complex man … It is impossible to place him in the contemporary categories of the Left … He is so obviously a syndicalist that you wonder why

16 *Glasgow Herald*, 18 October 1982.
17 *Glasgow Herald*, 5 November 1980.
18 *Reid about Poland*, Scottish Television.

you never noticed this before ... Apart from his homespun brand of syndicalism he is a rather old fashioned type of fundamental socialist. To Arthur the revolution is just around the corner if only people, particularly Labour Leaders, would open their eyes and look ... he is no dogmatist and belongs to no hard-nosed Left sect and is his own man.[19]

However, rather than be a crusading voice for the miners, Reid turned into one of the strike's fiercest critics. His fire was directly aimed at his 'friend' of 25 years, Arthur Scargill, in a manner that outdid the right-wing tabloid press. He variously described Scargill in pejorative terms referring to him as 'Barnsley's Lenin', 'the Ayatollah', a deluded individual with an unquenchable thirst for power and self-aggrandisement; traits he also found in his other bête noir, Margaret Thatcher. Speaking to Tam Dalyell MP, Reid remarked:

> Those two deserve one another ... She has closed her mind to the possibility of being wrong; Scargill never admitted to having any doubts at all. He has that frightening certitude, like Mrs Thatcher. Although they are both apparently poles apart, politically, philosophically and ideologically, they are both dogmatists. The difference is that she has the whole state machine at her disposal.[20]

Why did he arrive at such a jaundiced view of Scargill in particular, and the strike in general? First, according to Neil Kinnock:

> Reid hated Scargill from their time in the YCL because Jimmy had to lead people of all political persuasions and none. Jim was *leading* people, taking political risks, taking personal risks. Arthur was on a conveyor belt because the Yorkshire miners were dominated by communists – and they were good people. Arthur was another on that conveyor belt from his time as an apprentice electrician. So it *was* about differences in politics but Jimmy hated people that threw their weight around. Arthur had never taken those personal risks but still felt he had the right – the obligation – to tell others how to lead their lives. Jimmy wasn't the only one who had told me this.[21]

19 *Glasgow Herald*, 5 October 1982.
20 *Independent*, 11 August 2010.
21 N. Kinnock, interview with McKinlay.

He saw what he called 'Scargillism' as an undemocratic attempt to seize power. In his article, in the right-wing *Spectator*, he said that 'Scargillism is a contempt for working people, who are seen as pawns to be used by an elite as they plan and scheme revolutionary change. This aim justifies the means'.[22] Secondly, he condemned the violence of the picket line, contrasting it unfavourably with the peaceful work-in in 1971–2 on Clydeside. The violence he saw was the outcome of the failure to hold a ballot which meant spreading the strike through fear and intimidation, stating:

> I'm talking of the violence of miner against miner – of people being beaten up in their own homes by thugs masquerading as trade unionists. I recoil in horror at scenes of a miner's home being daubed 'Scab'. Into my mind floods visions of Jewish homes being defaced in the Germany of the thirties.[23]

Thirdly, the strike was damaging to the prospects of the election of a Labour government in particular, to the wider labour movement in general, and a complete disaster for the National Union of Mineworkers. As Reid put it:

> Arthur Scargill is the best thing that's happened to Mrs Thatcher since General Galtieri invaded the Falklands. ... the strike in the coal industry is unquestionably damaging to the labour movement. It will destroy the National Union of Mineworkers as an effective fighting force for the rest of the century. It will damage trade unionism in general and alienate millions. It places in jeopardy any chance of a revival of the electoral fortunes of the Labour Party. Only the extent of the damage is in question. It might even prove disastrous.[24]

Many people on the left shared Reid's view on the potentially calamitous nature of the strike and the fact that the miners, given the preparations made by the state to keep the lights on by ensuring the movement of coal to the power stations, would lose, but said nothing. However, there were more critics than friends. James Airlie, his one-time comrade in arms, although agreeing that the failure to hold a ballot was a fatal error, was scathing about the timing and the tone of his 'disgraceful

22 *Spectator*, 13 October 1984.
23 *New Society*, 17 January 1985.
24 *New Society*, 17 January 1985.

attacks' on the miners' leaders. Above all, Airlie emphasised that Reid 'represents no one'.[25] He went further, saying: 'it is a disgrace to be seen to be stabbing the miners in the back when they are fighting virtually for their lives. When it comes from a man with the background of Jimmy Reid it defies my understanding'. Scottish miners' leader Mick McGahey was 'utterly disgusted' with Reid, dismissing him contemptuously as 'broken Reid' – something hard to take, as McGahey had been 'Uncle Mick' to his daughters.[26] Dennis Skinner, Labour MP for Bolsover, christened him 'Jimmy Weed'.[27] Jim Sillars of the SNP, in an interview, remarked: 'he should have said nothing' even if he was 'right'.[28]

Reid answered his critics by arguing that it was more important to speak out than to remain silent, as this would seem to condone the suicidal tactics of Scargill, with all the disastrous consequences this held for the miners and the labour movement. As he put it:

> I find that reasoning peculiar. It's like watching loved ones careering towards the precipice, and waiting till they are smashed up and bleeding on the rocks below and telling them, 'I knew you heading for this, but as an act of solidarity I decided not to say anything'. Scargill is capable of bringing down the whole labour movement, and there is too much at stake for a cowardly and squalid silence.[29]

One can admire Reid's courage in speaking out against the strike as he must have been aware that it would provoke a backlash from some of those on the British left. As the doyen of Scottish journalism, the late Ian Bell, remarked: Reid 'is now despised in many parts of the Labour movement'.[30] Indeed, he was 'devastated' by the intense criticism, especially from former comrades. Close friend and colleague Ross Wilson said that he was 'never more alone, politically and personally'.[31] To compound his sense of devastation his mother Isa died in Vale of Leven Hospital on 24 September 1984. Given the bond that had developed between mother and son it must have been difficult for Reid to continue

---

25 *Marxism Today*, May 1985, 47.
26 R. Wilson, interview with McKinlay (2018).
27 I. Bell, 'Reid between the Lines', *Observer*, 22 April 1990.
28 J. Sillars, interview with Knox (2016).
29 *New Society*, 17 January 1985.
30 Bell, 'Reid between the Lines'.
31 Wilson, interview with McKinlay (2018).

his campaign against Scargill. However, private grief remained private. Publicly, for the first and only time, Reid encouraged by others, perhaps those around Kinnock, thought that his personal authority, derived from his leadership role in the UCS work-in, gave him the right, perhaps the responsibility, to speak out. He had allowed himself to be persuaded that only he had the political and moral authority publicly to criticise Scargill. But all it did was to alienate his old comrades and help undermine the miners' leaders and their struggle. However, was he correct in his analysis of the miners' strike and in his predictions for the labour movement in Britain?

Enough time has elapsed to view the miners' strike of 1984–5 with some objectivity, although it is appreciated that for many displaced miners and their relatives the emotions are still raw. Part of the problem with Reid's approach to the strike was that it depicted the conflict in terms of high politics. It was the battle of wills between Arthur Scargill and his brand of revolutionary socialism versus Margaret Thatcher, the iron lady, the high priestess of neo-liberalism. Thus, it was a personal as much as an ideological struggle. This meant that community and the role of women became mere footnotes in Reid's analysis, if indeed he ever considered them. However, new research has placed greater emphasis on the role of community in the making and maintaining of the strike. Even before the strike broke out some 50 per cent of Scottish miners were in dispute with their pit managers.[32] In England, in the Yorkshire coal field, miners at the Manvers, Cadeby, Silverwood, Kiverton Park and Yorkshire Main collieries were already on unofficial strike on separate issues before the area NUM called for official action.[33] Moreover, there was still in place an overtime ban that had been instituted in November 1983 in protest against the offer of a 5.2 per cent pay increase.

It could be argued that the miners' leaders were being railroaded into a national strike whether they wanted one or not; that the push was coming from the periphery rather than the centre, for under the NUM constitution local associations were granted a great deal of autonomy, particularly after the 1978 wage agreement which marked a shift from national parity to a return to regional incentive payments in the industry. Indeed, Scargill attempted to kick-start the full strike by allowing each

---

32 J. Phillips, *Collieries, Communities and the Miners' Strike in Scotland, 1984–85* (Manchester, 2012), 7.
33 J. Winterton and R. Winterton, *Coal, Crisis, and Conflict: The 1984–85 Miners' Strike in Yorkshire* (Manchester, 1989), 81–2.

region to call its own strikes, imitating his predecessor Joe Gormley's strategy over wage reforms. After two weeks of calling for a strike some 80 per cent of miners had walked out, making holding a national ballot a futile exercise. In any case, to call a ballot would, it was argued, have been unfair to workers in less-prosperous coalfields, as, in the words of the newly elected secretary of the NUM Peter Heathfield: 'It cannot be right for one man to vote another man out of a job'.[34] Although in saying that it has to be remembered that the NUM had previously held three ballots on a national strike, all of which rejected the proposal (55 per cent voted against in January 1982 and 61 per cent voted against in both October 1982 and March 1983), which must have had a major bearing on the decision not to ballot individual members. However, during the strike there was little in the way of national co-ordination by the NUM leadership; in fact, the only nationally co-ordinated action was the mass picket of the Orgreave coking plant in South Yorkshire, which led to violence between police and pickets on a huge scale. Thus, by shifting the focus from high politics to the localities, a much more nuanced and sophisticated understanding of the strike can be developed, in contrast to Reid's one-dimensional psychodrama between Scargill and Thatcher.

Then there is the role of the Tory government to consider. Reid recognised that Thatcher wanted 'vengeance' for the humiliation inflicted on the Heath government by the miners in the 1974 dispute.[35] In a speech to the Tory Party's right-wing 1922 Committee, she said: 'In the Falklands, we had to fight the enemy without. Here the enemy is within, and it is more difficult to fight, and more dangerous to liberty'.[36] In his book *The Secret War against the Miners*, Seumus Milne argues that it was a 'fairy tale' that Scargill ordered the action. He argues that it was in fact incited deliberately by the government. First, by the provocative appointment to chairman of the NCB of union-busting Ian MacGregor, who although a Scot born in Kinlochleven had spent a large part of his business career in America. MacGregor, whose mentor had been the Port Glasgow shipbuilder Sir James Lithgow, was regarded as having been responsible for turning around British Steel from one of the least efficient

---

34 Phillips, *Collieries*, 5. On this issue, see also V.L. Allen, 'The Year-Long Miners' Strike, March 1984–March 1985: A Memoir', *Industrial Relations Journal*, 40 (2009), 282.
35 *New Society*, 17 January 1985.
36 A.J. Richards, *Miners on Strike: Class Solidarity and Divisions in Britain* (Oxford, 1996), 117.

steel-makers in Europe to one of the most efficient, bringing the company into a near profit. However, this was achieved at the expense of a halving of the workforce in only two years and overseeing a 14-week national strike of steel workers in 1980, which until the miners' action in 1984 was the longest strike undertaken by any group of workers since the end of the Second World War. On hearing of the appointment of MacGregor, John Cummings, the Labour MP for Easington, County Durham, said: 'He wants to take away our independence and our cultural heritage, our village life and our club life. All this is our heritage, and I'm not prepared to let him take my heritage away from me'.[37] Then, by announcing without the usual process of consultation with the NUM the closure of Cortonwood colliery, Yorkshire, and six days later giving notice of a further closure of 20 pits, and 20,000 more redundancies – MacGregor forced the NUM to act, for if it delayed further there would have been more closures.[38] As one South Wales miner put it: 'When the strike did come, it was motivated by the Government as far as I'm concerned. Because they knew, they had everything they wanted in their favour: stocks of coal, plenty of oil, [and] plenty of gas'.[39] Another Yorkshire miner said that strike action in these circumstances was the 'only weapon we had really. If not, they'd have run riot. We had no option'.[40] It was ironic that the Minister in charge of making the preparations to defeat the miners was none other than Nicholas Ridley, who had tried to close down the UCS consortium in the early seventies. He had written a report in 1977, which was leaked to *The Economist*, on how to prepare for a battle with the trade unions.[41] It was clear that the Tory government had been preparing for a showdown with the unions for some time.

To many in the labour movement, Reid's interventions in the dispute, as the historian Jim Phillips points out, 'comforted its opponents and divided its supporters'.[42] The journalist Jack McLean said that 'many journalists and indeed his former comrades in the Labour Movement … felt that his frequent intemperate outpourings in the Tory gutter press

---

37 J. Spence and C. Stephenson, '"Side by Side with Our Men?" Women's Activism, Community, and Gender in the 1984–1985 British Miners' Strike', *International Labor and Working-Class History*, 75 (2009), 68–84.
38 S. Milne, *The Enemy Within: The Secret War against the Miners* (London, 1995), 18.
39 Richards, *Miners on Strike*, 111.
40 Richards, *Miners on Strike*, 112.
41 Milne, *Enemy Within*, 9–10.
42 Phillips, *Collieries*, 4.

against Arthur Scargill was nothing short of Government propaganda'.[43] But did the strike destroy the future electoral prospects of the Labour Party as he predicted? The evidence would suggest it had little impact, as the Conservative vote held steady during the 1983, 1987 and 1992 general elections at around 42 per cent of votes cast, while the Labour vote, although faced with challenges from the Liberals, the Social Democrats, and in Scotland by the SNP, rose from 27.6 per cent in 1983 to 34.4 per cent in 1992. The strike also did little to alter the status of Arthur Scargill, who continued to enjoy the support of the bulk of the membership; he was made life president in 1985. Not only that, in the aftermath of the strike he was voted in a poll of 11- to 24-year-olds in Britain as a hero alongside Martin Luther King and John F. Kennedy.[44] Indeed, one of the questions unanswered by Reid and other critics was how could a deluded Scargill convince thousands of miners to remain on strike for over a year? Were the miners equally deluded? Indeed, the decision to call off the strike by the National Executive of the NUM was only carried by three votes.

Scargill was also correct in his prediction that if the strike was lost the coal industry would go the way of other heavy industries. He had stated during the strike that there was a long-term strategy to close over 70 pits. Not only did the Government deny this, but MacGregor wrote to every member of the NUM claiming that Scargill was deceiving them by making this allegation and that there were no plans to close any more pits than had already been announced. Cabinet Papers released in 2014 indicate that MacGregor did indeed wish to close 75 pits over a period of three years.[45] Between March 1984 and March 1992, and despite Scargill's defiant claim that 'The fight to save pits will go on',[46] the number of pits fell from 170 to 50 and the workforce contracted from 181,000 to 46,000. By early 1994, there were only 17 deep mines left in Britain, employing fewer than 11,000 miners.[47] The result was the social and economic annihilation of mining communities the length and breadth of the country; even the non-striking districts such as Nottinghamshire were not immune to the programme of closure. Formerly prosperous communities were plunged

43 J. McLean, *Hopeless but Not Serious: The Autobiography of the Urban Voltaire* (Edinburgh, 1996), 158.
44 Milne, *Enemy Within*, 32.
45 BBC News, 3 January 2014.
46 M. Jacobs, 'End of the Coal Strike', *Economic and Political Weekly*, 20 (1985), 443–4.
47 Richards, *Miners on Strike*, 2.

into poverty and despair. A 1994 study by the Coalfield Communities Campaign, based on a survey of 900 ex-miners, demonstrated the degree of that despair. It found that more than 50 per cent of ex-miners were still out of work more than a year after being forced from the pit. Some of them were on retraining schemes, but the majority remained unemployed. Of those who were working, the survey showed that almost half had taken pay cuts.[48] One only needs to tour the former mining villages and towns of Ayrshire and Fife to appreciate the social devastation that has resulted from the loss of employment. Alcoholism, drug taking, petty thieving and high divorce rates are the consequences. Thus, it was not the strike per se that led to the decline of the NUM and mining in general, but the government's plan to shift energy creation from coal to gas and nuclear power. Reid had argued during the UCS work-in the social rather than the economic case for keeping the yards open, but he failed to make this argument in the case of the miners.

On the question of violence on the picket line he chose to attack with justification some of the hard-line treatment of miners refusing to strike, but had little to say on police violence. The violence was extensive, as Professor Victor Allen, secretary of the unofficial Miners' Forum, points out:

> Pickets in general carried no weapons. Sometimes they tried to stop the movement of cars with their hands, but in the main, they simply used their voices. The police who used truncheons, dogs and horses to inflict punishment and generate fear largely determined the means, the extent and the intensity of the violence. There were many instances of pickets being kicked after being thrown to the ground, of the windscreens of pickets' cars being smashed by crowbars, and, after Orgreave, of riot police rampaging through Yorkshire villages, breaking into houses and damaging family property in pursuit of pickets. It was state sponsored vandalism. The treatment of the strikers was gratuitously violent while their attitude to women supporters was crudely and offensively sexist. One woman later recorded that the police had called them 'Scargill's slags'.[49]

The degree of police violence was recognised in 1991 when the South Yorkshire Police force paid out compensation amounting to £425,000 to

---

48 BBC, *Inside Out*, 2 February 2004.
49 Allen, 'The Year-Long Miners' Strike', 283.

39 miners, represented by Bhatt Murphy Solicitors, who were arrested during the picket at the Orgreave coking plant. This was for 'assault, false imprisonment and malicious prosecution'.[50] Other less well known, but no less bloody battles between pickets and police took place in other parts of the country; for example, in Maltby, South Yorkshire in September 1984, where 6,000 pickets were met by 700 policemen in full riot gear.[51]

While Reid was correct to point to the fact that the workers had voted for the UCS work-in (although not for him and the other stewards as leaders), that every week a mass meeting was held of all those involved to decide on the best way forward and that this level of consultation maintained the solidarity of those taking part in the work-in.[52] However, there were major differences between the two struggles. First, the miners' strike was a national rather than a local action, involving 180,000 men rather than under 10,000 in Clydebank; secondly, given the numbers involved and the geographical spread of mining districts, weekly ballots were impossible at a national level; thirdly, the UCS workers were paid a weekly wage and never faced the same privations of the miners, many of whom were starved back to work; fourthly, they did not face the same violent provocations from the police that the miners faced, and neither did they experience the level of negative reporting from the tabloid press, which demonised Scargill, whereas it had previously lionised Reid; and, finally, the miners faced a government far more resolute in pursuit of victory than that of Heath. Thus, it seems rather disingenuous to offer comparisons between two entirely different disputes.

What led to the failure of the miners' strike was not as Reid claims the refusal to hold a ballot: that was a side issue highlighted by the media and government to undermine the resolve of the strikers; the reasons lie elsewhere. First and foremost is the determination of the Thatcher government to defeat the miners using the full panoply of resources at its disposal: coercive – the police – and economic – the withdrawal of social security benefits for striking miners and their families. But it was not simply a political struggle, it was also an environmental one with the government intent on shifting the supply of energy from the contentious coal industry to nuclear power and gas. A leaked Cabinet memo of November 1979 showed clearly that: 'A nuclear programme would have the

---

50 Bhatt Murphy Solicitors, London. See https://www.bhattmurphy.co.uk/about-bhatt-murphy.
51 BBC News, 21 September 1984.
52 Letter to *The Times*, 26 May 1984.

advantage of removing a substantial portion of electricity production from the dangers of industrial action by coal miners and transport workers'. In this sense the coal strike was itself part of the government's environmental strategy. The Tories were determined not only 'to reduce the size of the coal industry and to replace it with nuclear power but to break the back of the miners' union in the process'. Nigel Lawson, Chancellor of the Exchequer, explained the government's purpose when he described the huge £4 billion cost of the strike (a sum much greater than the intended savings from pit closures) as a 'worthwhile investment for the good of the nation'.[53]

The other fatal weakness was internal; and was the product of the differing histories and traditions of the various coal fields. The NUM had a decentralised regional structure, and certain regions historically were more militant than others. Scotland, South Wales and Kent were militant and had some communist officials, whereas the Midland counties of Derbyshire and Nottinghamshire were traditionally much less strike prone. During the 1972 and 1974 strikes the miners had been united in their demand for across-the-board wage increases. However, as mentioned above, the introduction in 1978 of area incentive wage schemes led to major cracks in that solidarity. Those working in coal rich seams were earning more with less effort than those miners in loss-making pits in places like Scotland and South Wales. Thus, when a national strike was called to defend jobs and communities there were already observable divisions among miners, which the government must have been aware of, and were more than willing to exploit. The failure to mount national strikes in 1982 and 1983 were ominous signals of what the future might hold if one was declared.

The divisions within mining communities were also mirrored in the wider trade union movement. In 1972 and 1974, the miners had the support of workers in transport, the docks, steel and those employed in power stations; in 1984–5 that support was decidedly patchy in its distribution. The TUC appeared paralysed with fear about breaching Tory anti-trade union laws which prohibited key forms of supportive industrial action, such as sympathetic strikes. Other individual trade unions, excepting railway workers, seafarers and key sections of the TGWU, did not respond to the NUM call for support, and in some cases, as with the leaders of the electricians' union, opposed the miners in their struggle.

There were of course mistakes made by the NUM leadership, particularly as to the timing of the strike. Although heavily pushed

---

53 Jacobs, 'Coal Strike', 443–4.

from the periphery, the leadership could have kept negotiations going with the NCB until the autumn, as the worst time to have a coal strike was in spring and summer, particularly with 2.5 million tons of coal stockpiled at Britain's power stations: enough for a 'UK-wide power endurance of twenty-eight weeks'.[54] Then there was the failure to settle with the NCB in October 1984 when the pit deputies were prepared to support the strike and MacGregor announced the sacking of any deputy who refused to cross NUM picket lines. This provided the basis for a settlement as all pits were legally required to have on site a deputy where men were working underground. While McGahey was prepared to settle, Scargill was in no mood to compromise and thus the dispute rumbled on and on towards predictable defeat. By 27 February 1985, 46.7 per cent of Scottish NUM members were working; on 3 March, the dispute was called off.[55] Scargill had put the politics of the strike before the economics of striking in his desire to bring down the Tory government. If he had a major fault, then it was clearly his commitment to principle over pragmatism.

While mistakes were made by the NUM, they do not vindicate Reid; his analysis was flawed, and his predictions were wrong. All his interventions did was to earn him the contempt of certain sections of the left. At the 1985 Scottish Trades Union Congress the miners' delegate, Jim McCafferty, won a round of applause from delegates when he said he was sure 'everyone present shared his "contempt" for the morality which the former UCS work-in leader had exhibited in his opinion column during the pit strike';[56] however, Reid was simply articulating the position of his close political ally and long-time friend, the Labour leader Neil Kinnock. Kinnock's strategy was to distance himself from the strike and the picket line violence, while at the same time criticising the government for its handling of the dispute. This was the line adopted by Labour's shadow cabinet, in contrast to the Party's NEC, which gave 'unequivocal support to the miners'. Kinnock only infrequently and 'discreetly' visited the picket line, although he went along to Wylfa power station in North Wales where his brother-in-law was organising support for the pickets.[57] He came under increasing attacks from the left in the Party for his reticence and

---

54 D. Stewart, 'A Tragic Fiasco? The 1984/5 Miners' Strike in Scotland', *Scottish Labour History*, 41 (2006), 39.
55 Stewart, 'A Tragic Fiasco?', 44–5.
56 *Glasgow Herald*, 11 March 1985.
57 E. Jones, *Neil Kinnock* (1994), 64.

refusal to attend miners' rallies. As far as Tony Benn was concerned, the 'Labour leadership has totally failed to support the working class when in struggle'.[58] In an article in the *Guardian*, Reid fiercely defended Kinnock from attacks from those critics within the Labour Party.[59] Later, in his column in the *Daily Record*, he attacked left MPs who viewed Kinnock as 'lightweight', saying:

> I resent the malicious attacks on Neil Kinnock which suggests he is a lightweight leader. It just isn't true. He has intellectual depth, wide-ranging interests, firmly held beliefs which haven't hardened into the futility of dogma. He also has courage and all the qualities to be an outstanding leader of the Labour Party.[60]

In an interview with the journalist, Ajay Close, some ten years on, the point was made that in criticising Scargill's stewardship of the miners' strike 'the Labour leadership was cheering him all the way, and even encouraged him to publish the same sentiments in the *Guardian*, guaranteeing the widest possible circulation'.[61] However, the emphasis on the failure of the NUM to hold a ballot led him to support one aspect of the widely condemned industrial relations reforms introduced by the Thatcher government – that is, holding a ballot before a strike could take place: 'Trade union ballots are here to stay, and maybe in the long run the best thing that has happened to British trade unionism'.[62] Thus, he was prepared to sign away one of the most effective weapons the trade union movement possessed – the lightning strike: something which management or government could not prepare for.

The relationship between Reid and Kinnock forged in difficult circumstances of the miners' strike was to grow closer during the fight to expel Trotskyist groups like Militant Tendency that had infiltrated the Labour Party in the 1970s. For Reid, one of the appeals of Labour was the diversity of opinion tolerated inside the Party. This was a strength, argued Reid, that should not be diluted. In a long, often rambling interview with Michael Foot, he attacked Militant as Leninists who shared the Labour right's instinctive opposition to dissent: 'Democratic socialism embraces dissent. A corporate body that prohibits internal dissent cannot be a vehicle for

---

58   Quoted in Jones, *Kinnock*, 69.
59   *Guardian*, 16 July 1984.
60   *Daily Record*, 3 February 1986.
61   *Spectrum*, 27 March 1994.
62   *Daily Record*, 20 January 1986.

socialism. The right of dissent is not a liberal luxury. Dissent produces new truths'.[63]

Although Reid held no position of authority or power within the party, he used his position as a journalist to excoriate the political pretensions of the hard-line leftists, saying:

> Trotskyism could be defined as a retarded branch of Leninism ... living in a country (Russia) with a tiny working class and a massive even more backward peasantry ... their concept of political change was based on seizing and not winning power ... That the tortuous organisational methods and political structures emanating from such circumstances should be advanced as a model for the labour movement in Britain ... is on the face of it absolutely absurd ... Trotskyism ... is essentially an ideology of the alienated middle class ... how could such a ridiculous and tiny sect actually win control of ... certain constituency parties? The main responsibility lies with those Labour MPs and councillors who deliberately enclosed the party in their wards and constituencies to a small rump of supporters that would guarantee their continued domination of the local political machine.[64]

With the proscription of the Trotskyist leader of the Liverpool Council, Derek Hatton, in 1986, the Militant threat began to fade, but it took the decisive defeat of Tony Benn in the Labour Party leadership contest in 1988 by Kinnock finally to put an end to such entryist tactics by the far left. The innocuous but inclusive Rose motif had become the party symbol, replacing the Red Flag; the move of Labour to the centre ground of British politics was under way and would, as we will see, be realised first in the election of John Smith as leader and, after his untimely death in May 1994, in the election of Tony Blair as his successor two months later.

Reid not only attacked the Trotskyists and their entryist tactics but what he considered to be the 'Loony Left'. This was a rainbow coalition of feminists, gay and ethnic minorities linked to the Labour Party, who in the 1980s, particularly in London, began to challenge the dominant white, male political culture. Their political methods were controversial and it allowed the right-wing press, such as the *Daily Mail*, to ridicule their activities and by extension the Labour Party itself. A number of journalists wrote stories designed to discredit the leader of the Greater

---

63 Michael Foot, interview with Jimmy Reid (n.d.).
64 *Glasgow Herald*, 27 September 1982.

London Council (GLC) Ken Livingstone ('Red Ken') and the 'Loony Left', claiming (falsely), for instance, that the Council forced its workers to drink only Nicaraguan coffee in solidarity with that country's socialist government; that Haringey Council leader Bernie Grant had banned the use of the term 'black bin liner' and the children's rhyme 'Baa Baa Black Sheep' because they were perceived as racially insensitive. However, despite the vitriol heaped upon him by the tabloids, Livingstone did much to assist minority groups in London, including appointing the Ghanaian barrister Paul Boateng as the first black head of the Metropolitan Police Committee: policies that laid the basis of London becoming an electoral stronghold for Labour. The GLC was disbanded by the Tory government in 1986; but after a brief time as an MP, Livingstone was elected as first mayor of London in 2000.

Reid felt that while the causes were worthwhile their methods increasingly made Labour unelectable. Proof for him was the loss of Greenwich, in south-east London, which Labour had held since 1945, to the Social Democrats, in a by-election in February 1987 just prior to the general election. But in criticising these groups one cannot help feeling that his education and training in the CPGB rendered him unable to understand or constitutionally to cope with these alternative ways of politicking. As he put it: 'I don't like dressed down dungareed lassies with rounded steel-framed specs. Nor clever-dick, middle-class culture-vultures whose pretentiousness is only exceeded by their ignorance'.[65] In his dislike of the new Labour politics, Reid almost parroted the 'loony' mantra of the right-wing press, as for him the 'Loony Left' was a peculiarly London phenomenon and made up:

> of rich middle-class revolutionaries, salon Socialists from Belsize Park and other such havens of the well-to-do. The rest are a motley collection including some who took diplomas in sociology as mature students and read a smattering of philosophy ... Their campaigns against racism are conducted in such nonsensical terms as to antagonise potentially supportive white workers. They propagandise for gay rights by alienating heterosexuals. The struggle to end the undeniable injustice to women in our still male-dominated society is undermined by the shrillness of their voices which often degenerate into a barely disguised hatred of all men. They campaign against the bomb with such hysteria

---

65 *Daily Record*, 22 December 1986.

as to frighten people into the camp of the warmongers ... Their superficial analyses of complex questions are insulting ... Their half-baked juvenile ideas have nothing to do with Socialism or Labour politics ... [Labour] will lose the election in the south-east of England unless it somehow manages to smash the power and influence of the loony left in London.[66]

Perhaps it was because of his formative experiences in the politics of the left that he had always viewed the middle class with suspicion. The CPGB was a predominantly working-class political party; its members and its leaders were of the working class and while there were the odd intellectual members such as Palme Dutt, they were always viewed as suspect and unreliable. For the CPGB, Marxism was a lived experience rather than a theoretical exercise. Reid, in a later, but no less revealing, piece on Salman Rushdie's novel *Satanic Verses*, which was made the subject of a fatwah by radical Muslims and was publicly burnt, attacked the *Guardian* and the Foreign Minister Geoffrey Howe for attempting to appease the Islamists, quoting with approval a 'Cockney stalwart of the Labour movement', who said: 'When the chips are down, never trust the middle-class liberal intellectuals, particularly those who live in and around London, for they are assuredly 22 carat cowards who missed out on backbone'.[67]

By the mid-1980s, Reid's reputation as a journalist had grown, and the tabloid press began to take an interest. In 1986, a sports journalist and friend then working for the *Sun*, Ken Gallagher, told him that Australian-born Kelvin MacKenzie, editor of the paper, was keen to have a word with him. They 'met in a hotel restaurant near the Embankment'. According to Reid:

> Kelvin wanted me to work for him as a columnist. Free to write what I wanted ... I discussed the proposition with Neil Kinnock ... Neil wanted me to accept for they desperately wanted a friendly voice within the tabloid ... But Neil had decided that it would be prudent to explain everything to (Robert) Maxwell, who promptly exploded. The upshot was that I was to stay put as they didn't want to antagonise the owner of the Mirror Group ... I wrote to ... MacKenzie and briefly explained ... He wrote back saying the offer still stood ... The outcome was that I ended up writing for the *Mirror* and the *Record* at a time when contracted to

---

66 *Daily Record*, 23 February 1987.
67 *Sun*, 7 March 1989.

the production of television documentaries was a bit of a bind ... Neil's fear of antagonising Maxwell, who he thought was mad, was perfectly understandable, given the hostility to Labour of all the other mass circulation papers. But the issue (of press power) had to be faced sooner or later, and not just by Labour.[68]

At the *Record*, Reid, on a salary allegedly in excess of £50,000,[69] campaigned against warrant sales, singling out Labour councils for particular criticism. Under the Law of Diligence (a law peculiar to Scotland), someone in arrears of rent or rates could be subject to public auctions of their household goods by sheriff's officers to erase some, if not all, of their debts. These debt collectors appointed by the court were permitted to enter a debtor's home and poind (put a value on) items, which would be subject to a later, public, sale under warrant. It was a law aimed at the poorest in Scottish society and Reid saw its implementation as an affront to socialist values, saying, 'Neil Kinnock makes great play about socialist morality based on love and compassion. Yet, as he speaks, the Labour chairman of finance (Tony Worthington) in Strathclyde defends and uses a law which is totally devoid of love and compassion'.[70] Reid and his wife had themselves experienced an attempted warrant sale at their home. On Friday, 3 October 1986, 'two men came to my door with a notice from the Strathclyde Regional Council. The Sheriff Principal had authorised Sheriff's Officers to "poind, seize and secure" my furniture unless we paid, within four days, £16 rates arrears. Owed from ... 1982'. Reid wrote: 'We know nothing of these arrears ... [and] I will pay nothing until someone proves to me that I owe anything'.[71] Three years later it was being used extensively by Labour councils to punish those refusing to pay the Poll Tax; actions that Reid viewed as 'unforgiveable'.[72] The practice was abolished in 2001 by the Scottish parliament following cross-party support for a private members' bill introduced by Tommy Sheridan of the Scottish Socialist Party.

Reid was promoted by Maxwell from the *Record* to the *Mirror*, grandiosely announced by the latter in typically vainglorious manner:

---

68 Reid, *As I Please*, 53–4; *Glasgow Herald*, 19 October 1995. However, it may have been 1985 as the Diary column in the *Glasgow Herald* for 11 March mentions that Reid had been approached by the *Sun* 'with a view to his writing a political column'.
69 *Glasgow Herald*, 11 March 1985.
70 *Daily Record*, 13 August 1986.
71 *Daily Record*, 6 October 1986.
72 *Sun*, 4 July 1989.

'Publisher Robert Maxwell is pleased to announce that Jimmy Reid ... will be joining the Daily Mirror to write his own column'.[73] The editorial staff were incredulous when Maxwell decided to put Reid's column on industrial and political affairs on page two of the Saturday edition, a part of the paper normally reserved for leisure.[74] However, editorial changes to an article he had written incensed him and he threatened to resign. A compromise was reached between the editor of the paper and Reid: the latter received a 'grovelling' apology, in return the editor remained in post. Editorial interference was becoming more common and the final straw for Reid was when an article attacking Thatcherism was spiked; it was suggested that it was the result of an intervention from the management of the Mirror Group. Reid worked for a few more weeks, filing his last copy towards the end of April 1987, before moving to the newly launched *Scottish Sun* by invitation from its first editor, Jack Irvine, over a boozy lunch in Glasgow. Irvine had calculated that the *Sun* needed a quintessentially Scottish voice if it was to entice the *Daily Record* readers to desert their morning print fix and the iconic Reid more than fitted the bill.[75] This time he did not even consult Neil Kinnock;[76] the Poll Tax, party modernisation and Scottish home rule became areas of major disagreements between the two men and led to their estrangement – so much so that in 1997 he refused an invitation to a fund-raising dinner that Kinnock was to speak at, 'denouncing him as the man who abandoned Clause IV'.[77]

Taking Rupert Murdoch's shilling without a hint of a pang of conscience,[78] was for some on the left a step too far, and constituted to them a great betrayal of all that Reid up till then had stood for. As Ian Bell put it:

> It was all too typical of the man, who seemed unable to grasp the distinction of a principled defence of his integrity and hiring himself out to a newspaper group which is blind to the word and which, moreover, has done most in the past twenty years to destroy all that he once stood for.[79]

73 R. Edwards, *Goodbye to Fleet Street* (London, 1988), 244.
74 Edwards, *Goodbye to Fleet Street*, 244.
75 J. Irvine, interview with Knox (2016).
76 *Glasgow Herald*, 15 June 1986.
77 K. MacAskill, *Jimmy Reid: A Scottish Political Journey* (London, 2017), 263.
78 Irvine, interview with Knox.
79 *Observer*, 22 April 1990.

His former UCS comrade and friend Sammy Gilmore put it more forcefully, saying: 'He works for the dirtiest, lousiest, scabbyist newspaper proprietor in the world'.[80]

Gilmore delivered a commonly held verdict of those on the left over the quality of the journalism in the tabloid, but Reid proved himself to be no puppet or token leftie of Rupert Murdoch. His column in the *Sun* continued to follow the same trajectory as it had done in the Labour-leaning *Daily Record*, pointing out the pretentiousness of the middle-class intellectual and commenting on the trivia of everyday life and the odd sporting event. This went down well with the *Sun* management, but what did not go down so well was the fact that he pulled no punches when it came to attacking the Thatcher government.

Reid, as we have seen, drew a distinction between the paternalism of Tories, such as his old boss David Robertson, and old school 'one-nation' Tory politicians like Harold Macmillan and Iain Macleod, and the bare-knuckle free-market values of Thatcherism. He saw the former as compassionate and the latter as unkind and callous and wasn't afraid to say so: 'Thatcher and Thatcherism have fused together into an overall impression – insensitivity, hardness, even cruelty'.[81] Moreover, he passionately defended the right to free speech and attacked the Tory government for politicising the media and the civil service. As far as Reid was concerned it was the duty of a journalist to hold those in power to account. All this was known to MacKenzie, but on Irvine's advice he offered Reid a column in the national edition at a much greater salary and access to a readership of approximately four million per day. However, it wasn't really surprising given the *Sun*'s support for the Tories that his column lasted barely a year before it was pulled. According to Irvine, MacKenzie grew frustrated and tired of Reid's continued attacks on Thatcher. After three successive weeks in late 1989 of criticising the Iron Lady, MacKenzie, in his trademark pugnacious and colourful language, declared to Irvine: 'I'm fucking fed up, can he not write about something fucking else?' On the fourth week, and on the advice of Irvine, Reid complied with the request and filed a different kind of copy. However, a week later he was back on the attack, leading an exasperated MacKenzie to say to Irvine: 'fuck it, dump him'. And he was duly informed by Irvine over the telephone that he was dumped, to be replaced at the *Scottish Sun* by the former Labour MP turned Scottish nationalist Jim Sillars.[82]

80 *Guardian*, 31 August 1988.
81 *Daily Record*, 21 May 1986.
82 Irvine, interview with Knox.

His sacking did not unduly worry Reid, as he had other means of making a good living. His reputation as a no holds barred, punchy and controversial columnist naturally led to frequent appearances on television. He had, of course, been a guest on talk shows in the 1970s and 1980s, such as *Parkinson*, and had popped up as a talking head on various documentaries, but in the succeeding decade he made the transition to having his own show. One of the most popular was *Reid about Scotland*, shown on Scottish Television (STV) and co-written with the intellectual left-wing nationalist Tom Nairn, author of the hugely influential book *The Break-up of Britain* (1977). The programmes were presented as a travelogue, aimed at a popular audience, but nevertheless provided insights into Reid's interpretation of national identity, of what made the Scots, their landscape, their culture and traditions so unique. The underlying theme of the programme was the phoney versus the real Scotland. It was an attack on the tartan tack, 'the hail to us whaes like us' mentality, the dewy-eyed Kailyard view of the Scottish Highlands: in other words, the commercialisation of national identity. To Reid, Scotland may have been a small country that had punched above its weight in terms of its contribution to world civilisation, but it was still a society marked by inequality, poverty and unemployment and that the true Scotland lay with the working people whose sacrifices in war and peace had made the nation what it is today.

The more controversial programmes related to the Soviet Union. In a certain sense, much of Reid's print and television journalism in the decades after 1976 represent his attempt to come to terms with his own development as a Marxist and communist as well as with the nature of the Communist Party in Britain and in the Soviet Union. In 1972, when Reid first visited the Soviet Union as a guest of the ruling elite, he was feted as a hero. When he returned in October–November 1987, as a broadcaster and journalist for the programme *Reid about the USSR*, the situation had changed. His reason for returning was to witness at first hand the USSR during the period of Perestroika. Reid and a Scottish TV crew spent eight weeks filming extensively and talking to ordinary people the length and breadth of the USSR from Kazakhstan to Latvia and Georgia. According to Anita Cox, the production assistant on the programme, some things shocked Reid. First, the cold. When he had been there in 1972 it had been an exceptionally warm summer and, typical of the Scots, Reid complained of the heat! During October–November, the temperature was never higher than minus 10 Celsius. It was so cold that while covering the 70th anniversary celebrations of the Russian Revolution, standing near to Lenin's tomb in Red Square, in the freezing conditions his jaw kept locking. Secondly, he was 'shocked at the disrepair of the country'. Nothing seemed to work, whether it was a television or a phone, and there was little in the shops to buy or to eat in restaurants. The privation of the Russian people was brought home to him when he interviewed a leading heart surgeon in Moscow. After the interview, Reid and his crew were invited back to his tiny one-bedroomed flat, which he shared with his wife and teenage daughter; he also had been on the waiting list for a car for six years. To Reid, 'the country was 20 years behind the West economically'.[83] Thirdly, he was shocked that Stalin was still venerated by ordinary Russians. Standing in the Stalin Museum in Gori, Georgia, he stood open-mouthed while Georgians openly displayed their reverence for the former dictator. But he was less shocked and more moved by the openness and generosity of the people of the Soviet Union and their history. In a cemetery in Leningrad it was so cold that the jackets of the crew iced up. That discomfort failed to prevent Reid and his crew being moved to tears by the narrative of a one-legged female survivor of the siege of the city by the Nazis during the Second World War.[84]

On his return to Britain, Reid was called to the Admiralty for a debriefing,[85] which was not unusual for journalists returning from the USSR, although he was under no compulsion to accede to the request. What that concerned is locked away in the secret vaults of the security services, but shortly after this he was invited to address 'a black-tie dinner in the Royal Artillery mess, Woolwich, with about forty flag generals and air officers. The letter was from Lt General Sir Anthony Walker, KCB, and Deputy Chief of Defence Staff'. His memories of national service had coloured his views of the brass hats as a bunch of weak-minded, chinless, public school, boy wonders – so it was with some trepidation that he agreed to speak. However, he was pleasantly surprised: 'The dinner was splendid', which one might expect, but less expected was the discourse: 'an intelligent discussion. There were no Blimps. Instead there was intelligence and a firm grasp of the complexities of a deadly critical situation in the USSR'.[86]

What, then, of the trajectory of Reid's journalistic career and politics in the decade after 1979? Undoubtedly, his was a tale of personal success,

---

83 *Scotsman*, 23 May 1988.
84 A. Cox, interview with Knox (2015).
85 B. Atherton and L. Atherton, interview with Knox (2015).
86 Reid, *Power without Principles*, 50–1; *Glasgow Herald*, 5 October 1995.

in which he gained – or perhaps regained – a significant platform in, first, Scottish and, for a period, British politics. But the close alignment of a deep personal morality and a coherent Marxist world view that characterised his politics during the UCS crisis evaporated during the 1980s. There was no sense in which Reid deepened his personal philosophy through, for instance, asking what 'democracy' might mean in different organisational settings. Far from Thatcher's use of state power provoking a development in his understanding of state theory, he regressed to a consistent and sometimes wearisome attack on Thatcher as an individual. The moral outrage that lay behind his early conversion to Marxism remained intact into his middle years but now without a theoretical understanding, or a party discipline, to give it focus and consistency. To bridle against the pretensions of intellectuals inside the CPGB in the 1970s was about maintaining the Party's close identification with and its roots in popular struggles. By the late 1980s, to reprise such sentiments in the right-wing press was to become complicit in a wider narrative that equated expertise with elitism. Again, there is no sense that Reid reflected on his popular instincts and how they might contribute to the neo-liberal agenda on sale for 50p in the *Sun*. Career success also came at some personal cost as former political allies fell away and friendships became strained or broken: a process which was compounded by his stance on the worker occupation of the American multi-national Caterpillar company's tractor-making factory in Tannochside, Uddingston, North Lanarkshire, in January 1987.

As the former leaders of the legally dubious work-in at the UCS yards in 1971–2, both Airlie, as a member of the NEC of the AEU, and Reid, as a journalist, in 1987 were advising workers occupying the factory, to prevent its closure and relocation, to obey the law and end their occupation of the plant. As Reid put it: 'I tell you this: if you continue. I'm convinced that your campaign will disintegrate … in a matter of days … I'm absolutely and utterly convinced of it'. The workers failed to heed the advice, one occupier saying that: 'right now the union … is taking my livelihood away from me. Because we'll have nothing to bargain [with]'.[87] John Gillen, another one of the occupiers, stated it more forcibly:

> The AEU will continue to support the dispute. They don't support the dispute at the moment because it's illegal. So, if we go out on

---

87 See J. Foster and C. Woolfson, *Track Record: The Story of the Caterpillar Occupation* (London, 1988), 200–1. For film footage of Reid's and Airlie's statements, see the Caterpillar Workers' Legacy Group Digital Archive.

the street, there is only one way of preventing stuff coming out and in ... it's a *mass picket*. And we all know what happens to mass pickets. The first thing that's going to happen is the AEU are going to say – *that's* illegal. We can't support that. So, with a position of six of us taking our turns standing there, water running out of our arse, waving at lorries as they go by, waving at the staff as they go in in the morning – talk about the *continuation will kill us*? We're stone dead the minute the occupation ends. Everybody knows that. [italics in the original][88]

The occupation ended after 103 days, on Sunday, 26 April. It was called off after the Caterpillar company obtained an eviction order and managers were allowed through the gates the following day. Everything was cleared from the site by October, including plant and machinery, men and women.[89]

The shift from the politics of resistance to the more pragmatic politics of compromise was a measure of how far Reid at this time had travelled to the centre ground of British politics. His relationship with Kinnock was the catalyst in this transformation, and through him Reid was able to exert a fair amount of influence in Labour Party circles and in the media. However, that was about to end following the unexpected defeat of Kinnock in the 1992 general election, which led to his resignation as party leader. Reid was otherwise minded, accusing, in a letter to *The Times*, the 'union barons' and 'some members of the shadow cabinet' of hatching a plot to oust Kinnock from leadership.[90] Whether this was true or not a new leadership emerged committed to a social market economic agenda in which the party and its history and its values were refashioned. In practice, this involved a shift to the centre right of politics by Labour, a development which was to have a major political impact on Reid. He experienced almost a road to Damascus episode in which he rediscovered his old values; something that took him on new and for him surprising political pathways. That journey reminds us that, politically, Reid was never static, his politics were constantly evolving even if they lacked the theoretical rigour of his time in the CPGB. But despite this he would not be forgiven by old comrades for his stance on the miners' strike and for his willingness to take Murdoch's shilling.

---

88   Foster and Woolfson, *Track Record*, 202.
89   *Glasgow Evening Times*, 19 February 2014.
90   *The Times*, 18 April 1992.

8

Reborn

The surprising defeat of Labour by the Tories in the 1992 general election called for the election of a new leader, the mantle of which fell on John Smith. However, his tenure was tragically cut short when he died from a heart attack in May 1994, and was replaced by Tony Blair. Under Blair, Labour underwent a political metamorphosis from a left-wing party to a centre-right one, repudiating in the process past cherished principles and policies, such as Clause Four of the constitution which committed it to the 'common ownership of the means of production'. Nationalisation was out and the free market, or social market as Blair would have it, was in. The intention was to allow a strongly deregulated market to flourish using the extra wealth it generated to fund improvements in public services – it became known as 'New Labour'. The question is how far would Reid, given his political record during the 1980s, coalesce with Blair's new vision for Labour's future?

In a revealing encounter with the late Tam Dalyell MP as they both left the funeral of John Smith, the former asked Reid who he was going to vote for in the forthcoming leadership contest. Dalyell said he was giving his vote to John Prescott, while Reid replied saying he was in favour of Margaret Beckett, then acting leader of the Labour Party. Thus, from the outset, there was opposition expressed by Reid to Blair and this only intensified as time wore on and the New Labour agenda was rolled out. As far as Reid was concerned:

> New Labour from the start, was not so much a disappointment as a disaster. It accepted the Thatcherite economic strategy which meant it couldn't possibly tackle the social degradations of the Thatcher years. In fact, New Labour locked itself into an inexorable economic system that would intensify these degradations. New

Labour is able to do things no Tory government would have got away with.[1]

Some of the party faithful, particularly in Scotland, who, although unhappy regarding Labour's political direction under Blair, clung on to the hope that Gordon Brown, erstwhile editor of *The Red Paper on Scotland* (1975), once Prime Minister, would reverse the slide towards the right. Reid had no truck with this fanciful thinking, saying:

> I don't think New Labour can be changed, power is now too centralised in the party. Talk of Gordon Brown leading the fight to resurrect Labour principles is risible. He was and is a major player in turning Labour into a party of the Right ... Brown is now the darling of the City. The fire in his belly was extinguished years ago. Oh what a blessing it would be to have an independent Scottish Labour Party free of Tammany Hall.[2]

In spite of his misgivings over the leadership, Reid agreed to campaign for Labour in Govan during the run-up to the general election of 1997. However, he made it clear from the start that he would 'voice criticisms of New Labour', which was surprisingly accepted by the local constituency party. At a meeting, he articulated the thought that after the formation of a New Labour government 'the political fight for the future of Britain would take place within the Labour Party itself'. Then, as he put it, 'the excrement hit the fan. From on high New Labour barred [him] from speaking at any other meetings. [He] didn't care. What [he] said was true ...'.[3] In fact, Reid had already made his mind up regarding his future in the Labour Party three months before the general election, 'having become convinced the man [Blair] and those around him were essentially Thatcherites'.[4] As it turned out, Labour won the election by a landslide and Blair was duly elected Prime Minister, with Brown Chancellor of the Exchequer. But as if to bear out Reid's views on the Thatcherite nature of New Labour, the first politician sought out by Blair was the Iron Lady herself. Indeed, according to Thatcher, Tony Blair and New Labour was her greatest political achievement.[5]

1   Reid, *Power without Principles*, xi–xii.
2   Reid, *Power without Principles*, 361; *Herald*, 6 January 1999.
3   Reid, *Power without Principles*, 245; *Herald*, 3 December 1997.
4   Reid, *Power without Principles*, 271; *Herald*, 11 March 1998.
5   *Independent*, 8 April 2013.

However, in Govan, the election was marred by allegations of electoral fraud. The successful Labour candidate, multimillionaire businessman Mohammad Sarwar, along with his co-accused Mumtaz Hussain, another Glasgow businessman, was accused by the *News of the World* only a few days after his victory of bribing an independent candidate standing against him, Badar Islam, as well as adding to the register of electors the names and false qualifying addresses of at least four people. Despite declaring his innocence, claiming that the £5,000 given to Badar was a loan not a bribe, Sarwar was suspended by the Labour Party and deprived of the right to represent the party at any level, being permanently 'paired' by the Whip's Office as a technical justification of his non-appearance in the Commons. After two years he was finally exonerated at the High Court in Edinburgh and re-elected MP for Govan in the 2001 general election. But even before the 1997 election had taken place there had been acrimony within Labour ranks over who should be put forward as Prospective Parliamentary Candidate (PPC), with allegations being bandied about regarding vote-rigging and racism. The Govan Labour Party's choice was Mike Watson, who had seen his constituency of Glasgow Central disappear owing to boundary changes. Under party rules, Watson should have been awarded the new Govan constituency, but a neighbouring MP, Jimmy Dunnachie, whose constituency was also altered in boundary changes, declared his intention to seek selection. His decision triggered a contest which created the opportunity for Sarwar to throw his hat into the ring. Ill health forced Dunnachie to withdraw from the contest, leaving the Sarwar and Watson camps to go head to head for the nomination during the bitter years 1995 to 1996. The *Herald* stated that it was 'a time of extraordinary mud-slinging, and some of Watson's supporters were accused of going over the top. But accusations of dirty tricks cut both ways, with allegations of mass sign-ups into the party of members of the Asian community'.[6] In the first ballot, Watson emerged victorious, but only by the narrowest of margins – one vote. There was 'fury in the Sarwar camp' and the Labour Executive ordered a rerun of the election, which was held six months later, and which Sarwar won comfortably by 82 votes.[7] Such was the bitter aftertaste within the Govan party that Watson's supporters refused to campaign for Mr Sarwar in the run-up to the general election.[8]

6   *Herald*, 29 March 1999.
7   *Herald*, 29 March 1999.
8   *Scotsman*, 29 March 1997.

As a member of the Govan Labour Party, Reid had 'supported' and 'campaigned' for Sarwar's selection as PPC.[9] He used his column in the *Herald* to condemn the Govan Labour Party and extend sympathy for the accused, saying: 'I believe Mohammad Sarwar is more sinned against than sinner'.[10] As far as Reid was concerned:

> The Labour Party in Govan stinks. It has stunk for many years ... If Mr Blair, Government and the Labour Party are wise they should dissolve the whole machine and expel the pack of them ... What we see is the old Tammany Hall world of labour corruption in west central Scotland ... Labour in Glasgow Govan ... is divorced from its own people, the party is pledged to serve.[11]

Sarwar was in his view stitched up by New Labour and left hung out to dry:

> The serious allegations against Sarwar came only days after the election. He was accused of corruption, electoral fraud, and goodness knows what. Having investigated previous allegations against him that were proven to be false – that's what brought me into the case in the first instance – I presumed his innocence until or unless his guilt was proven. Blair took the opposite view. He presumed his guilt until his innocence was proven. That was nearly a year ago and neither a civil nor criminal case has been brought to court.
>
> If Sarwar is guilty of fraud and corruption then let him be driven from public life. But if he is innocent, then some people have their sins to answer for, and answer they must. The only alternative to his guilt is that he was stitched up, and if this is the case the culprits will be found in the ranks of New Labour. I'm convinced New Labour has a vested interest in postponing a conclusion, or would want to find Sarwar guilty of something, almost anything. Justice doesn't matter. The man and his family don't matter. The prestige of the leader is all that matters. And yet again there is this resonance of Stalinism in the thirties. The arrogance of New Labour apparatchiks apparently knows no bounds.[12]

---

9 *Herald*, 3 March 1999.
10 *Herald*, 3 December 1997.
11 *Herald*, 27 May 1997.
12 *Herald*, 8 April 1998.

Although he was not personally close to Sarwar, Reid did not come forward to endorse him as a PPC without first checking out his record as an employer in the cash and carry sector, which he found to be exemplary. He was informed by Davie Stark, chairman of the Scottish Labour Party and trade group officer for the TGWU's food and drinks division, that Sarwar was the only cash and carry employer in the west of Scotland who recognised and negotiated with a trade union and actually paid above the going rate.[13] He also spoke at a number of morale-boosting rallies on behalf of Sarwar eventually going on to give evidence for the defence at his trial in February and March 1999 at the High Court in Edinburgh. To him the Sarwar case was not simply an injustice to an individual party member, it was also another example of the control freakery favoured by the New Labour leadership and symptomatic of the degree to which party had become centralised. As far as he was concerned, 'Democracy in the party has been effectively destroyed'.[14] This worrying development he saw extending into the new Scottish devolved parliament in Edinburgh, which from the outset, he argued, lacked proper autonomy and was 'enmeshed in Westminster's culture'.[15] The 'new' consensus politics promised at the opening of the Scottish parliament was for Reid nothing more than chimera:

> When Blair became leader I believed it was too late to stop Scottish devolution without tearing apart the Scottish Labour movement. But his grasp of what it really means is, as with many other things, extremely superficial. To him it meant a Scottish Parliament that he could control as he controls Westminster; a Welsh Assembly that would endorse his agenda without a quibble; a London Mayor that would do his bidding without a qualm. It was assumed he would control all areas of government in Britain through his command of the Labour Party machine in Britain.
>
> To do this he had first to destroy Labour's traditional democracy based on a federal system of autonomous, self-governing, affiliated units. This has been more or less accomplished. Labour's National Executive now plays second fiddle to the leader's office; all regional officials are appointed in London. The Scottish Labour Party is still considered a region of UK Labour, and not a nation;

---

13 Information from Brian McGeachan.
14 *Herald*, 30 December 1998.
15 *Herald*, 10 April 2000.

devolution an' a' an' a'. The UK Labour Conference is relegated to an annual theatrical production, orchestrated for television, crammed with cheerleaders; it pays excessive homage to the leader, and his supporting thespians. The branches are stripped of effective power. Amorphous policy groups create an image of democracy without substance. The only relationship encouraged is that between the leader and the led, with nothing in between to curb his authority.[16]

To maintain an iron grip on personnel and policy, New Labour acted to control the selection of parliamentary candidates for the first Scottish elections. It was a case of jobs for the boys and girls, as long as they sung from the New Labour hymn sheet. The task was given to Rosemary McKenna who was 'virtually appointed, nay anointed, New Labour's candidate for Kilsyth and Cumbernauld, by Tony Blair himself. The sitting MP, Norman Hogg, had been re-adopted. At the eleventh hour Norman was told to get lost, or words to that effect. Who told him? Who knows?' According to Reid, she was instructed by the Scottish Executive to draw up a list of 200-plus potential candidates. A list of 229 names was faxed to London and when returned sixty names had been deleted. 'The list of 169 was made public last week. It is full of Blairites, leaving constituency parties without a real choice', and includes her daughter and friends of Gordon Brown, such as Douglas and Wendy Alexander.[17] Thus, he concluded, that 'those who had been accepted as Labour candidates for the Scottish Parliament had all been approved by New Labour brass hats in London. Without their approval they wouldn't have been on the list'.[18]

According to Reid, those with the courage to speak out against the New Labour project faced non-selection as candidates, or were demoted, or sacked. He raised the case of dissenters such as Dennis Canavan in Scotland, and Rhodri Morgan in Wales, both long-standing campaigners for devolution. The latter was a critic of New Labour's attempts to introduce internal markets in public services, and, as such, was brushed aside twice in his attempt to become the (then titled) First Secretary for Wales in favour of more government-friendly candidates. In Scotland, Dennis Canavan, when the first elections to the Scottish Parliament were held in 1999, was rejected by the New Labour leadership as an official Labour candidate, in

---

16 *Herald*, 22 November 1999.
17 *Herald*, 17 June 1998.
18 *Herald*, 8 March 1999.

spite of the fact that he enjoyed the support of 97 per cent of local party members in Falkirk West.[19] Rejection led him to stand as an Independent, an act which led to his expulsion from the party. Canavan had the last laugh, as he won his seat with almost 55 per cent of the vote, the largest majority of any Member of the Scottish Parliament in the 1999 Scottish election.

However, it was not only the drift towards what might be best described as democratic centralism (a concept that Reid was certainly familiar with) that undoubtedly troubled him, but just as much was the ease which Labour leaders felt in the company of big business: 'New Labour is in thrall to big business, from Bernie Ecclestone to Geoffrey Robinson, the Institute of Directors to the CBI. They listen to them more than all the other social and civic organisations in this country put together. Labour Ministers now move in these circles. They think as their very wealthy friends do; try to ape their lifestyles'. The Secretary of State for Business, Peter Mandelson, later provided some support for Reid's view when he remarked that 'we [Labour] are intensely relaxed about people getting filthy rich'.[20] This was in stark contrast to New Labour's attitude towards the trade union movement:

> New Labour is going to oppose a European law that would give employees the right to be consulted on redundancies by their employers. And so the trail of betrayals continues. Why unions should be giving money to this mob baffles me ... [Indeed] In the next few weeks trade unions in Scotland will be handing over £250,000 to New Labour to help pay expenses for the Scottish Parliament elections. Public-sector unions will be giving money to a party that is cutting the throats of their members through depressed wages and redundancies.[21]

Thus, for Reid, it was a case of rewarding the rich and punishing the poor, and 'That's why many can't vote New Labour. I'm one of them'.[22]

Scottish Blairites were not slow to attack Reid. Councillor James McCarron, of Glasgow City Council, condemned him for his criticisms of Tony Blair, saying: 'I do not know what party Jimmy Reid belongs to but as far as I am concerned as a Labour Party member, good riddance.

---

19 *Herald*, 22 November 1999.
20 *Observer*, 21 December 2008.
21 *Herald*, 18 November 1998.
22 *Herald*, 17 June 1998.

The fact that he is no longer involved in Labour Party politics is among the best news received in Scottish politics for some time'.[23] Alex Gallagher, Chairman of the Largs Labour Party, was also critical, accusing him of hypocrisy:

> Jimmy Reid is critical of Tony Blair for his supposed dealings with Rupert Murdoch? But who used to write a column for Mr Murdoch's *Sun* when that paper was so ferociously anti-Labour that it could claim with some justification that it was 'The Sun Wot Won It' for the Tories? And who gave short shrift to those who had the temerity to suggest that this lucrative pastime might be seen as a teensy-weensy sell-out? Drivel can be spouted in any journalist's column, whatever the paper, whoever the paymaster.[24]

However, for Reid, staying in the Labour Party meant 'voting for the Iraq war, PFIs (private finance initiatives) economic policies that I fundamentally disagree with'. But as a political activist he had to ask himself some fundamental questions: 'What am I to do? What is the next step?'[25] Lenin had asked the same question in his 1902 pamphlet, *What is to be done?* There were a few possibilities open to Reid to continue an active political role. One option was to join the Scottish Socialist Party (SSP), which had been formed in 1988 from the remnants of the Scottish Socialist Alliance, a broad-based set of left-wing organisations. The Alliance turned itself into a political party in order to contest the first elections to the new Scottish Parliament in 1999, which saw Tommy Sheridan, then convenor of the SSP, and an outspoken opponent of the Poll Tax, elected on the Regional or List vote in Glasgow. Hugh Kerr, the recently expelled Labour MEP, arranged for Reid to meet Sheridan for lunch in the upmarket Rogano restaurant in Glasgow to discuss in a discreet manner the electoral prospects of the SSP and the hope that Jimmy would give it a 'favourable mention in his column, which he duly did'.[26] Indeed, he stated that, 'if the choice were between New Labour and the SSP I would vote for the latter'.[27] It was in some ways an unlikely alliance since Sheridan was a Trotskyist and a former member of Militant

---

23 Letter to *Herald*, 7 October 1999.
24 Letter to the *Herald*, 2 April 1998.
25 'Jimmy Reid on New Labour or SNP'. See https://www.youtube.com/watch?v=6AHnnpD4fEo.
26 *Guardian*, 12 August 2010.
27 *Herald*, 4 November 1998.

Tendency: a philosophy and an organisation that Reid had vehemently attacked in his newspaper columns. However, Sheridan, in the course of a lunch consisting of fine food and wine, and a few brandies, consumed by Kerr and Reid, was able to reassure him that the SSP was going to be a modern, open and undogmatic political party far removed from the historical sectarianism that had frustrated past attempts to unify the left in Scotland.[28] In spite of the SSP pulling off a remarkable coup in the 2003 Scottish elections, winning six seats, it was not enough. Reid decided that his future political home was to be elsewhere. It was a remarkable piece of foresight on his part as the SSP imploded in 2006 when Sheridan was accused by the *News of the World* of allegedly attending a swingers' club in Manchester and engaging in extra-marital affairs. The court case that followed saw the party disintegrate, with Sheridan eventually forming a rival left group – Solidarity.[29]

Another way of remaining active was print media. Along with other disillusioned members of the Labour Party, such as MEP Henry McCubbin, John McAllion MP and Roseanna Cunningham of the SNP, among others, he established the bi-monthly left-of-centre *Scottish Left Review* in 2000 – a not-for-profit publication which provided an inclusive, non-party forum for all the left in Scotland. The motivation for the *Review* was the concern Reid had along with others in the Scottish left that 'there had been significant changes taking place in the Scottish political scene. Labour traditionally home to the left, had dismayed many by embracing the free market and distancing itself from socialism'.[30] In spite of being a computer illiterate, according to Murray Ritchie, the political editor at the *Herald*, Reid saw the potential of the internet for mass communication and interaction at a low cost to put forward radical alternative policies and views. 'Jimmy, using his address book, convened a number of meetings and the *Scottish Left Review* was set up, primarily as a free, online magazine with printed copies available'. To one of the other founder members of the journal, Bob Thomson, 'His involvement and contacts were instrumental in keeping the magazine going in our early years. Ten years on, thanks to our readers, trade unions and individuals, the *Review* is going from strength to strength and providing that radical Scottish thinking which Jimmy envisaged and always practised himself'.[31]

28 H. Kerr, interview with Knox (2016).
29 *Guardian*, 13 August 2006.
30 *Herald*, 19 September 2000.
31 *Scottish Left Review*, 60 (2010).

The internet venture followed Reid's dismissal from the *Herald* in February 2001. According to the *Scotsman*'s media correspondent at the time, Simon Pia, the incoming editor, Mark Douglas Home, whom he had never met, sacked him by telephone while he was in Paris following the Scottish rugby team: an outing organised by Ernie Walker of the Scottish Football Association that included 'flights, a nice hotel room, a day at the races and a posh dinner',[32] as he reminded him at his 70th birthday celebrations in Haggs Castle Golf Club in Glasgow. The alleged reason was his piece on John Reid's (Scottish Secretary of State for Scotland at the time and a lapsed communist) misuse of parliamentary funds for party political/electoral purposes.[33] A report on the matter was issued on the Friday before Christmas and Reid used it to pen a damning piece on his namesake 'only for it to be spiked' – the first time this had happened to him at the *Herald*. The Scottish Media Group which owned the *Herald* were sensitive to the loss of advertising revenue from New Labour which amounted to £100,000 in 1999, and Reid as its foremost high-profile critic had to go. The article was later published in the *Guardian* on 26 January 2001.[34] As Reid put it:

> Members of the select committee had split along party lines. The majority are Labour … If the verdict had been guilty, Mr Reid would have had to resign and all hell would have been let loose in the run-up to the election: for New Labour this was something to be devoutly avoided. The select committee of MPs ruled the allegations not proven.[35]

Reid found himself working almost immediately for the *Herald*'s Scottish rival the *Scotsman*, thanks to the good offices of his friend and broadcaster David Scott,[36] as well as Alex Salmond who also left the *Herald* to work for its rival as racing correspondent, carrying on where he left off as Tony Blair's and New Labour's staunchest critic.

However, in 2005, Reid joined the SNP which was quite a remarkable step for him to take given his political history and his clash with the

---

32 *Scotsman*, 16 July 2002.
33 Elizabeth Filkin, the Parliamentary Commissioner for Standards, received a complaint regarding Reid and after an investigation found against him. However, the Select Committee on Standards and Privileges disagreed, arguing that her evidence wasn't robust enough.
34 *Scotsman*, 12 February 2001.
35 *Guardian*, 26 January 2001.
36 Scott, interview with McKinlay.

Nationalists in Dundee in 1979. Reid could argue that he had been a consistent supporter of self-government for the Scottish people throughout his active political life. In an article in Communist Party paper the *Morning Star* as far back as February 1968 he was calling for a political initiative to unite the 'great mass of the Scottish people around the demand for a Scottish parliament'.[37] However, he did not support the idea of separation. Giving Scots more control of their affairs was not the trigger to tear up the 1707 Treaty of Union and the formation again of an independent sovereign state. He also did not see the SNP as the vehicle to bring about home rule for Scotland: that task was for 'the most powerful force in Scottish life, the Scottish labour movement'. But, as he recognised, the Scottish labour movement had not given the question of nationalism serious consideration in the second half of the twentieth century.[38] In the decades after the Second World War Labour had declared itself to be a Unionist Party and it was through the agency of the British state, rather than a Scottish Assembly, that the modernisation of the socio-economic framework of the country was to be achieved. Scottish Labour's old demand for home rule had dissipated as Scots embraced enthusiastically a new form of British citizenship engineered by the creation of the welfare state and the wide-ranging programme of nationalisation by the Attlee governments of 1945–51.

But things were changing politically as slowly a realignment of the left in Scotland rallying around a radical nationalist agenda began to take place. From 1967, when Winifred Ewing of the SNP won Hamilton, Labour's safest seat in Scotland, in a by-election, the two-party system of Labour versus Tories was in trouble as the Scots reasserted their sense of national identity. Reid to his credit spotted the dangers for Labour in Scotland and advocated that: 'the main task for the Scottish Left was to win the Scottish Labour Movement for a policy of Home Rule in the form of a Devolved or Independent parliament in Edinburgh'. But his call was to fall on deaf ears, which effectively meant that 'The custodianship of Scotland's Nationalist aspirations literally fell into the hands of the Nationalists'.[39] At this point, Reid saw the SNP and separatism as 'infantile' and said so when he stood against Gordon Wilson in Dundee East in 1979.[40] However, as he became more estranged from New Labour,

---

37 Reid, *Reflections*, 73.
38 Reid, 'Not Scared to Be Ourselves', 6–7.
39 Reid, 'Not Scared to Be Ourselves', 6–7.
40 *Advertiser and Courier*, 18 April 1979.

his views on independence began to change quite radically. Following the 1992 general election, he wrote:

> What I can't understand is how Westminster MPs, including Labour MPs, can support the right of self-determination for Croats and Bosnians but not for Scots. How some of them will support a referendum on Maastricht but not for Scots to determine how they would like to be governed. If sovereignty is the name of the game then what about our sovereignty?[41]

This did not mean unequivocal support for the SNP as the party of independence. As Reid explained: 'I have believed for years that Scotland, in common with all nations, had an absolute right to self-determination and that in any referendum on this issue I would vote for independence, but I still distrusted the SNP. I believed, and still do, that nationalism and a rightist mentality is a deadly concoction that is not to be trusted'.[42] But by September 2001 he had no longer 'any qualms about the SNP'. The decision of the latter to turn itself from a centre-right to a centre-left party removed any lingering doubts on Reid's part. In the wake of the looming conflict in Iraq, Reid gave public notice of his likely defection to the SNP by agreeing to sign the nomination papers of the SNP candidate Jim Mather in the Argyll and Bute constituency from his home in Rothesay. Moreover, he threw his weight behind the pairing of Alex Salmond and Nicola Sturgeon for leadership of the SNP, and the former was able to produce an open letter signed by Reid to that effect.[43] By 2006, he along with Alasdair Gray and Christopher Harvie in a joint declaration stated that: 'We accept the view of Tam Dalyell – an honourable opponent who in some respects we agree with – that devolution was a motorway to independence without an exit. It is time to go down it, making our own decisions and not blaming others when things go wrong'.[44]

Perhaps this shift towards the SNP was the reason why his column at the end of 2002 was pulled by the *Scotsman*. From 1995, the paper had been under the ownership of the right-wing and highly reclusive Barclay brothers, and in 1996 it was they who appointed the equally right-wing former

---

41 Reid, *Power without Principles*, 9; *Glasgow Herald*, 8 July 1992.
42 *Scotsman*, 24 September 2001.
43 *Herald*, 9 August 2004.
44 Christopher Harvie, Jimmy Reid and Alasdair Gray, 'Scottish Independence? No Fear!', *Open Democracy*, 30 November 2006. See https://www.opendemocracy.net/en/scottish_independence_4141jsp.

Sunday Times editor Andrew Neil to oversee their publishing interests. As editor -in-chief, Neil appointed Iain Martin, the paper's former political editor, as editor, and Fraser Nelson who took over the latter's role. This brought the editorial staff into alignment with the owners: all were on the right of the Conservative Party. The new troika may have viewed a left-wing columnist being critical of Blair and New Labour as being one thing, but to have a high-profile, pro-SNP columnist, particularly with the Holyrood elections taking place the following year, was another, and must have sat rather uncomfortably with the Unionist editorial line of the *Scotsman*. Although it may also have been a decision taken on medical grounds, as when returning from the funeral of Arnold Kemp, former editor of the *Glasgow Herald*, in Edinburgh, Reid had a stroke on 19 September 2002 on a railway platform inside Glasgow's Queen Street Station. Reid recalled the comedian Billy Connolly phoning him from California only to put the receiver down without saying a word as he feared that Reid's 'speech might have been affected'.[45] However, while he suffered no brain damage, from then on, his mobility was somewhat impaired, and he relied on his walking stick to get around. As such he tended to avoid public spaces that had no banisters, having lost consciousness after falling at Hampden Park watching a Scottish international football match.[46] But, as usual with Reid, he turned the condition to his advantage, using the stick as a prop: waving at people who recognised him or stamping the ground when he wished to emphasise a point.[47] Rather than a symbol of frailty, the stick became a positive affirmation of continuing involvement in, and passion for, life. Even a few minor heart attacks following the stroke failed to dampen his enthusiasm. Thus, his medical condition seems an unlikely explanation behind his sacking since he was still producing copy for the paper after his stroke, and as we will see he remained very active politically.

Reid returned to public life to protest against the Iraq war and took part in anti-war rallies. On 30 November 2004, he spoke at the long-running Conversation Pieces at the Royal Concert Hall, Glasgow, which was a sell-out. Questioned by radio presenter Iain Anderson, he covered the Iraq war, the Northern Ireland Peace Process, New Labour under Blair, and whether Scotland's parliament had the potential for further autonomy in the future,[48] which went to show that physical disability had not

45 *Glasgow Evening Times*, 20 October 2007.
46 *Glasgow Evening Times*, 20 October 2007.
47 Information from Brian McGeachan.
48 Information from Brian McGeachan.

diminished his interest and mastery of home and world affairs. Margo MacDonald, reporting on the occasion, stated that Reid announced his formal membership of the SNP, remarking that he was 'back on top form':

> a legend in his own lifetime, all twinkling eyes, good humour and with the hacks in the palm of his hand, dominating the SNP press conference. The TV cameras recorded more than is normal on these occasions. The newspaper snappers circled, ducked and dived, trying to capture on camera his larger than life, yet Puckish, personality.[49]

He was also at his combative best when speaking out against the Labour government's intention to close the last remaining merchant shipyard on the Lower Clyde – Fergusons of Port Glasgow – by awarding a contract for two fisheries protection vessels to a Polish firm. The Scottish Executive claimed that it was being forced under European Union procurement rules to place the order with the lowest bidder, a yard in Gdansk, Poland. However, Fergusons claimed that it would have to close unless it got the order and lodged a complaint with the European Commission that the Baltic option was being unfairly subsidised.[50] A mass letter campaign was orchestrated in protest from Port Glasgow residents to the then Labour First Minister of Scotland, Jack McConnell. A month later Reid flew to Brussels with Bruce McFee and Alyn Smith, two SNP MEPs, to lobby for the Ferguson yard. The venture was successful in part as the order was split between the Clyde and Gdansk yards and Fergusons was saved from closure. However, Reid's interaction with the European Union did not end there. Later that year he was invited to contribute to a public hearing on the future of the European social model held in London on 19 and 20 October and chaired by Francis Wurtz, President of the European United Left – Nordic Green Left group. The central question in the debates was whether one supported a market-dominated Europe or a more social Europe. Among the many speakers, the current Labour Party leader Jeremy Corbyn 'called for a global anti-privatisation movement and a movement against governments that fail to take account of the social aspect', while Reid argued 'that the socio-economic model should be adaptable and service the social objectives of society as a whole'.[51] Only a broken rib incurred after a fall in his home in early February 2007 on the

---

49 *Scotland on Sunday*, 24 April 2005.
50 *Herald*, 18 July 2005.
51 Agence Europe AGE, Europe Daily Bulletin.

Isle of Bute prevented him from leading a Pensioners for Peace blockade of the Faslane naval base at Gare Loch.[52] Thus, Reid was far from being a spent force and was still a highly respected figure among the European left.

By the time Reid had left the *Scotsman* and joined the SNP he was in his early seventies. Some Labour activists saw his resignation as an act of betrayal given the high profile the historical Jimmy Reid had on the Scottish left. He answered his Labour critics by saying: 'I have waited a long time to see forces emerging within the New Labour Party that would bring the party back to its roots ... But I have been waiting in vain and with every year that passes, Tony Blair and New Labour move further to the right. They are now indistinguishable from the Thatcherite Tories'.[53] Reid had once again done it his way. However, the fallout from his defection was nothing compared with leaving the CPGB – that still had the capacity to elicit raw emotion. Nowhere was this better dramatised than at the funeral of James Airlie, his one-time comrade and close friend, who had died on 10 March 1997, at the age of 60, following a six-month battle with cancer. The estrangement of the two men must have been painful for Reid. It was rumoured that they had an altercation during a chance meeting in the street; an encounter that marked the end of their friendship. Harsh words were exchanged, stopping short of blows. Privately, Reid was enraged by Airlie's quiet departure from the Communist Party in 1991 to join the Labour Party; an act which smacked of hypocrisy given the stance the latter had taken on Reid's decision to join in 1978. He was not invited to give the funeral oration that was instead performed by Campbell Christie, General Secretary of the STUC. Arnold Kemp, of the *Glasgow Herald*, wrote that the funeral attended by hundreds was on a first come, first served basis. 'Outside is Jimmy Reid, Airlie's co-leader in the 1971–2 work-in ... rubbing shoulders [in the rain] with an old acquaintance Robert Courtney Smith, the UCS liquidator. Together they listen to the oration ... which avoids Reid's name almost as much as they snub God ... Only the oration by Christie ... mentioned Reid's role in an event (work-in) that defeated Edward Heath'.[54] While he must have been saddened at the snub he had received it is clear that Airlie was still fondly remembered by Reid. He said of him, 'he was a smashing bloke, a dear friend ... It was bloody delightful to have known him'.[55]

---

52 *Herald*, 15 February 2007.
53 BBC News, 20 April 2005.
54 Kemp, *Confusion to our Enemies*, 137–8.
55 Kemp, *Confusion to our Enemies*, 138.

The people who were important in his working and political life were embraced in the 2007 official portrait of Reid by the artist Barry Atherton which hangs in the People's Palace, Glasgow. The front row in an overcrowded painting of figures in the labour movement past and present, family and important international political opponents (such as Thatcher and George Bush) were, in order of importance: James Airlie, Tony Benn, Hugh Scanlon and Bob Dickie. This was the same group of men (minus Vic Feather of the TUC) who, linked arm-in-arm, had led the monster UCS demonstration through the streets of Glasgow back in 1971. It remained the case that UCS rather than any other moment in a controversial political life was paramount in Reid's memory. It was his defining historical moment and afforded him a guaranteed place in the pantheon of the Scottish left.

Atherton's portrait was not the only visual representation of Reid. In 1999, the sculptor Kenny Hunter was commissioned by the curator of the Scottish Portrait Gallery James Holloway to produce a work of a political figure of his choice. Thus the artist was chosen but not the subject. In a conversation with his mother she brought up the possibility of a bust of Jimmy Reid, which immediately struck a chord with him. Hunter was not interested in providing an intimate sculpture of Reid but one that would reflect his working-class background – his humble origins. This ruled out the traditional bronze statue in favour of a modernist work in bright red (the colour of the shipyards) fibre glass, placed on an ordinary table rather than a grand plinth. No one would be expected to look up to Reid; he was, like them, ordinary, but his story was that ordinary people can do extraordinary things with their lives. Although Reid was enthusiastic, Hunter claims that his 'family did not go out of their way to congratulate him'. At the launch in the portrait gallery Michael Forsyth, formerly Tory Secretary of State for Scotland, placed his wine glass on the table holding the bust of Reid only to given a verbal shot across the bows by the man himself.[56] The alternative to the everyman image in Hunter's work is Andrew Hay's portrait in Elder Park Library, Govan, which depicts Reid as a colossus of thought and action.

Prior to his stroke, Reid left his home at 3 Newark Drive, Glasgow for a Victorian villa, Bishop Lodge, overlooking Rothesay Bay and the harbour, on the Isle of Bute, in November 1998. As he told his wife when he inspected his new home, 'it was what he had always wanted, to wake up each morning to a view of his beloved Clyde'.[57] There he could indulge

---

56 K. Hunter, interview with Knox (2015).
57 *Scotsman*, 11 August 2010.

his passions for Burns's poetry and cricket, as well as taking his responsibilities of the Chieftain of the Bute Highland Games seriously. He died on 10 August 2010 of a brain haemorrhage at Inverclyde Royal Hospital, Greenock. Death was something Reid had contemplated since his stroke. In an interview with the journalist Kenneth Roy seven years earlier he said it was something that he 'didn't have any fear' of.[58] After a private service in Rothesay, his hearse was ferried to Weymss Bay and then driven into Glasgow for a secular funeral service at Govan Old Parish Church on 19 August. The cortège passed the BAE Systems Surface Ships yard in Govan, one of the shipyards saved after the collapse of UCS, where hundreds of workers gathered outside in tribute. The Scottish vernacular poet Rab Wilson caught the Govan mood when he wrote:

> The Finnieston Crane shuid dip its jib the day,
> Bow its heid lik the fowk wha thrang these streets,
> Lulled tae a hush, as Jimmy Reid cams hame.[59]

The funeral service at Govan Old Church was attended by notable figures from the world of politics and show business including Ed Balls, Ed Miliband, Gordon Brown, Alex Salmond, Sir Alex Ferguson and Billy Connolly. The *Scotsman* described the day's events as follows:

> The day began with a ceremony at the United Church of Bute, where Reid had lived out his final years, taking delight in the daily view of the Clyde. While the heroes of classical literature he so enjoyed crossed the River Styx after death, Reid crossed the River Clyde as the funeral cortege boarded a ferry to the mainland, while 50 people lined the pier. The cortege later travelled, under police escort, to Glasgow where workers at Govan shipyard lined part of the road. Reid's coffin, with roses on top, was carried into the church led by a piper. Flowers spelt the words 'papa' and 'dad' in the hearse. While the coffin arrived and was in place at the front of the altar at 12:55pm, the service did not begin until exactly 1:30pm as had been stated, as Reid believed in the courtesy of punctuality. In the front row was his wife Joan and three daughters, Eileen, Shona and Julie, as well as his grandchildren.[60]

---

58   *Scottish Review* 2003 (reprinted June 2017).
59   *Herald*, 19 August 2010.
60   *Scotsman*, 20 August 2010.

The tributes immediately followed his death as political figures fell over themselves in praise of the 'best MP Scotland never had'. Alex Salmond, First Minister of Scotland, said of him: 'Jimmy Reid was Clyde-built. He has been Scotland's great rallying figure over the last four decades and was one of the few Scottish political figures who can genuinely say that they provoked real change for the better in society – always addressing both a Scottish and international audience. He was a warm, humorous and generous human being.'[61] From the left, Tony Benn declared him: 'a great figure of the labour movement ... He built a really powerful and proud and self-confident group of people who decided to take over the yard and make it work. In the end, it came to a conclusion and the yard did continue'.[62] From New Labour, Gordon Brown said: 'Jimmy will always be remembered for the inspired and disciplined way he fought for the shipyard industry and the fact there is still a shipbuilding industry in Scotland today is in large measure because of the inspirational campaigns that he waged'.[63] As far as the Scottish press was concerned, his death marked the passing of an era – the end of the 'self-improved politicised working man'.[64]

But perhaps the most moving tributes of all came from the ordinary working men and women whose memory of him endured and by whom he was revered and esteemed. A letter to the *Guardian* published shortly after his death captured the inspirational Reid who literally changed lives:

> I was a 13-year-old at High Storrs school in Sheffield in 1973 and I had the dubious pleasure of having to attend our speech day. On stage were the Halle Orchestra which, as a Pink Floyd fan, I was barely able to appreciate. What I had not expected was that the keynote speaker would have such an influence on me. I had no idea who Jimmy Reid was and only later did I fully appreciate him. He spoke with passion and he delivered his 'rat race' speech to an audience of school children and their parents that was stunned into silence by his brilliance. That I still tingle as a 50-year-old at the thought of it is testament to the fact. He helped form my political beliefs and I mourn his passing. (Simon Gair, Bumpstead, Suffolk)[65]

---

61 *Scotsman*, 11 August 2010.
62 *Scotsman*, 11 August 2010.
63 *Scotsman*, 11 August 2010.
64 *Guardian*, 1 January 2011.
65 *Guardian*, 16 August 2010.

George Brechin, who as a student had helped Reid get elected as Rector of Glasgow University, said that he was 'simply the most impressive man he had ever met', and many shared his feelings.[66]

However, in all this maelstrom of words, eulogies and hangers on to his memory and reputation, it is easy to lose sight of the fact that many of those loudest in their praise were opposed to the values held, and the politics practised, by Reid. As Ian Bell put it:

> They damn your every belief while you live. When you pass away they form a queue to heap praise on your distinguished memory. Jimmy Reid would have been amused, I think, by some of the eulogies compiled beneath his name last week. He had a sense of humour, after all … He was being remembered for an argument. The irony – not one he would have overlooked – is that his argument is anathema still to the sort of people who last week garlanded his name with tributes. It is anathema now, more than ever.[67]

One of his long-time friends and political allies, Jim Sillars, said he could not bring himself to attend Reid's funeral. As he stated in a letter to his widow, it would have been difficult to listen to eulogies from those in the socialist and trade union movement who had 'ill-used him'; that 'a fair number of those working men going into the service had not voted for him when it really mattered', whether for trade union office or parliament.[68] At least his Trotskyist opponents from way back in his days in the CPGB remained consistent in their criticism of him. They claimed that 'Reid's legacy is not to be celebrated, but it must be learned from. He was a key figure in the ranks of Stalinism and the trade union and Labour bureaucracy – the central forces responsible for the continued survival of capitalism in Britain'.[69] Although the Trotskyist verdict may induce some suppressed mirth that the left is all that is keeping capitalism going in Britain, there is a feeling that they like Reid have had their moment. If we, as Martin Kettle suggests, accept that Reid's career was marked by 'isolated successes amid wider failures', then he remains a 'dazzling tribune'

---

66   Brechin, interview with Knox.
67   *Sunday Herald*, 15 August 2010.
68   Sillars, interview with Knox.
69   Steve James, 'Jimmy Reid, Stalinist Union Leader Who Betrayed Scottish Shipyard Struggle, Dies at 78', *World Socialist Web Site*. See https://www.wsws.org/en/articles/2010/08/reid-a25.html.

for a world that no longer exists: heavy industry, trade union power, communism.[70] However, Reid never stopped battling against poverty and inequality; the memories of his childhood were always present, guiding him in this struggle. His journey from the left to the centre of British politics and from there to a radical nationalism only served to emphasise that he was an individual, an outsider, a man of restless intellect who could never quite come to terms with the discipline and organisation needed to succeed in the cutthroat world of politics. Indeed, the former managing director of UCS, Ken Douglas, once said to him during the height of the work-in:

> 'You're no more a communist than I am; you're an idealist. And idealists make for hard negotiators. I recognise you as an idealist because that's what I am'. He laughed and left. A few weeks later he said to me that he'd been thinking over what I'd said about him being an idealist, not a communist, and that he agreed with me.[71]

Idealism was perhaps Reid's most important legacy; indeed, reflecting on death he said that 'I want to know that my life has advanced the cause of decency and social justice just a wee bit, and that will make me feel comfortable'.[72] Those concerned to carry on the fight for a more equal society can find in Reid their inspiration not just as historical memory but also practically through the work of the Jimmy Reid Foundation, the only left-wing think tank in Scotland, which was established after his death by friends and admirers attached to the *Scottish Left Review* in 2011 to continue the legacy of the radical political thinking his life represented.

---

70 *Guardian*, 12 October 2010.
71 K. Douglas, interview with McKinlay (2014).
72 *Scottish Review* (June 2017).

Bibliography

Manuscript Sources

Admission Register, Glasgow City Archives (D-ED7/218/2/4).
Amalgamated Engineering Union, District Committee Minutes, Glasgow City Archives, Mitchell Library.
BBC Transcript, 'Jimmy Reid – The Campaign Leader', 1 January 2002, Glasgow University Archives (ACCN3717/16/5).
Clyde Employers' Association, Correspondence, Glasgow City Archives, Mitchell Library.
Clyde Shipbuilders' Association, Glasgow City Archives, Mitchell Library.
Communist Party biography project, British Library, London.
Communist Party of Great Britain Archive, People's History Museum, Salford.
Communist Party of Great Britain, Papers, Working Class Movement Library, Manchester.
Communist Party of Great Britain, Scottish Papers, Glasgow Caledonian University.
Gordon Wilson Papers, University of Dundee (MS 315/3/3).
J. Reid, unpublished autobiography (2006), Glasgow University Archives, Mitchell Library.
Jimmy Reid Collection, Glasgow University Archives.
Lamb Collection, Dundee Central Library.
Poor Relief, Govan, Glasgow City Archives, Mitchell Library (D-HEW17/546. Nos. 72561, 72562, 72563, 72564).
Robert Courtney Smith Papers, Glasgow University Archives (ACCN3613/1/5).
Scottish Engineering Employers' Association, Glasgow City Archives, Mitchell Library.
Upper Clyde Shipbuilders' Collection, Glasgow University Archives.
Willie Thompson Collection, Glasgow Caledonian University Archives.

Newspapers and Periodicals

Challenge
Clydebank Press
Daily Mirror
Daily Record
Daily Worker
Dundee Courier
Glasgow Evening Times
Glasgow Herald
Glasgow University Guardian
The Guardian
The Herald
The Independent
Morning Star
New Society
The Observer
The Scotsman
Scottish Catholic Observer
Scottish Left Review
The Spectator
The Sun
Sunday Herald
The Times
Tribune

Pamphlets

Criminal Statistics (1930), United Kingdom Parliamentary Papers, Cmd 3963.
R. Faber, 'The 1968 Czechoslovak Crisis: Inside the British Communist Party', Socialist History Society Pamphlet, 5 (1996).
J. Foster, 'The 1971–72 Work-in Revisited: How Clydeside Workers Defeated a Tory Government', *Our History*, New Series, Pamphlet No. 9 (London, 2013), 1–36.
Glasgow City Council, *Education Handbook* (1947).
Scottish Trade Union Council, *Annual Reports* (1960, 1970, 1980).
Youth in Overalls, Clydeside apprentices' four-page celebratory newspaper (1952).

Books

D. Aaronovitch, *Party Animals: My Family and Other Communists* (London, 2016).
K.J.W. Alexander and C.L. Jenkins, *Fairfields: A Study in Institutional Change* (London, 1970).
J. Allison, *Guilty by Suspicion: A Life and Labour* (Glendaruel, 1995).
G. Andrews, *End Games and New Times: The Final Years of British Communism, 1964–1991* (London, 2004).
F. Beckett, *Enemy Within: The Rise and Fall of the British Communist Party* (London, 1995).
T. Benn, *Office without Power: Diaries 1968–1972* (London, 1988).
D. Betteridge, *A Rose Loupt Oot: Poetry and Song Celebrating the UCS Work-in* (Middlesbrough, 2011).
N. Bosanquet and P. Townsend (eds), *Labour and Inequality: A Fabian Study of Labour in Power, 1974–79* (London, 1980).
D. Butler and D. Kavanagh, *The British General Election of February 1974* (London, 1975).

B. Caine, *Biography and History* (London, 2010).
J. Callaghan, *Cold War, Crisis and Conflict: The CPGB, 1951–68* (London, 2003).
C. Cockburn, *Crossing the Line, Being the Second Volume of Autobiography* (London, 1958).
C. Collins, *Language, Ideology and Social Consciousness: Developing a Sociohistorical Approach* (Aldershot, 1999).
A. Davies, *City of Gangs* (London, 2014).
R. Davies, *The Kenneth Williams Diaries* (London, 1994).
P. Donnelly, *Govan on the Clyde* (Glasgow, 1994).
H.M. Drucker, *Breakaway: The Scottish Labour Party* (Edinburgh, 1978).
J. Eaden and D. Renton, *The Communist Party of Great Britain since 1920* (Basingstoke, 2002).
R. Edwards, *Goodbye to Fleet Street* (London, 1988).
R. Ferguson, *George Macleod: Founder of the Iona Community* (London, 2001).
T. Ferguson and J. Cunnison, *The Young Wage-Earner: A Study of Glasgow Boys* (Oxford, 1951).
S. Fielding, *Labour: Decline and Renewal* (Tisbury, 1999).
J. Foster and C. Woolfson, *The Politics of the UCS Work-in: Class Alliances and the Right to Work* (London, 1986).
———. *Track Record: The Story of the Caterpillar Occupation* (London, 1988).
B. Fowkes, *Eastern Europe, 1945–1969: From Stalinism to Stagnation* (London, 2000).
T. Gallagher, *Glasgow: The Uneasy Peace* (Manchester, 1987).
R. Glasser, *Growing up in the Gorbals* (Thirsk, 2001).
E. Heath, *The Course of My Life* (London, 2012).
E.J. Hobsbawm, *Interesting Times* (London, 2002).
B.W. Hogwood, *Government and Shipbuilding: The Politics of Industrial Change* (Farnborough, 1979).
M. Holroyd, *Bernard Shaw* (London, 2011).
G. Hughes, *In Search of a Way: Two Journeys of Spiritual Discovery* (London, 1986).
———. *Walk to Jerusalem: In Search of Peace* (London, 1991).
I. Jack, *Before the Oil Ran Out: Britain, 1977–86* (London, 1987).
L. Johnman and H. Murphy, *British Shipbuilding and the State: A Political Economy of Decline* (Liverpool, 2002).
———. *Scott Lithgow: Déjà Vu All Over Again! The Rise and Fall of a Shipbuilding Company* (Liverpool, 2005).
S. Johns, *Reformism on the Clyde: The Story of UCS* (London, 1973).
E. Jones, *Neil Kinnock* (London, 1994).
T. Judt, *Postwar: A History of Europe since 1945* (London, 2005).
J. Kay, *Red Dust Road* (London, 2010).
J. Kemp (ed.), *Confusion to Our Enemies: Selected Journalism of Arnold Kemp* (London, 2012).
R. Kenna, *Heart of the Gorbals* (Ayr, 2004).

J. Klugmann (ed.), *Dialogue of Christianity and Marxism* (London, 1968).
——. *The Future of Man* (London, 1970).
W.W. Knox, *Industrial Nation: Work, Culture and Society in Scotland, 1800–Present* (Edinburgh, 1999).
D. Kogan and M. Kogan, *The Battle for the Labour Party* (London, 1982).
K. Laybourn and D. Murphy, *Under the Red Flag: A History of Communism in Britain, c.1849–1991* (Stroud, 1999).
K. MacAskill, *Jimmy Reid: A Scottish Political Journey* (London, 2017).
B. McGeachan, *Jimmy Reid: From Govan to Gettysburg* [one-act stage play] (Glasgow, 2007).
P. McGeown, *Heat the Furnace Seven More Times* (Motherwell, 1967).
J. McGill, *Crisis on the Clyde: The Story of Upper Clyde Shipbuilders* (London, 1973).
S. McGinty, *This Turbulent Priest: A Life of Cardinal Winning* (London, 2003).
J. McLean, *Hopeless but Not Serious: The Autobiography of the Urban Voltaire* (Edinburgh, 1996).
J. Mahon, *Harry Pollitt: A Biography* (London, 1976).
J. Medhurst, *That Option No Longer Exists: Britain, 1974–1976* (London, 2014).
J. Melling, *Rent Strikes: People's Struggle for Housing in West Scotland, 1890–1916* (Edinburgh, 1983).
J. Melling and A. McKinlay (eds), *Management, Labour and Industrial Politics in Modern Europe: The Quest for Productivity Growth during the Twentieth Century* (Cheltenham, 1996).
S. Milne, *The Enemy Within: The Secret War against the Miners* (London, 1995).
K. Morgan, *Harry Pollitt* (Manchester, 1994).
K. Morgan, G. Cohen and A. Flinnet, *Communists and British Society, 1920–1991* (London, 2007).
D. Morley, *Gorgeous George: The Life and Adventures of George Galloway* (London, 2007).
M. Parkinson, *Parky: My Autobiography* (London, 2009).
J. Phillips, *Collieries, Communities and the Miners' Strike in Scotland, 1984–85* (Manchester, 2012).
——. *The Industrial Politics of Devolution: Scotland in the 1960s and 1970s* (Manchester, 2008).
N. Rafeek, *Communist Women in Scotland: Red Clydeside from the Russian Revolution to the End of the Soviet Union* (London, 2008).
A.J. Reid, *United We Stand: A History of Britain's Trade Unions* (London, 2004).
J. Reid, *As I Please* (Edinburgh, 1984).
——. *Power without Principles: New Labour Sickness and Other Essays* (Edinburgh, 1999).
——. *Reflections of a Clyde-Built Man* (London, 1976).
A.J. Richards, *Miners on Strike: Class Solidarity and Divisions in Britain* (Oxford, 1996).
R. Samuel, *The Lost World of British Communism* (London, 2006).
A. Sayle, *Stalin Ate My Homework* (London, 2010).

R. Seifert and T. Sibley, *Revolutionary Communist at Work: A Political Biography of Bert Ramelson* (London, 2012).
A. Slaven and H. Murphy, *Crossing the Bar: An Oral History of the British Shipbuilding, Ship Repairing and Marine Engine Building Industries in the Age of Decline, 1956–1990* (Liverpool, 2013).
T.C. Smout, *A Century of the Scottish People, 1830–1950* (London, 1986).
B. Starrett, *The Way I See It* (Glasgow, 2013).
C. Stevens, *Born Brilliant: The Life of Kenneth Williams* (London, 2011).
P. Thompson, *The Voice of the Past: Oral History* (Oxford, 1978).
W. Thompson, *Good Old Cause: British Communism, 1920–1991* (London, 1992).
R. Vinen, *National Service: Conscription in Britain, 1945–1963* (London, 2014).
G. Wilson, *SNP: The Turbulent Years, 1960–1990* (Stirling, 2009).
J. Winterton and R. Winterton, *Coal, Crisis, and Conflict: The 1984–85 Miners' Strike in Yorkshire* (Manchester, 1989).

Articles and Chapters in Books

V.L. Allen, 'The Year-Long Miners' Strike, March 1984–March 1985: A Memoir', *Industrial Relations Journal*, 40 (2009), 278–91.
R. Baird, 'Housing', in *The Third Statistical Account of Scotland: Glasgow*, eds J. Cunnison and J.B.S. Gilfillan (Glasgow, 1958), 448–74.
L. Baston, 'The Age of Wilson, 1955–79', in *The Labour Party: A Centenary History*, eds B. Bravati and R. Heffernan (Basingstoke, 2000), 87–111.
R.K. Brown, 'From Donovan to Where? Interpretations of Industrial Relations in Britain since 1968', *British Journal of Sociology*, 29 (1978), 439–61.
A. Clark, '"And the Next Thing, the Chairs Barricaded the Doors": The Lee Jeans Factory Occupation, Trade Unionism and Gender in Scotland in the 1980s', *Scottish Labour History*, 48 (2013), 116–35.
C. Collins, 'Developing the Linguistic Turn in Urban Studies: Language, Context and Political Economy', *Urban Studies*, 37 (2000), 2027–43.
P. Deery, 'The Secret Battalion: Communism in Britain during the Cold War', *Contemporary British History*, 13 (1999), 1–28.
D. Denver and J. Bochel, 'The Political Socialization of Activists in the British Communist Party', *British Journal of Political Science*, 3 (1973), 53–71.
C. Efstathiou, 'E.P. Thompson, the Early New Left and the Fife Socialist League', *Labour History Review*, 81 (2016), 25–48.
D.B. Forrester, 'MacLeod, George Fielden, Baron MacLeod of Fuinary (1895–1991)', *Oxford Dictionary of National Biography* (2004) www.oxforddnb.com/view/10.1093/ref:odnb/9780198614128.001.0001/odnb-9780198614128-e-49886.
J. Foster, 'Upper Clyde Shipbuilders 1971–2 and Edward Heath's U-Turn: How a United Workforce Defeated a Divided Government', *Mariner's Mirror*, 102 (2016), 34–48.

T. Green, 'The Leicester Conference on Oral History: Four Impressions', *Oral History*, 1 (1971), 7–10.
R. Hay and J. McLauchlan, 'The Oral History of Upper Clyde Shipbuilders: A Preliminary Report', *Oral History*, 2 (1974), 45–58.
L. Hunter, 'The Scottish Labour Market', in *The Economic Development of Modern Scotland*, ed. R. Saville (Edinburgh, 1985), 163–82.
M. Jacobs, 'End of the Coal Strike', *Economic and Political Weekly*, 20, 9 March 1985.
J. Kay, 'Non-Stop Party', in *Children of the Revolution*, ed. P. Cohen (London, 1977), 32–42.
N. Lorentzen, '"You Can't Fight for Your Jobs and Just Sit There": The Lee Jeans Sit-in', in *Fighting Closures: De-Industrialisation and the Trade Unions, 1979–1983*, eds H. Levie, D. Gregory and N. Lorentzen (London, 1984), 43–62.
S. Ludham, 'Norms and Blocks: Trade Unions and the Labour Party since 1964', in *The Labour Party: A Centenary History*, eds B. Bravati and R. Heffernan (Basingstoke, 2000), 220–45.
J. McGoldrick, 'Crisis and the Division of Labour: Clydeside Shipbuilding in the Inter-War Period', in *Capital and Class in Scotland*, ed. T. Dickson (Edinburgh, 1982), 143–85.
——. 'Industrial Relations and the Division of Labour in the Shipbuilding Industry since the War', *British Journal of Industrial Relations*, 21 (1983), 197–220.
A.B. McHardy, 'The Economics of Crime', *Juridical Review*, 14 (1902), 45–58.
A. McKinlay, 'Jimmy Reid: Fragments from a Political Life', *Scottish Labour History*, 46 (2011), 38–53.
——. 'Management and Workplace Trade Unionism: Clydeside Engineering, 1945–1957', in *Management, Labour and Industrial Politics in Modern Europe: The Quest for Productivity Growth during the Twentieth Century*, eds J. Melling and A. McKinlay (Cheltenham, 1996), 174–86.
H. Murphy, 'Labour in the British Shipbuilding and Ship Repairing Industries in the Twentieth Century', in *Shipbuilding and Ship Repair Workers around the World: Case Studies, 1950–2010*, eds R. Varela, H. Murphy and M. Van der Linden (Amsterdam and Chicago, 2017), 47–116.
T. Nairn, *The Break-up of Britain: Crisis and Neonationalism* (London, 1977).
P. Payne, 'The Decline of Scottish Heavy Industries, 1945–1983', in *The Economic Development of Modern Scotland, 1950–1980*, ed. R. Saville (Edinburgh, 1985), 79–113.
R. Penn, 'Trade Union Organisation and Skill in the British Cotton and Engineering Industries, 1850–1960', *Social History*, 8 (1983), 37–55.
J. Reid, 'Not Scared to Be Ourselves', *Scottish Left Review* (November/December 2007), 6–7.
E. Reid, 'The Lessons My Father Taught Me', *Sunday Herald*, 6 July 2014.
——. 'To Russia with my Dad, Jimmy Reid', *Scottish Review* (June/July 2014), 2–5.

P. Ryan, 'Apprentice Strikes in the Twentieth-Century UK Engineering and Shipbuilding Industries', *Historical Studies in Industrial Relations*, 18 (2004), 1–63.

——. 'The Embedding of Apprenticeship in Industrial Relations: British Engineering, 1925–65', in *Apprenticeship: Towards a New Paradigm of Learning* (1999), eds P. Ainsley and H. Rainbird (London, 1999), 41–60.

R. Samuel, 'Class Politics: The Lost World of British Communism, Part Three', *New Left Review*, 165 (1987), 52–91.

J. Spence and C. Stephenson, '"Side by Side with Our Men?" Women's Activism, Community, and Gender in the 1984–1985 British Miners' Strike', *International Labor and Working-Class History*, 75 (2009), 68–84.

D. Stewart, 'A Tragic Fiasco? The 1984/5 Miners' Strike in Scotland', *Scottish Labour History*, 41 (2006), 34–50.

M. Waite, 'Sex 'n' Drugs 'n' Rock 'n' Roll (and Communism)', in *Opening the Books: Essays on the Social and Cultural History of British Communism*, eds G. Andrews, N. Fishman and K. Morgan (London, 1995), 210–24.

B. Warren, 'The British Road to Socialism', *New Left Review*, 63 (1970), 27–41.

R. Wishart, 'An Introduction to the UCS Crisis', in J. Reid, *Reflections of a Clyde-Built Man* (London, 1976), 77–83.

Oral Testimonies

James Airlie
Jack Ashton
Barry Atherton
Linda Atherton
Sammy Barr
Ian Borthwick
George Brechin
Janey Buchan
Douglas Chalmers
James Cloughley
Davie Cooper
Anita Cox
Tam Dalyell
Pat Devine
Bob Dickie
Margaret Easedale
Michael Foot
John Foster
George Galloway
Andrew Gilchrist
George Grieg

Nan Grieg
Andrew Hay
Kenny Hunter
Jack Irvine
John Kay
Stephen Kelly
Hugh Kerr
Neil Kinnock
Ian Leggat
John McAllion
John McAuley
Brian McGeachan
Diane McGoldrick
Jim McGoldrick
Margaret McGowan
Willie McKelvey
Gordon McLennan
Ruby McNicol
Raymond Mennie
Betty Meth
Alex Murray

Mike Park
Bridget Prentice (née Corr)
Stuart Purdie
John Quigley
Eileen Reid
Jimmy Reid
Joan Reid
David Scott
Freddie Shiack
Jim Sillars
Robert Courtney Smith
George Tasker
Bob Thomson
Willie Thompson
Davie Todd
Davie Torrance
James Whyte
Charles Woolfson
Igor Yurgens

Unpublished Theses

G. Andrews, 'Culture, Ideology and Strategy of the Communist Party of Great Britain 1964–1979' (PhD, Kingston University, 2002).
S. Bruley, 'Socialism and Feminism in the Communist Party of Great Britain, 1920–1939' (PhD, University of London, 1980).
A. Mills, 'Worker Occupations, 1971–1975: A Socio-Historical Analysis of the Development and Spread of Sit-ins, Work-ins and Worker Co-Operatives in Britain' (PhD, University of Durham, 1982).
W. Styles, 'British Domestic Security Policy and Communist Subversion: 1945–1964' (PhD, University of Cambridge, 2016).
M. Waite, 'Young People and Communist Politics in Britain, 1920–1991: Aspects of the History of the Young Communist League' (M.Phil., University of Lancaster, 1992).
C. Woolfson, 'Working-Class Culture: The Work-in at Upper Clyde Shipbuilders' (PhD, University of Glasgow, 1982).

Broadcast Media

BBC News (21 September 1984).
BBC News (20 April 2005).
BBC Scotland News (19 August 2010).
Class Struggle: Film from the Clyde. Cinema Action documentary (1977) https://vimeo.com/ondemand/32096.
Daddy's Girl, BBC Radio Scotland (2008).
Inside Out, BBC One television (2 February 2004).
It's Your Line (3 December 1971).
Jimmy Reid: My Britain, ITV (1992).
The Likes of Jimmy Reid, BBC (August 1975).
Maritime History, BBC (2003).
Moscow Gold (1992), Glasgow University Archives (ACCN 37/17/16/5).
Moscow Gold, rough draft (1992), Glasgow University Archives (ACCN 3717/16).
Moscow Gold, final draft (1992), Glasgow University Archives (ACCN 3717/16/8).
Open University, *Decision-Making in Britain*, BBC television (11 July 1976).
A Place in My Mind, BBC Radio Scotland (7 June 1998).
Reid about Poland, Scottish Television (1990).
Reid about Scotland, Scottish Television (1990).
Reid about the USSR, Scottish Television (1987).
Scottish Legends, Scottish Television (2003).
Strike – Jimmy Reid, BBC Radio Scotland (30 September 2008).
When the Eyes of the World Were on the Clyde, J. Lloyd, BBC Radio 4, *Archive on Four* (2011).

Index

Acts of Parliament
   National Service Act (1948) 64
   Housing Finance Act (1972)
     172
Adams, Gerry 196
Airlie, James 1, 103, 104, 128, 160,
   238
   boilermakers 91–2
   Caterpillar strike 220–1
   death 13, 237
   friendship with Reid 165
   funeral 13, 237
   1984 miners' strike 201–2
   personality 110–11
   UCS work-in 108, 122, 124, 131,
     132
Alexander, Douglas 228
Alexander, Wendy 228
Allen, Victor 207
Allison, Jimmy 177, 191
   Alternative Economic Strategy
     (AES) 179–80
Amalgamated Engineering Union
   (AEU) 41, 43–4, 49
   apprentices' strike 52, 56
Amalgamated Union of Engineering
   Workers (AUEW) 159–61, 162
Anderson, Iain 235
Arnot, Robin Page 166
Ascherson, Neil 171

Ashton, Harry 75
Ashton, Jack
   Hungarian Uprising 75–6
   Reid's organisational skills 110
   Reid's resignation 166
Atherton, Barry 238

Badar, Islam 225
Baggott, Maurice 131
Balls, Ed 239
Bambridge, Anthony 124
Barclay, William 140
Barr, Sammy 1, 95, 132–3
Beckett, Margaret 223
Bell, Colin 182
Bell, Ian 216–17
   miners' strike 202
   Reid obituary 241
Belsham, Ronald 120
Benn, Tony 238
   CLPD 178
   Labour leadership 180, 212
   1984 miners' strike 211
   Reid 1, 190, 240
   UCS 97, 98, 107, 119, 135
Berlinguer, Enrico 198
Blair, Tony 4, 212, 223–4, 237
Boateng, Paul 213
Borthwick, Ian 190–1
Boy Scouts 33

Boyd, John McFarlane 159, 161
Brechin, George
   rector campaign 140, 146–7
   Reid's character 241
British Polar Engines (BPE) 47–8, 68
British Road to Socialism (BRS) 4, 47, 67–8, 93, 167–8, 180
Britten, Benjamin 198
Brown, Gordon 1, 4, 139, 146, 224, 239–40
Buchan, Janey 182
Bullock, Alan 135
Burns, Emile 38, 47
Burns, Robert 142
Butler, Rab 188
Byrne, J.T. 56

Cairns, Robert 182
Calder, Bob 153, 157
Caldwell, Martin 140
Callaghan, Jim 180, 186
Callaghan, John 75, 85
Cameron, James 69
Campaign for Labour Party Democracy (CLPD) 178–9
Campaign for Nuclear Disarmament (CND) 82–3, 197–8
Campbell, Johnny 70
Canavan, Denis 228–9
Carroll, Mary 19
Castle, Barbara 98–9
Castro, Fidel 87
Caterpillar strike 220–1
Catholic Church
   1974 general election 153–5
   social programme of 154
Ceaușescu, Nicolae 87
Celtic Football Club 197
Central Dunbartonshire 149, 177
Challenge 61–2, 82
Charles, Prince 195
Chicago gangs 16–17
Chisholm, Daniel 182–4

Christie, Campbell 237
Clements, Dick 176–7
Close, Ajay 211
Cloughley, Jimmy 8
   UCS work-in 132
Clyde Employers' Association (CEA)
   blacklisting 45–6
Clydebank
   blitz 34
Clydebank Labour Party 156–7
Clydebank Press 149
Clydebank Town Council (CTC) 90, 149
   charges against Reid 157–8
   opposition to 1972 Housing Act 172–3
Clydeside Apprentices' Committee 52–3
Coalfields Communities Campaign 207
Cockburn, Claude 69
Cohen, Gerry 69
Cole, Bob 165
Collins, Chik 105–6
Communist Historians' Group 74
Communist Party of Great Britain (CPGB)
   apprenticeship 45
   CND 82–3
   Clydebank 152
   Cuban missile crisis 86–7
   Czechoslovakia 87–8
   democratic centralism 79, 175
   divisions 93–4
   Dundee 182–3
   elections 68, 156–7
   employees 89–90
   Eurocommunism 175
   female membership 85–6
   foundation 2
   fraternity 62–4
   1972 Housing Act 172–3
   Hungarian Uprising 73–7

Index 253

Marxist education 91
membership 41, 83, 92
Reid's resignation 165–6
respectability 83–4
Soviet Union 4, 11, 67, 75, 87–8, 167, 169, 171–2, 218
Stalinism 67, 73–4, 83
UCS work-in 113–15, 134, 136
Communist Party Shipbuilding Branch (CPSB)
divisions within 132–3
membership 90, 136
strategies 90, 104–5
Confederation of Shipbuilding and Engineering Unions (CSEU) 49, 56
Connolly, Sir Billy 235, 239
Conroy, Harry 190
Conservative Party
economic strategy 97–8
electoral support 206
industrial strategy 98–9
1984 miners' strike 204–5, 208–9
paternalism 188–9
Cooper, Davy 90, 114, 164
Corbyn, Jeremy 196, 236
Corr, Bridget 146
Cox, Anita 218–19
Cox, Idris 73, 168
Cox, Nora 73
Crawford, Stewart 104
Crime 24
Cripps, Sir Stafford 178
Cummings, John 205
Cunningham, Roseanna 231

Daily Herald 55
Daily Mail 195, 212
Daily Mirror 215–16
Daily Record 211, 215–16
Daily Worker 36, 39, 44, 72, 82
Hungarian Uprising 73–4
Reid's resignation 163
Soviet financial backing 78–9

Dalmuir 177
Daltrey, Roger 85
Daly, Lawrence 74
Dalyell, Tam 190, 223, 234
Darling, Alastair Lord 181
Davies, Barney 82
Davies, John 99, 102, 108, 116, 123, 125
Day, Robin Sir 140
deindustrialisation 86
Delors, Jacques 161
Department of Trade and Industry (DTI) 101
Dewar, Donald 191
Dickie, Bob 105, 108, 112, 131, 238
Dimbleby, Jonathan 77
Dougan, Tom 162
Douglas, Dick 49, 52
Douglas, Ken 102, 122, 242
Dubček, Alexander 87
Dundee 182–90
Dundee Courier and Advertiser 187, 189
Dundee District Council
corruption in 183
Dundee East 185–6, 189–90
Dundee Labour Party
divisions within 182–3, 190
Dundee West 189
Dunnachie, Jimmy 225
Dutt, Palme 88, 174, 214
Dylan, Bob 85

East Dunbartonshire 148–9
Ecclestone, Bernie 229
Economic League 52
Eden, Douglas 185
Eden, Sir John 113
Edinburgh Festival 194
Elder Park Library 32
European Economic Community (EEC) 161
Ewing, Winnie 233

Falber, Rueben 78–9
Feather, Vic 119, 121
Ferguson, Sir Alex 32, 239
Fergusons of Port Glasgow 236
Ferry, Alex 49, 52
Flint, Professor David 100
Foot, Michael 69, 198, 211
Forsyth, Michael 238
Foster, John 89, 91, 108
Fraser, William (Lord Strathalmond) 124
Friedan, Betty 85
Fryer, John 123

Gair, Simon 240
Gall, Gregor 1
Gallacher, Willie 70, 83
Gallagher, Alex 230
Gallagher, Ken 214
Galloway, George
   opposition to Reid 182–3
Garscadden 182
Gdansk 198, 236
general elections
   1945 35, 68
   1964 81–2, 148
   1970 148–9
   1974 149–50, 156
   1979 182–90
   1992 221, 223
   1997 224
Gibb, Andrew 26
Gilchrist, Archibald 121–2
Gillen, John 220–1
Gilmore, Sammy
   Reid's journalism 217
   UCS work-in 95
Glasgow Herald (later *The Herald*) 55, 187, 189–90, 193, 196, 199, 225, 231–2
Glasser, Ralph 18
Glen, Sir Alexander 102
Glen (Reid's dog) 53, 80

Gollan, John 67, 69, 82, 92
   death 164
Gorbals
   economic structure 16
   gang culture 16–17
   housing 16–18
   mortality rates 21
Govan 15, 27–8, 35–6, 57
   civic pride 16
   economic structure 28
   housing conditions 27–8
Govan Labour Party 224–6
Govan Old Parish Church 35, 239
Govan Shipbuilders Limited 121–2
Graham, Stan 82
Grand Hotel, Brighton 193
Grant, Bernie 213
Gray, Alasdair 234
Greater London Council (GLC) 212–13
Green, Tony 5
Greenwich by-election 213
Greer, Germaine 85
Grieg, George 78, 89–90
Grossart, Angus 121
Guardian 1, 4, 149–50, 172, 198, 211, 214, 232, 240

Haddow, Charlotte 182
Hain, Peter 177
Hamilton, John 157
Harbin, Wayne 134
Hardie, Keir 83
Hart, Finlay 71–2, 82, 165–6
Harvie, Christopher 234
Hatton, Derek 212
Hay, Andrew 238
Hayward, Ron 184
Healy, Denis 4, 180
Heath, Sir Edward 97, 108
Heathfield, Peter 204
Heffer, Eric 191

Henderson, Arnold 71, 82, 152
Hepper, Anthony 96
Herbison, Margaret (Peggy) 142
Hobsbawm, Eric 74, 84
Hogg, Norman 228
Holland, Stuart 179
Holloway, James 238
Home, Mark Douglas 232
Howe, Sir Geoffrey 214
Hoxha, Enver 87
Hughes, Gerry 140–2
Hungarian Uprising 67, 73–4
Hunter, Kenny 238
Hussain, Mumtaz 225
Huxley, Julian 198
Hyde, Douglas 75

Ingersoll, Robert 27
Iona Community Mission apprentices' strike 54
Irish Republican Army (IRA) 196
Irvine, Jack 216–17
Islam, Badar 225
Isle of Bute 238–9

Jack, Ian 83, 108
Jacques, Martin 84
James, Steve 241
Jefferies, Jim 73
Jimmy Reid Youth Brigade 81–2
Johns, Stephen 145
Johnston, Tom 32, 34

Kay, Jackie 62–3
Kelly, Stephen 176, 178
Kemp, Arnold 235, 237
Kerr, Hugh 80–1, 230–1
Kerrigan, Peter 70, 163, 175
Kettle, Martin 1, 241–2
Khrushchev, Nikita 67, 79, 83
Kinnock, Neil 174, 176–7, 198, 200, 210–12
Klugmann, James 143

Labour League of Youth (LLY) 37
Labour Party
    divisions 178–80
    infiltration 179
    1945 landslide 35
    New Labour 4, 223, 229
    social profile 179
    votes for 206
Labour Party (Scotland)
    opposition to Reid 190, 229–30
    selection process 228
Laird, Sir Gavin 49, 159–62
Lawson, Sir Nigel 209
Lee Jeans work-in 127
Leggatt, Ian 184
Lennon, John 119
Lessing, Doris 198
Lithgow, Sir James 204
Livingstone, Ken 213
Lloyd, A.L. 17–18

McAllion, John 231
McAlpine, Alastair 186
McAuley, John 182, 184
McCafferty, Jim 210
McCarron, James 229–30
McCartney, Hugh 149, 156, 186
McCartney, Wilf 69
McConnachie, Elaine 120
McConnachie, John 120
McCubbin, Henry 231
McCulloch, Karl Marx 58
McConnell, Jack 236
MacDonald, Alexander 102
MacDonald, David 102
MacDonald, Margo 236
McEwan, George 112
McFee, Bruce 236
McGarvey, Dan
    Catholicism 121
    Marathon Oil 125, 134–5
McGahey, Mick 159, 166, 202, 210
McGeachan, Brian 190

MacGregor, Ian 204, 206, 210
McKelvey, Willie 182–3
McKenna, Rosemary 228
MacKenzie, Donald 81
MacKenzie, Kelvin 214–15, 217
MacKenzie, Roddy 120
McKinlay, Adam 120–1
Mclean, Hamish 25
Mclean, Jack 205–6
Mclean, John 43
MacLellan, Robert 121
McLennan, Gordon 75–7, 114, 173–4
MacLeod, Rev George Fielden
  career 35
  Iona Community 35
  rector 146
  Youth Parliament 36
MacLeod, Ian 188, 217
MacLeod, Rev John 35
MacMillan, Harold 189, 217
McShane, Harry 43, 68
Maltby, 208
Mandelson, Peter 229
Manifesto Group 184
Marathon Oil
  closure 136–7
  employment 131, 135
  industrial relations 131–2, 134–5
Marquez, Gabriel Garcia 5
Martin, Iain 235
Marxism 47
Marxism Today 84
Mather, Jim 234
Matthes, George 68
Maxton, James 5
Maxwell, Robert 214–16
Meth, Betty 60–1
MI5 6, 126–7
Miliband, Ed 239
Militant Tendency 211–12
Miller, Jonathan 32
Milne, Seumus 204

1984 miners' strike 7
  causes of 203–4
  comparisons with UCS 208
  end of 210
  legacy 207
  picket and police violence 207–8
Mitchell, Juliet 85
Montford, Arthur 147
Moore, John 165
Moore, Tom 183
Morgan, Kevin 164
Morgan, Rhoddri 228
Morley, David 189
Morning Star 82, 175, 233
Moscow 219
Moss, John 69
Motherwell, Elizabeth 25
Murdoch, Rupert 216–17
Murphy, Jack 75
Murray, Alex 145, 173–4

Nairn, Tom 218
National Coal Board (NCB)
  coal stocks 210
  pit closures 204–6
National Service 64–6
National Union of Journalists 193
National Union of Mineworkers (NUM)
  see also 1984 miners' strike
  divisions within 204, 209–10
  regional structure 203–4, 209
NATO (North Atlantic Treaty Organisation) 197
Neil, Andrew 235
Nelson, Fraser 235
New Left 84
New York Times 142
News of the World 225, 231
North British Locomotive Company 56
North East Debating Society (NEDS) 182–3

Old Age Pensions 68
Ono, Yoko 119
oral history 5–7

Park, Eric 42–3, 52, 57
Parkhouse, Geoffrey 181
Parkinson, Michael 142, 147–8
Parkinson (show) 147–8
Phillips, Jim 205
Pia, Simon 232
Pollit, Harry 67–8, 70–2, 77, 175
  death 79
  Stalinism 70, 79
Prescott, John 223
Presley, Elvis 85
Purdie, Sam 131

Ramelson, Bert 114–15
Rangers Football Club 27
Ratcliffe, Alexander 25–6
Reid, Eileen 84–5, 88–9, 126, 163, 171, 239
  Soviet Union 73–4, 170–2
Reid, Isabella
  death 202–3
  family role 20–1, 25
Reid, Jimmy
  AEUW 159–62
  Airlie, James 90, 111–12, 165, 237
  Alienation Address 142
  apartheid 197
  apprentices' strike 49–60
  apprenticeship 41–3, 47–9
  Caterpillar 220–1
  Clydebank Town Council 149, 157–8, 172–3
  CND 197–8
  CPGB (Scotland) 92–3, 173–4
  Cuban missile crisis 86–7
  Czechoslovakia 87–8, 169
  death 239
  early childhood of 2, 15, 21–2, 31, 33–4

  education 30, 32
  European Economic Community (EEC) 161
  Falklands War 195
  funeral 239
  1974 general election 3, 149–57
  1979 general election 4, 182–90
  Glen 53, 80
  Gollan, John 67, 69, 164
  health 126, 235–6
  1972 Housing Act 172–3
  journalism 4, 193–4, 214–17, 231–3
  Kinnoch, Neil 174, 176–7, 198, 210–11, 214–16, 221
  Labour Party (Broad Left) 181
  Labour Party (joining) 176–7
  leaving the CPGB 163
  legacy 242
  London 69, 73
  Loony left 213–14
  Marathon Oil 131–2
  marriage and fatherhood 72–3
  Marxism 38, 81, 169, 194, 220
  1984 miners' strike 199–211
  Murdoch, Rupert 216
  National Service 64–6, 219
  nationalism 176, 187–8, 232–4
  New Labour 4, 223–4, 227–9, 237
  Northern Ireland 195–7
  old age pensions campaign 68–9
  oratorical skills 117–18
  Parkinson (show) 147–8
  Poll Tax 215
  Pollitt, Harry 67, 70–1, 79–80, 163
  popular culture 84–5
  rector 128, 139–47
  Reid about Poland 199
  Reid about Scotland 218
  Reid about the USSR 218–19
  religion 26–7, 140–3

royalty 195
Sarwar, Mohammad 225–7
Scargill, Arthur 199–203, 206
Sectarianism 196–7
social life 33, 59
Solidarity 198–9
South Africa 197
Soviet Union 169–70, 218–19
stockbroking 36, 38–40
television career 217–19
Thatcher, Lady Margaret 200, 217
Thatcherism 217
Tory paternalism 217
Trotskyism 181, 211–12
University of Glasgow 128, 139–47
UCS work-in 95–137
Young Communist League (YCL)
   3, 39, 48, 60–2, 69, 81–2
Youth parliament 36–7
Jimmy Reid Foundation 1, 242
Reid, Joan 2, 239
   communism 72, 165
   marriage 72–3
Reid, John 181, 232
Reid, Julie 239
Reid, Leo 18–19
   casual employment 20
   childhood 19
   death 89
   gambling 20, 24–5
   poor relief 20
   politics 35
Reid, Michael 18–19
Reid, Shona 239
Richmond, John 43
Ridley, Sir Nicholas
   1984 miners' strike 205
   UCS 98, 125
Ritchie, Murray 231
Robens, Alfred 102
Robertson, David 38–40, 217
Robinson, Sir Geoffrey 229
Ross, Eernie 189

Ross, Willie 102–3
Rowbotham, Shelia 85
Roy, Kenneth 17
Royal Air Force (RAF) 64
Rushdie, Salman 214
Russell, Bertrand 198
Ryan, Paul 48

Salmond, Alex 1, 232, 239–40
Samuel, Raphael 62
Sands, Bobby 196
Sarwar, Mohammed 225–7
Scanlon, Hugh 119, 160, 238
Scargill, Arthur 7, 159, 206, 210
Scarman Report 195
Scotsman 232, 234–5, 237, 239
Scott, David 165, 232
Scottish Catholic Observer (SCO)
   1974 general election 154–5
Scottish Daily Express 193
Scottish Left Review 231, 242
Scottish Media Group 232
Scottish National Party (SNP) 5, 182,
   233
   bringing down Labour government
      186
   electoral prospects 187
   1979 general election 189
   smear campaign 189–90
Scottish Precision Castings (SPC)
   41–2
Scottish Protestant League 25–6
Scottish Socialist Alliance 230
Scottish Socialist Party (SSP) 230
Scottish Trade Union Congress
   membership 86
   UCS 108
Second World War 33–4
Sectarianism
   Church of Scotland 26
   Clydebank 156
   Glasgow 25–6
   labour market 42

Service, John 125
Shakespeare, R.W. 125–6
Sharp, Ian 118
Shaw, George Bernhard
  impact on Reid 26–7, 31
  religious views 27
Sheridan, Tommy
  News of the World 231
  Scottish Socialist Party 230–1
Sherriff, John 'Jock'
  description 44
  industrial relations 44–6
  mentoring Reid 46–7, 65
shipbuilding
  demarcation 103
  Fairfields' experiment 103–4
  nationalisation 128, 136
  post-war difficulties 86, 95–6
  unemployment 20, 29
Sillars, Jim
  funeral of Reid 241
  1984 miners' strike 202
  Scottish Labour Party 176
  Scottish Sun 217
Sinn Fein 196
Skeffington-Lodge, Tom 184
Skinner, Denis 202
Smith, Alyn 236
Smith, Jock 71, 163
Smith, John 223
Smith, Sir Robert Courtney 8, 13, 110, 237
  appointment 100
  role as liquidator 100–1, 108, 128–30
  shipyard closures 100
Sochi 170–1
Social Democratic Alliance 185
solidarity 198–9
South Yorkshire Police
  police violence 207–8
Soviet Union 83, 218–19
Spencer, Lady Diana 195

Stalin, Joseph 79, 188, 219
Stark, Davie 227
Starrett, Bob 112
Steinen, Gloria 85
Stenhouse, Sir Hugh 121–2
Stewart, Sir Ian 97, 104
Stewart, W. Rennie 186–7
Strathclyde Regional Council 215
Strauss, George 178
Sturgeon, Nicola 234
Sun 4, 214–17
Swankie, Emily 72–3, 165
  National Union of Unemployed Workers 2
Swankie, Joan
  see Reid, Joan
Swankie, John 72

Tanner, Jack, 54–5, 58
Tasker, George 153
Taylor, Teddy 142, 185
Thatcher, Lady Margaret 188–9, 203–4, 224
Thompson, Bob 231
Thompson, Edward Palmer 198
Thompson, Grant 152
Thompson, Willie 78, 81
Thorndyke, Sybil 82
Times 125–6, 155, 168, 184–5, 221
Titan Crane 137
Todd, Davie 166
Torrance, Davie 104
  Fairfields 104
  UCS work-in 137
Trade Union Congress (TUC) 127
  1984 miners' strike 209
Transport and General Workers' Union (TGWU) 183
  1984 miners' strike 209
Tribune 162, 175, 177–8, 181
Troops Out Movement 196

UCS work-in
　Airlie/Reid leadership 111–13
　boilermakers 130–3
　CPGB 113–14
　donations 120
　drink culture 118–19
　government u-turn 124
　humour 113
　idea of 105–6
　JSSCC 109–10, 115, 122, 131
　levy 106, 131
　lobbying parliament 108
　no 'bevvying' speech 117
　organisation 109
　police 120–1
　politics 109
　Right to Work demonstration 119
　workforce 134
UiE 137
unemployment
　Clydebank 102–3
　Scotland 29
　shipbuilding 20, 29
Upper Clyde Shipbuilders (UCS) 1
　formation 96–7
　financial position 97, 99–101, 124
　opposition 97

Walesa, Lech 198
Walker, Sir Anthony 219
Walker, Ernie 232
warrant sales 215
wars
　Falklands 195
　Iraq 235
　Korean, 95
Watson, Mike 225

Weir, Sir William 43
Weirs of Cathcart 42–3, 46
Wheatley, John 5
Whittingham, Brian 137
Whittock, David 182
Whyte, Jim 63
Williams, Kenneth 147–8
Williams, Shirley 185
Wilson, Colin 73
Wilson, Gordon
　career 186
　1979 general election 186
Wilson, Harold 180
Wilson, Rab 239
Wilson, Ross 202
Winning, Cardinal Thomas
　career 153–4
　death 155
　1974 general election 154–5
Wishart, Ruth 125
Women's Liberation Movement 85
Wood, Wendy 189
Woolfson, Charles 8
Worker's Educational Forum 33
Workers' Open Forum 37–8
Worthington, Tony 215
Wrigglesworth, Ian 184
Wurtz, Francis 236

Yarrow, Sir Eric 98
Young Communist League (YCL) 3, 39, 69
　apprentices' strike 61–2
　conformity 82, 84
　membership 60–1, 80–1, 84, 105
Younger, George 172
Youth Parliament 36
Yurgens, Igor 171